מסורה

The ArtScroll Series®

Rabbi Nosson Scherman / Rabbi Meir Zlotowitz

General Editors

GROWING

Published by

Mesorah Publications, ltd

by

Rabbi Abraham J. Twerski, M.D.

FIRST EDITION
First Impression . . . July 1992

Published and Distributed by
MESORAH PUBLICATIONS, Ltd.
Brooklyn, New York 11232

Distributed in Israel by
MESORAH MAFITZIM / J. GROSSMAN
Rechov Harav Uziel 117
Jerusalem, Israel

Distributed in Europe by
J. LEHMANN HEBREW BOOKSELLERS
20 Cambridge Terrace
Gateshead, Tyne and Wear
England NE8 1RP

Distributed in Australia & New Zealand by
GOLD'S BOOK & GIFT CO.
36 William Street
Balaclava 3183, Vic., Australia

Distributed in South Africa by
KOLLEL BOOKSHOP
22 Muller Street
Yeoville 2198, Johannesburg
South Africa

THE ARTSCROLL SERIES ®
GROWING EACH DAY
© *Copyright 1992, by* MESORAH PUBLICATIONS, Ltd.
4401 Second Avenue / Brooklyn, N.Y. 11232 / (718) 921-9000

ISBN:
0-89906-579-1 (hard cover)
0-89906-580-5 (paperback)

Printed in the United States of America by Noble Book Press Corp.
Bound by Sefercraft Quality Bookbinders, Ltd., Brooklyn, N.Y.

∾§ Publisher's Foreword

When Rabbi Dr. Abraham J. Twerski's *Living Each Day* was published, it ignited a firestorm of gratitude and searching on the part of untold numbers of readers. People called and wrote about how it had become an indispensable part of their lives, how it gave them ideas for the day, strength for its challenges, respite from the stress and rigors of life.

We are proud, therefore to publish this successor volume. *Growing Each Day* does exactly what its title implies. It throws down a new challenge for each day in the calendar, and provides ideas and inspiration to meet and overcome it, to grow and prosper in spiritual strength and self-esteem. For, as Rabbi Twerski often says, self-esteem is the key to all personal growth.

Life is hard, and the world is crowded with people who find it harder than they can bear, because they are overwhelmed by tasks and responsibilities and challenges and problems and goals and handicaps and . . . and . . . and . . . That accounts for the proliferation of "self help" and "how to" books that attempt to deal with the mounting frustrations and demands of everyday life. But they don't seem to work. Perhaps solutions forged in the crucible of the present are not enough; perhaps the past has more to teach us than the champions of modernity like to acknowledge.

In addition, there are countless people who are very satisfied with themselves, and with good reason. Though their student days are behind them, they maintain a Torah schedule, often juggling many other obligations to do so. But, imperceptibly, the old sense of challenge and aspiration weakens and falters. Lacking is the incentive to meet each day head on and utilize it as if it were the only day available.

Chiddushei HaRim put it masterfully: "If not now — when?" (*Avos* 1:14). Every moment is a new "now" with its own potential, and it will never come back. The next moment has its own mission. If we waste a "now" — when can we ever make up the loss? There is nothing more tragic than a backward look at wasted days, months, years, or at time that was expended without having purchased sixty minutes on the hour. Fortunes have been spent on tinsel; time, too, is a treasure not to be wasted, not to be lived without its own morsel of growth.

Rabbi Abraham J. Twerski is one of those rare people who has learned how to help others master life. He grew up in a home where people could come for warmth, comfort, and guidance whenever they needed it; where no one screened calls and where there were no office hours or answering machines. His father was a Talmudic scholar and Chassidic leader who succeeded uniquely in nurturing the learning and values of his Torah heritage in Middle America. To his children he bequeathed the fertile soil of eternity, and it was in that soil that their subsequent learning, training, and experience took root and flourished.

A major component of that heritage is its perspective on life. The Torah's message and the philosophy of its great exponents speak to us all. In a stressful, often chaotic age, we need their wise counsel and mellowing experience. If we can deal intelligently with the present, then we will manage to repent what we must of the past and lay the groundwork for the future.

In this book, Rabbi Twerski shines the searchlight of the past on the present, on today — to help us survive today, because if we can grow and be productive today, we will be better able to welcome and conquer tomorrow. The author mines rich lodes of wisdom and slices them into daily portions. For each day of the year, he selects a pithy saying from the Jewish classics, flavors it with thoughtful, incisive comments, and ends with a resolution for the day. This book succeeds on many levels. It is good reading. It gives strength and insight. It relieves anxiety and broadens horizons. It provides a Torah perspective. And it accomplishes all this without demanding special training or scholarship from the reader. The book is accessible to everyone, and it will be a rare reader indeed who will not benefit from it, day by day.

Growing each day is no easy matter nowadays, but *Growing Each Day* will make it much more enjoyable, pleasant and worthwhile.

❈   ❈   ❈

Rabbi Twerski began his rabbinical career by assisting his father who was the founder and spiritual leader of Congregation Beth Yehudah in Milwaukee. Today he is president, and gives daily *shiurim,* at the Lubavitcher Center in Pittsburgh.

In 1954, Rabbi Twerski entered the medical profession. From 1965 to 1985 he served as Clinical Director of Psychiatry at St. Francis Hospital in Pittsburgh.

Currently, he is Medical Director of Gateway Rehabilitation Center, an institution he founded in 1972 for the treatment of alcoholism and other substance-abuse addictions; Associate Clinical Professor of Psychiatry at the University of Pittsburgh School of Medicine; and often is a guest lecturer in various schools and hospitals.

Rabbi Twerski has also authored many books and articles on Torah topics, as well as works on various facets of psychology and psychiatry.

We express our appreciation to Rephael Waldman who edited this volume with skill and sensitivity to its message.

✎ Introduction

The last charge of Moses to the Israelites begins with, "You are standing *this day* before your God" (*Deuteronomy* 29:9). In the chapter that follows, Moses uses the word *hayom*, "this day," no less than eleven times. Yet each sentence would appear to be complete without reference to "this day." The repetition of this term must be significant.

Moses told the Israelites that the fulfillment of the Divine Will was not a superhuman task. To the contrary, "It is extremely close to you, to achieve it in your heart and your mouth" (ibid. 30:14). However, if we look at the totality of Torah with its 248 positive commandments and its 365 restrictive commandments, to which were added the rabbinic decrees, and with the emphasis on character refinement, which is by Torah ethics, it appears that the required self restraint and sacrifice required constitute a formidable challenge. How then could Moses say that this is so simple to accomplish?

Truthfully, Jewish observance is not at all formidable if one does not try to do everything at once. The character refinement which Torah requires must be achieved gradually. Rabbi Moshe Chaim Luzzato's monumental ethical work, *Path of the Just,* is based on a program of self development consisting of ten progressive levels, and Luzzato cautions us not to try to attain the ultimate level too rapidly.

Moses prefaced his assertion that success is simple by saying "this day" — for it *can* be achieved if we take it in manageable portions, one day at a time. Hence, he repeats the term "this day" numerous times. The theme of "one day at a time" was also manifested in the miracle of the manna, which was provided in daily portions. The cryptic phrase that "Abraham grew old well on in years" (*Genesis* 24:1) may also mean that the Patriarch achieved the ultimate in spirituality by living his life "one day at a time."

Perhaps the statement that the Patriarch Jacob waited for his beloved Rachel for seven years, but that this lengthy period seemed to him like "*singular* days," (*Genesis* 29:20) is also understandable in this light. How can it be that a separation from his bride to be of seven years appeared to be as if only a few days? The Torah may be telling us that the long period of waiting was tolerable because Jacob did not confront it as a period of seven years, but approached it only "one day at a time." Although they may not have been *few* days, they were *singular* days.

That is why Moses stressed, "The *mitzvah* I instruct you *this day* is not beyond you (*Deuteronomy* 30:11).

In *Living Each Day*, I presented a collection of thoughts on prayer and excerpts from Torah literature, to serve as sources of *daily* inspiration. In this book, *Growing Each Day*, I again draw on the infinite resources of Torah literature, this time drawing inferences as to how we may implement these ideas in our daily lives. By doing something each day, we break down the challenge of character development and refinement into manageable units, and the task is no longer formidable.

Perfecting any given trait is not a one-time task, and as one continues to advance in character improvement, it will become evident that there is further room for growth in any particular trait. Hence, the message of *Growing Each Day* is not exhausted at the end of a year, because the traits that were improved upon in the past year can now be elevated to an even higher level of perfection.

It is my hope that by approaching our spiritual and character growth one day at a time, we will merit that which the Torah relates of the Patriarch Abraham, who "came with the days, and God blessed Abraham with all" (*Genesis* 24:1).

GROWING EACH DAY

**First Day of
Rosh Hashanah**

Sept. 28, 1992
Sept. 16, 1993
Sept. 6, 1994
Sept 25, 1995
Sept 14, 1996
Oct. 2, 1997

*From
our
Prayers*

זֶה הַיּוֹם תְּחִלַּת מַעֲשֶׂיךָ זִכָּרוֹן לְיוֹם רִאשׁוֹן כִּי
חֹק לְיִשְׂרָאֵל הוּא מִשְׁפָּט לֵאלֹקֵי יַעֲקֹב

This day is the beginning of Your works, a memoriam for the first day. For it is an ordinance for Israel, a judgment for the God of Jacob (*Machzor of Rosh Hashanah*).

This day is the beginning of God's works? Rosh Hashanah marks the day on which man was created, which was the sixth and last day of Creation. Rather than being the beginning of the Divine works, it was the *end*. When man came into being, the earth, the sun, moon, stars, galaxies, rivers, oceans, mountains, vegetation, and all forms of life were already in existence.

The message is quite clear. An artist may spend days and weeks assembling all the materials he needs for his painting, but the actual work does not begin until he touches the brush to the canvas. All that preceded was indeed essential to the work, but was not the work itself.

We are told here that the work of Creation begins with man. Everything else in the universe, from the tiniest sub-atomic particle to the greatest galaxy, is but preparatory to man. Man is thus the essence of the entire universe and the goal of all Creation.

This places an awesome responsibility upon man. He cannot live his life like the sub-human species, because they are merely appurtenances in a universe that makes man's existence possible. As the ultimate purpose of Creation, therefore, man must search for the purpose of his existence and how he can best achieve it, because all else in the universe is the means, whereas he is the end.

Because man is the end of Creation, he is the *beginning* of God's works.

NOTES

_____
_____
_____
_____
_____
_____
_____
_____
_____
_____

Today I shall . . .

. . . try to search for the meaning of my existence, and dedicate myself to finding and fulfilling the purpose for which I was created.

And **You open the book of recollections,** *Prayers*
and it reads on its own, and the seal of
each person's hand is therein *(Machzor of
Rosh Hashanah).*

*Second Day of
Rosh Hashanah*
Sept. 29, 1992
Sept. 17, 1993
Sept. 7, 1994
Sept. 26, 1995
Sept. 15, 1996
Oct. 3, 1997

The Baal Shem Tov taught that a person must be
extremely cautious not to pass harsh judgment on others.
"It is yourself that you are judging," said the Baal Shem
Tov.

When the prophet, Nathan, rebuked King David following the Bath-Sheba incident, he related the parable of a
wealthy man who owned abundant livestock, and who
robbed a poor neighbor of his one and only lamb. David
was outraged at this terrible injustice, and in his anger
exclaimed, "I swear by God, that man is deserving of
death!" Nathan then said, "You are that man!" (*II Samuel*
12:1-5).

God knows that personal interest makes us oblivious to
the significance of our own misdeeds, so He contrives to
make us observe in others actions and behavior similar to
our own. How we react to our own acts as we see them in
others determines how God will judge us. If we are
considerate and lenient in our judgment, and give others
the benefit of doubt, allowing them the broadest latitude of
circumstances that might have caused them to behave
improperly, then God will judge us with equal leniency. But
if we are self-righteous and quick to condemn others, we
will be judged with equal severity.

On the Days of Judgment, the books of our deeds are
opened, and they "read on their own"; i.e. our actions
speak for themselves. "And the seal of each person's hand
is therein"; i.e. we have rendered our *own* judgment on our
actions by the way we reacted to similar actions when we
observed them in others. God merely carries out the
judgments we have made on ourselves.

NOTES

_____

_____

_____

_____

_____

_____

_____

Today I shall . . .

. . . try to be considerate when judging other people's
behavior, remembering that there may be extenuating
circumstances that might account for their actions.

_____

_____

_____

TISHREI

3

תשרי

Fast of Gedaliah

[When 3 Tishrei
falls on the
Sabbath, the
fast is observed
on Sunday.]

Sept. 30, 1992
Sept. 18, 1993
Sept. 8, 1994
Sept. 27, 1995
Sept. 16, 1996
Oct. 4, 1997

NOTES

From our Prayers

כְּרַחֵם אָב עַל בָּנִים כֵּן תְּרַחֵם עָלֵינוּ

As a father is merciful toward his children, so may You be merciful to us
(Selichos).

As children of God, we have the right to plead for mercy, just as we would expect a human father to be kind and compassionate with his errant child. Actions that might elicit stern judgment from strangers do not provoke a similar reaction from one's father. In praying for Divine forgiveness for our misdeeds, we are therefore not asking for the extraordinary, but simply for the natural response of a father toward a child. Even if our actions deserve rebuke, we ask that the discipline should be tempered by paternal compassion.

But if we ask to be treated as children, we must relate to God the way the Torah expects a child to relate to a parent, with respect and reverence. We cannot expect a parent-child relationship to be one-directional.

The Talmud speaks harshly of someone who profanes that which is sacred, going so far as to deny him a share in the eternal world, even though he may have performed many *mitzvos* (*Ethics of the Fathers* 3:15). This is because although no one is perfect, and while sins can be forgiven if one is irreverent toward holiness and lacks the respect for God that should characterize a child-parent relationship, such a person may forfeit forgiveness. For example, halachic authorities sharply criticize one who converses during the prayer services, for while this is not a Biblical transgression, it indicates disrespect for the Divine Presence.

During these days of penitence, as we recite the prayer, *Avinu Malkeinu* (our Father, our King), we should give thought to the concept of reverence for our Father.

Today I shall . . .

. . . try to behave in a manner that befits a child of God.

4 / GROWING EACH DAY

זָכְרֵנוּ לְחַיִּים מֶלֶךְ חָפֵץ בַּחַיִּים וְכָתְבֵנוּ בְּסֵפֶר *From*
הַחַיִּים לְמַעַנְךָ אֱלֹקִים חַיִּים *our*

R̲emember us for life, O King Who *Prayers*
desires life, and inscribe us in the book
of life, for Your sake, O living God
(*Amidah*, *Ten Days of Penitence*).

Oct. 1, 1992
Sept. 19, 1993
Sept. 9, 1994
Sept. 28, 1995
Sept. 17, 1996
Oct. 5, 1997

What is the meaning of *for Your sake?* How can the extension of life to a person be for the sake of God?

We might read the verse a bit differently. "Inscribe us into the book of a life that is lived for Your sake." In other words, we pray not only for life, but for a quality of life that is meaningful and purposeful, one that will be lived for the greater glory of God.

Some people find life boring, and it is little wonder that such people seek escape from its boredom. Some turn to intoxicating chemicals, and others to a quest for thrills and entertaining pastimes which, while not destructive, have no purpose except an escape.

But why should there be a need to escape? Why should life ever be boring? A person whose goal is to amass great wealth never tires of adding more to his already sizable fortune. If we have the kind of goal in life that allows us to add to it continually, we will never be bored.

Of course, we wish to be inscribed in the book of life, but it should be a life that we wish to be *in* rather than one that we seek to escape from.

NOTES

_____
_____
_____
_____
_____
_____
_____
_____
_____

Today I shall . . .

. . . try to enrich my life by living it according to the Divine will, bringing greater glory to His Name — and therefore greater meaning to my life.

Oct. 2, 1992
Sept. 20, 1993
Sept. 10, 1994
Sept. 29, 1995
Sept. 18, 1996
Oct. 6, 1997

From our Prayers

מוֹחֵל עֲוֹנוֹת עַמּוֹ מַעֲבִיר רִאשׁוֹן רִאשׁוֹן

He forgives the sins of His people, and passes them over, one by one ... (*Selichos*).

The Talmud states that if a person repeats a particular sin, he may be forgiven up to the third time, but not beyond that (*Yoma* 86b).

Before Yom Kippur, a *chassid* came to the chassidic master, Rabbi Bunim of Pshis'cha. The master reprimanded him for being remiss in the proper observance of a *mitzvah* and the man promised that he would be more diligent — but the following year, the same scene was repeated.

When the *chassid* again asserted that he would mend his ways, the Rabbi invited him to a game of chess. During the game, the Rabbi intentionally made a wrong move and asked permission to be permitted to retract the move. "You know the rule, Rabbi," the *chassid* said, "once you have removed your hand from the piece, the move is final." Nevertheless, he gave in. Later in the match the same thing happened, and the man said, "I am sorry, Rabbi, but you cannot keep on retracting moves. You must think *before* you move; once you have done so, it is final."

"Exactly, my son," the Rabbi said, "and if this is so in a game, how much more so in the serious business of life."

Just as there cannot be endless retractions in chess, so we must realize that some actions are final. Repeating the same sin after one knows it was wrong indicates an attitude of carelessness.

NOTES

Today I shall ...

... try to give serious consideration to my behavior and avoid repeating the mistakes of the past.

וּמַה הִיא הַתְּשׁוּבָה? וְיָעִיד עָלָיו יוֹדֵעַ תַּעֲלוּמוֹת *From* שֶׁלֹּא יָשׁוּב לָזֶה הַחֵטְא לְעוֹלָם *the*

And what does teshuvah consist of? *Sages* [Repentance to the degree] that the One Who knows all that is hidden will testify that he will never again repeat this sin (*Maimonides, Laws of Teshuvah* 2:2).

Oct 3, 1992
Sept. 21, 1993
Sept. 11, 1994
Sept. 30, 1995
Sept. 19, 1996
Oct. 7, 1997

"How can this be?" ask the commentaries. "Inasmuch as man always has free choice to do good or evil, to sin or not to sin, how can God testify that a person will never repeat a particular sin? Is this not a repudiation of one's free will?"

The answer to this came to me at a meeting of Alcoholics Anonymous, at which the speaker, a man who had been sober for twenty-one years, said, "The man I *was* drank. The man I *was* will drink again. But now I am a different man."

A sin does not occur in a vacuum. A person who is devout does not abruptly decide to eat *treifah*. A sin occurs when a person is in such a state that a particular act is not anathema to him.

Consequently, repentance is not complete if one merely regrets having done wrong. One must ask, "How did this sin ever come about? In what kind of a state was I that permitted me to commit this sin?"

True repentance thus consists of changing one's character to the point where, as the person is now, one can no longer even consider doing the forbidden act. Of course, the person's character may deteriorate — and if it does, he may sin again.

God does not testify that the person will never repeat the sin, but rather that his degree of repentance and correction of his character defects are such that, as long as he maintains his new status, he will not commit that sin.

NOTES

_____

_____

_____

_____

_____

Today I shall . . .

_____

. . . try to understand how I came to do those things that I regret having done, and bring myself to a state where such acts will be alien to me.

_____

_____

Oct. 4. 1992
Sept. 22, 1993
Sept. 12, 1994
Oct. 1, 1995
Sept. 20, 1996
Oct. 8, 1997

From the Scriptures

לֵב טָהוֹר בְּרָא לִי אֱלֹקִים וְרוּחַ נָכוֹן חַדֵּשׁ בְּקִרְבִּי

O, God, create for me a pure heart, and renew within me a just spirit (*Psalms* 51:12).

In 6 Tishrei we noted that true repentance consists of changing one's character to the point where one is no longer capable of repeating certain acts.

Some people may be frightened by the prospect of the emergence of a new personality. Generally we are most comfortable with the familiar, and the creation of a new personality is an excursion into the unknown. What is this new person going to be like? What kinds of likes and dislikes will he have? Will he still let me do the things I have enjoyed in the past, or will he be so restrictive that he will take all the fun out of living? How will people relate to this new person? Will my friends like him? Will my family accept him?

The anxiety about this unknown entity who may emerge may be so severe that a person may decide to remain just as he is. Even if one's present character is defective, there is at least the comfort of familiarity.

But one must have the courage of one's convictions. All growth carries a risk of discomfort. Newborn infants cry when they leave the security of the womb, and "growing pains" are a fact of life.

To avoid such pain by simply not growing should not be an option for a thinking person.

NOTES

_____
_____
_____
_____
_____
_____
_____
_____
_____

Today I shall . . .

. . . be courageous enough to discard faulty behavior patterns and allow a better "self" to emerge.

אַתָּה חֹפֵשׂ כָּל חַדְרֵי בָטֶן וּבֹחֵן כְּלָיוֹת וָלֵב *From*
You search one's innermost recesses and *our*
You examine one's motivations and the *Prayers*
emotions of the heart (*Machzor of Yom
Kippur*).

Oct. 5, 1992
Sept. 23, 1993
Sept. 13, 1994
Oct. 2, 1995
Sept. 21, 1996
Oct. 9, 1997

Rabbi Eliezer of Kozhnitz visited Rabbi Naftali of Rop-schitz and, noting that the curtains of the windows were drawn closed, he said, "There is something I do not understand. If you wish people to be able to look in, why do you draw the curtains? If you do not wish people to look in, what purpose is there for the window?"

Rabbi Naftali was stunned by the question. Rabbi Eliezer smiled and said, "I will tell you what the window is for. There may be someone whom you trust and who you know loves you, and you can then open the curtains and let him look in."

To some degree we are all secretive, and we close the curtains of the windows of our hearts and minds. We may have thoughts and feelings that we would not disclose to anyone. However, we can be comfortable that God knows our innermost secrets, because we are certain that He loves us and we can trust Him.

Our verbal expression of character defects adds nothing to God's knowledge of them, but serves to reinforce our own awareness that we can safely confide in God, and that He will help us in our quest to improve our character.

NOTES

_____
_____
_____
_____
_____

Today I shall . . .

. . . open my heart and mind to God, sharing with Him all that I think and feel, and ask Him to help me cleanse myself of improper thoughts and feelings.

_____
_____
_____

*Erev Yom
Kippur*
*[Eve of
Yom Kippur]*
Oct. 6, 1992
Sept. 24, 1993
Sept. 14, 1994
Oct. 3, 1995
Sept. 22, 1996
Oct. 10, 1997

*From the
Scriptures*

לַמְנַצֵּחַ מִזְמוֹר לְדָוִד בְּבוֹא אֵלָיו נָתָן הַנָּבִיא
כַּאֲשֶׁר בָּא אֶל בַּת שָׁבַע . . . הֶרֶב כַּבְּסֵנִי
מֵעֲוֹנִי וּמֵחַטָּאתִי טַהֲרֵנִי

For the conductor, a psalm of David.
When Nathan the Prophet came to
him, as he had come to Bath-Sheba . . .
Cleanse me abundantly from my sin,
and purify me from my transgression
(*Psalms* 51:1-4).

In this psalm of contrition, we hear David's heart-rending
plea for forgiveness and, indeed, Nathan informed him that
God had accepted his prayer and that he was forgiven (*II
Samuel* 12:13). What was it that earned David prompt
forgiveness? Rabbi Sholom Shachna of Probisch points to
the opening verse of the psalm: "When Nathan the Prophet
came to him, as he had come to Bath-Sheba." The depth of
David's contrition when the prophet reprimanded him was
no less intense than his earlier passion for Bath-Sheba.

During the Ten Days of Penitence, we confess our sins
and beat upon our breasts, but too often this is a mere
ritual. Even when we do understand the words we utter and
do regret having done wrong, the emotion accompanying
the regret is nowhere near the emotion that accompanied
the sin to which we confess. If we regret having offended
someone in the heat of anger, the pain of the awareness
that we committed a wrong is rarely of the same magnitude
as the anger that ignited our insult. Seldom do we shed
genuine tears while confessing our sins, something that
would occur spontaneously if our regret was both sincere
and profound.

Guilt can be as healthy and constructive as the pain we
feel when we touch something extremely hot, because the
discomfort of guilt will make us avoid repeating an
improper act, and this avoidance is what elicits forgiveness.
To accomplish this end, the pain of guilt must be as
profound as that of a burn, because only then do we stay on
guard not to be hurt again.

NOTES

_____
_____
_____
_____
_____
_____
_____
_____
_____

Today I shall . . .

. . . concentrate when reciting confession, so that my
resolve not to repeat sinful acts will be sincere and
profound.

עֲבוּר כִּי פָנָה יוֹם גוֹנְנֵנוּ בְּצֶדֶק יוֹשֵׁב כְּחֹם הַיּוֹם *From*

Because the day has passed, shield us by *our*
the merit of [the Patriarch Abraham] *Prayers*
who sat [at the door of his tent] in the heat
of the day [to welcome wayfarers] (*Genesis*
18:1) (*Ne'ilah* prayer).

Just prior to *Ne'ilah* (the concluding service of Yom
Kippur), one of the Chassidic masters ascended the *bimah*
(platform) and said tearfully, "My dear brothers and sisters!
God in His infinite mercy gave us the entire month of Elul to
repent, but we failed to take advantage of it. He gave us the
awesome days of Rosh Hashanah, when our standing in
judgment before the heavenly tribunal should have stimulated us to repent, but we neglected that opportunity. He
gave us the special grace of the Ten Days of Penitence, but
we let these pass too. All we have left now are a few
precious moments that are propitious for forgiveness.

"The Sages of the Talmud tell us that if a person enters a
marriage contract on the condition that he is a perfect
tzaddik, then it is binding even if he is known to be a
complete *rasha* (wicked person). Why? Because he may
have had one moment of sincere contrition that trans-
formed him from a complete *rasha* to a perfect *tzaddik*.

"Do you hear that, my dear brothers and sisters? All it
takes is one brief moment of sincere contrition! We have
the opportunity of that moment now. In just one moment
we can emerge totally cleansed of all our sins, in a state of
perfection akin to that of Adam in the Garden of Eden."

The rabbi wept profusely and uncontrollably. "Could we
be so foolish as to overlook such a rare opportunity? Let us
assist one another and join in achieving sincere repentance!"

Yom Kippur
[Yizkor]
Oct. 7, 1992
Sept. 25, 1993
Sept. 15, 1994
Oct. 4, 1995
Sept. 23, 1996
Oct. 11, 1997

NOTES

Today I shall ...

... take advantage of the Divine gift of forgiveness, and
make my resolutions of repentance sincere, so that the new
person that emerges will be unencumbered by the burdens
of the past.

Oct. 8, 1992
Sept. 26, 1993
Sept. 16, 1994
Oct. 5, 1995
Sept. 24, 1996
Oct. 12, 1997

From the Scriptures

צָמְאָה לְךָ נַפְשִׁי כָּמַהּ לְךָ בְשָׂרִי

My soul thirsts for You; my flesh pines for You (*Psalms* 63:2).

One Yom Kippur, after the *Maariv* (evening) services that ended the twenty-six-hour fast, Rabbi Levi Yitzchok of Berdichev exclaimed, "I am thirsty! I am thirsty!" Quickly someone brought him water, but the Rabbi said, "No! I am thirsty!" Hastily they boiled water and brought him coffee, but again he said, "No! No! I am thirsty!" His attendant then asked, "Just what is it you desire?"

"A tractate *Succah* (the volume of the Talmud dealing with the laws of the festival of Succos)." They brought the desired volume, and the Rabbi began to study the Talmud with great enthusiasm, ignoring the food and drink that were placed before him.

Only after several hours of intense study did the Rabbi breathe a sigh of relief and break his fast. The approaching festival of Succos with its many commandments — only five days after Yom Kippur — had aroused so intense a craving that it obscured the hunger and thirst of the fast.

It is also related that at the end of Succos and Pesach, festivals during which one does not put on *tefillin*, Rabbi Levi Yitzchok sat at the window, waiting for the first glimmer of dawn which would allow him to fulfill the *mitzvah* of *tefillin* after a respite of eight or nine days.

NOTES

Today I shall . . .

. . . try to realize that Torah and *mitzvos* are the nutrients of my life, so that I crave them just as I do food and water when I am hungry or thirsty.

Oct. 9, 1992
Sept. 27, 1993
Sept. 17, 1994
Oct. 6, 1995
Sept. 25, 1996
Oct. 13, 1997

Pursue the performance of even a "minor" mitzvah (*Ethics of the Fathers* 4:2).

How does one pursue a *mitzvah?*

Rabbi Moshe Leib of Sassov used to occupy himself with redeeming Jews from debtors' prisons. Usually, these people had been thrown into dungeons because they could not pay the rent demanded by the *poritz* (feudal lord). On one visit to such a prison, Rabbi Moshe Leib was unable to gain the release of a debtor, and gave up trying. He then saw another prisoner being flogged mercilessly, and he was able to get him released. Subsequently, he discovered that this latter person was not a debtor but one who was imprisoned for stealing.

"Well," said the Rabbi, "now you have been taught your lesson. After that flogging you will certainly never steal again."

"Why not?" the thief responded. "Just because I was caught this time does not mean that I will not succeed next time."

Rabbi Moshe Leib felt that these words were directed at him. Just because he had failed once to ransom a debtor, he did not have the right to resign himself to failure. He retraced his steps and renewed his efforts to redeem the debtor. Next time he might succeed.

That is what is meant by *pursuit* of a *mitzvah*. If a specific *mitzvah* eludes you, do not resign yourself, but pursue it until you overtake and fulfill it.

NOTES

Today I shall . . .

. . . renew my efforts to achieve things of which I had previously despaired.

Oct. 10, 1992
Sept. 28, 1993
Sept. 18, 1994
Oct. 7, 1995
Sept. 26, 1996
Oct. 14, 1997

From the Scriptures לְבִלְתִּי רוּם לְבָבוֹ מֵאֶחָיו וּלְבִלְתִּי סוּר מִן הַמִּצְוָה יָמִין וּשְׂמֹאול

. . . in order that his (the king's) should not be lifted above his brethren, and that he should not deviate from the commandment to the right or to the left (*Deuteronomy* 17:20).

The Torah requires that even one who is in a position of leadership and prominence must retain his humility. Moses and David are outstanding examples of leaders who were extremely humble.

How can one remain humble when one exercises great authority and is the recipient of homage and adulation? "Simple," said Rabbi Moshe of Kobrin. "If a king hangs his crown on a peg in the wall, would the peg boast that its extreme beauty drew the king's attention to it?"

While an organized society needs leaders, and in Judaism there is a need for *Kohanim* and Levites who have special functions, an intelligent person should never allow a particular status to turn his head and make him think that he is better than others. Nor should men consider themselves superior to women because they have certain *mitzvos* from which women are exempt, and women should not think that they must attain equality by rejecting these exemptions and performing these *mitzvos*. There is no need to attain something that one already has. Men and women, *Kohanim* and Levites, leaders and kings — we are all "pegs in the wall" which the King uses for His purposes as He sees fit.

True, we should always strive for that which is above us, but this means striving for greater wisdom and spirituality, and not for positions of superiority. The latter are not at all "above" us; one peg may be higher on the wall than another, but that does not make it a better peg.

NOTES

Today I shall . . .

. . . try to realize that I, like all other people in the world, am but an instrument of God, wherewith He wishes to achieve the Divine will.

From our Prayers

הִנְנִי מוּכָן וּמְזוּמָּן לְקַיֵּם מִצְוַת עֲשֵׂה **I am hereby ready and prepared to fulfill the positive commandment . . .** (*Siddur*).

Erev Succos
[Eve of Succos]
Oct. 11, 1992
Sept. 29, 1993
Sept. 19, 1994
Oct. 8, 1995
Sept. 27, 1996
Oct. 15, 1997

Erev Succos is a day on which Jews busily prepare for the commandments of the festival — building, covering, and decorating the *succah*, acquiring an *esrog* (citron) and the other three species, and the other preparations that are common to all festive days in the Jewish calendar. The commandments themselves are not performed until the festival begins, but the preparations occupy people for many days beforehand.

One of the Chassidic masters said that Satan once brought serious accusations against the Jews before God, stating that they had committed grievous sins and should be punished. Although the archangel Michael countered with bundles of *mitzvos* that Jews had performed, Satan argued that the *mitzvos* were insufficient to outweigh the sins. There was great danger that the heavenly tribunal would decree a harsh judgment against the Jews.

The archangel Michael then argued, "True, the Jews may have sinned, but this was because they were unable to resist temptation, and these were not premeditated acts. No one has ever preceded a sinful act by declaring, 'I am hereby ready and prepared to violate the prohibition written in the Torah.' It is only *mitzvos* that they perform with forethought and preparation, but never sins." This argument thwarted the evil plot of Satan.

We can see that as important as the performance of a *mitzvah* is, the effort in preparing for it may be even more important. On *Erev* Succos, when we adorn the *succah*, and we place the *esrog* in a beautiful container, and lovingly prepare for the festival, we show our dedication to the Divine *mitzvos*.

Today I shall . . .

. . . fully enjoy preparing for the Succos festival, and make joyful preparations an integral part of every commandment I perform.

NOTES

**First Day
of Succos**

Oct. 12, 1992
Sept. 30, 1993
Sept. 20, 1994
Oct. 9, 1995
Sept. 28, 1996
Oct. 16, 1997

*From the
Scriptures*

בְּסֻכֹּת תֵּשְׁבוּ שִׁבְעַת יָמִים . . . וְהָיִיתָ אַךְ
שָׂמֵחַ

Seven days shall you dwell in booths
(*Leviticus* 23:42) **. . . and you shall
only be rejoicing** (*Deuteronomy* 16:15).

Succos is the festival designated as זְמַן שִׂמְחָתֵנוּ, *the season
of our gladness.* Yet the commentaries state that one of the
symbolisms of the *succah,* a temporary hut, is that we
dwell in it for seven days to symbolize man's temporary
sojourn on earth for his average life span of seven decades
(*Psalms* 90:10).

Human mortality is a rather sobering thought; it is hardly
conducive to rejoicing. Most often we do not think about
our mortality, and when circumstances force us to face it,
we quickly dismiss it from our minds and go on acting as
though we will live forever.

How different Torah values are from secular values! The
Torah teaches us that there is an eternal life, a wholly
spiritual life, whose bliss is far greater than the human mind
can imagine. We are placed on this planet for our
ephemeral earthly existence only to give us an opportunity
to prepare for the eternal life.

The Torah teaches us to enjoy life, and if it restricts some
pleasures, it is because we should enjoy life in a manner
that befits a human being. Furthermore, our joy of living
should not be diminished by the awareness of our
mortality, nor need we deny it. The *succah* — the symbol of
our temporary stay on earth — is beautifully decorated, and
we enjoy our festive meals therein. Even our temporary
existence can be beautiful and happy, and our faith in the
eternal life should enhance that happiness.

NOTES

Today I shall . . .

. . . try to enjoy life as befits a spiritual person, knowing that
the true life of man is not the fleeting one, but that of
eternity.

וּלְקַחְתֶּם לָכֶם בַּיּוֹם הָרִאשׁוֹן פְּרִי עֵץ הָדָר *From the*

And you shall take for yourself on the *Scriptures*
first day the fruit of a (citron)
beauteous tree (*Leviticus* 23:40).

Second Day
of Succos
[In the Land
of Israel this
is the first day
of Chol Hamoed,
the intermediate
Days.]
Oct. 13, 1992
Oct. 1, 1993
Sept. 21, 1994
Oct. 10, 1995
Sept. 29, 1996
Oct. 17, 1997

Rabbi Mordechai of Nesh'chiz looked forward all year to the *mitzvah* of the Four Species on Succos. Since a fine *esrog* was costly and Rabbi Mordechai was hardly a man of means, he would accumulate small coins all year round, even depriving himself of food, in order to be able to afford an *esrog*.

A few days before Succos, Rabbi Mordechai joyfully took the money he had saved, and in high spirits, went off to buy the coveted *esrog*. On the way, he encountered a man sitting at the side of the road, weeping bitterly. He inquired as to the reason for the man's grief, and the latter told him, "Woe is to me! I earn my living with my horse and wagon, and this morning my nag died. How am I to feed my wife and children?"

"How much do you need to buy another horse?" Rabbi Mordechai asked.

The sum that the man specified was exactly the amount that Rabbi Mordechai had laboriously saved all year long for the *esrog*. Without giving it another thought, he gave his purse to the man. "Here, my dear man. Go buy yourself a horse."

After the man joyfully left with the money, Rabbi Mordechai said, "Oh well. All of Israel will be fulfilling the *mitzvah* of the Four Species with an *esrog*, but I will do so with a horse."

Rabbi Mordechai's sacrifice of his personal comfort all year round teaches us how precious is the *mitzvah* of the Four Species, but his final act teaches us that the *mitzvah* of *tzedakah* (charity) is even greater.

NOTES

Today I shall . . .

. . . try to realize the greatness of the commandment of charity, to make certain that another Jew has the means to survive.

TISHREI

17

תשרי

*Chol Hamoed
Succos*

Oct. 14, 1992
Oct. 2, 1993
Sept. 22, 1994
Oct. 11, 1995
Sept. 30, 1996
Oct. 18, 1997

*From
our
Prayers*

אֲזַמֵּן לִסְעֻדָתִי אֻשְׁפִּיזִין עִלָּאִין אַבְרָהָם יִצְחָק
יַעֲקֹב מֹשֶׁה אַהֲרֹן יוֹסֵף וְדָוִד

I welcome to my table the saintly guests,
Abraham, Isaac, Jacob, Moses, Aaron,
Joseph, and David (*Machzor of Succos*).

Why is Succos unique among all the festivals in that we invite the Patriarchs to share the celebration with us?

Succos is the חַג הָאָסִיף, *the festival of the harvest.* All the efforts that had been invested in the land — plowing, watering, fertilizing, weeding, pruning, and finally harvesting — have culminated in an abundant harvest, and we are now ready to enjoy the fruits of our labor.

God wants us to enjoy worldly goods, but to do so in a manner that befits a spiritual people, a kingdom of priests and a holy nation. While there are many laws that pertain to working the land and tithing its produce, these do not yet assure our spirituality. Much of the Torah does not relate to specific law, but consists of a narration of the lives of Seven Shepherds, whom we invite into our *succah,* as it were, because they are the role models whom we are to emulate. They were all people of means, yet their lives were dedicated to sanctity, and their worldly possessions did not distract them from their primary spiritual goals.

Each of them excelled in a particular attribute, although they all shared in each other's attributes. For example, Abraham's חֶסֶד, *benevolence,* included מַלְכוּת שֶׁבְחֶסֶד, *majesty of benevolence,* and David's מַלְכוּת, *majesty,* included *benevolence of majesty;* yet they and all the intermediate leaders were paragons of humility and self-effacement.

We invite the shepherds to our *succah* to remind us to fashion our lives after theirs.

NOTES

_____
_____
_____
_____
_____
_____
_____
_____
_____
_____

Today I shall . . .

. . . try to remember my roots, and incorporate my beautiful heritage into my daily activities.

שֶׁיְהֵא חָשׁוּב לְפָנֶיךָ מִצְוַת יְשִׁיבַת סֻכָּה זוּ כְּאִילוּ **From**
קִיַּמְתִּיהָ בְּכָל פְּרָטֶיהָ וְדִקְדּוּקֶיהָ וְתַרְיַ"ג מִצְוֹת **our**
הַתְּלוּיִם בָּהּ **Prayers**

May the mitzvah of sitting in the succah
be considered before You as though I
had fulfilled it with all its details and
specifications, and the six hundred thirteen mitzvos that are dependent on it
(*Machzor for Succos*).

*Chol Hamoed
Succos*
Oct. 15, 1992
Oct. 3, 1993
Sept. 23, 1994
Oct. 12, 1995
Oct. 1, 1996
Oct. 19, 1997

In what way are all six hundred thirteen *mitzvos*
dependent on the *mitzvah* of *succah*?

Rabbi Bunim of Pshis'cha said, "The *mitzvah* of *succah* is
so precious — because I enter into the *mitzvah* with my
entire person, even with my boots!"

All other commandments do not relate to the entire
body. We study with our eyes, mouth, and brain, eat
matzah with our mouths, listen to the *shofar* with our ears,
and wear the *tefillin* on the arm and head. When we enter
the *succah*, however, our whole body is enclosed within
the *mitzvah* and, as Rabbi Bunim pointed out, nothing that
is attached to us is excluded from the *mitzvah*, not even
one's boots.

Whereas total immersion into a *mitzvah* occurs physically only with *succah*, the concept of total involvement
should extend to all other *mitzvos*. Just as King David says
of prayer, *All my bones declare, "O, God, who is like unto
You?"* (*Psalms* 35:10), so with all *mitzvos*, the intensity of
performance should engulf one's whole personality. Indeed, one should feel that not only one's person, but
everything that one has is devoted to the Divine will.

The Kabbalists state that in addition to its manifest
meaning, "something we have been commanded to do or
not to do," the word *mitzvah* also means "joined," for one
attaches oneself to God by performing His will. Contact
with God should not be partial. When we relate to Him, we
should do so with the totality of our being. In this way,
succah teaches us how to perform all six hundred thirteen
mitzvos.

Today I shall . . .

. . . try to involve myself totally each time I pray, study
Torah, or perform any other mitzvah.

Chol Hamoed
Succos

Oct. 16, 1992
Oct. 4, 1993
Sept. 24, 1994
Oct. 13, 1995
Oct. 2, 1996
Oct. 20, 1997

From the וּלְקַחְתֶּם לָכֶם בַּיּוֹם הָרִאשׁוֹן פְּרִי עֵץ הָדָר
Scriptures And you shall take for yourself on the first day the fruit of a [citron] beauteous tree (*Leviticus* 23:40).

The *halachah* requires that an *esrog* must be הָדָר, *beautiful,* meaning that it must be free of blemishes. Even a minor defect may disqualify an *esrog.*

Why are the specifications for the *esrog* stricter than those for the other three species? Why is virtual perfection demanded only for the *esrog?*

The Midrash states that the leaf of the הֲדַס, *myrtle branch,* is shaped like the eye, and its use in the *mitzvah* of the Four Species symbolizes to us that we must dedicate our eyes to the service of God, and not allow them to gaze upon things that would tempt us to sin. The leaf of the עֲרָבָה, *willow branch,* resembles the lips, teaching us to guard our lips from speaking evil. The לוּלָב, *palm branch,* represents the spinal cord, which controls all our actions, symbolizing that they are all dedicated to fulfilling the Divine will. The *esrog* resembles the heart, for one's thoughts and feelings should be absorbed with sanctity.

Ideally, while sight, speech, and deed should be completely involved with holiness, a deviation in any of these areas may be an isolated phenomenon and may not affect the whole being. Not so with thought and feeling. They affect everything one does. The heart's devotion must be complete, and there is, therefore, a greater requirement that the heart be pure.

The *esrog,* which represents the heart, must therefore be הָדָר, completely beautiful, without the slightest defect.

NOTES

Today I shall . . .

. . . try to direct all my thoughts and feelings to fulfillment of the Divine will as expressed in the Torah.

כָּל הַפָּטוּר מִן הַסּוּכָּה וְאֵינוֹ יוֹצֵא מִשָּׁם אֵינוֹ *From*
מְקַבֵּל עָלָיו שָׂכָר וְאֵינָן אֶלָּא מִן הַדְּיוֹטוֹת *the*

All who are exempt from the succah *Sages*
[because of severe discomfort; e.g.
heavy rain or extreme cold] and do not
leave, do not receive reward for this and
are merely simpletons (*Shulchan Aruch
Orach Chaim, Ramah, 639:7*).

*Chol Hamoed
Succos*
Oct. 17, 1992
Oct. 5, 1993
Sept. 25, 1994
Oct. 14, 1995
Oct. 3, 1996
Oct. 21, 1997

How wise we would be to observe the way great Torah
personalities live, and see how their every move is
calculated to adhere to Torah teachings.

Rabbi Chaim Ozer Grodzenski of Vilna had a severe cold
one Succos and, because it was chilly in the *succah*, he ate
indoors. However, he had a guest for whom a meal was
served in the *succah*.

During the meal the guest was surprised to see Rabbi
Chaim Ozer come into the *succah* all bundled up with coat
and scarf. He asked the Rabbi why he had come out to the
succah, especially since he had already eaten in the house.

Rabbi Chaim Ozer explained, "If being in the *succah* is
distressful, then one is exempt from that particular *mitzvah*.
However, the *mitzvah* of *hachnasas orchim*, hospitality to a
guest, requires that the host join the guest at the table, so
that the latter should not eat in solitude. We do not find
that distress is an exemption for the *mitzvah* of hospitality.
Thus, although I ate in the house, I have come to sit with
you as part of the *mitzvah* of hospitality."

This is what Torah living is all about. Everything one does
must be carefully considered, so that it complies with
Torah principles.

NOTES

Today I shall . . .

. . . try to give greater thought to what I do, to make sure
that I am in compliance with Torah at all times.

Hoshana
Rabbah
Oct. 18, 1992
Oct. 6, 1993
Sept. 26, 1994
Oct. 15, 1995
Oct. 4, 1996
Oct. 22, 1997

From the
Scriptures

שִׁבְעַת יָמִים תָּחֹג לַה' אֱלֹקֶיךָ ... וְהָיִיתָ
אַךְ שָׂמֵחַ

Seven days shall you celebrate before
HASHEM, your God . . . and you shall
only be joyous (*Deuteronomy* 16:15).

Many people think of Judaism as being extremely
solemn, perhaps not realizing that the essence of Judaism is
simchah, joy, and that whatever solemnity there is, is in
reality a preparation for joy.

Rabbi Samson Raphael Hirsch points to a simple fact.
The Torah designates one day each for Rosh Hashanah and
Yom Kippur (the second day of Rosh Hashanah is of
Rabbinical origin), whereas Succos, the festival of rejoicing,
is of seven days' duration.

The Gaon of Vilna was asked which of the six hundred
thirteen *mitzvos* he considered the most difficult to
observe. He answered that it was Succos, because for
seven consecutive days a person must be in constant joy.
Regardless of what might occur during these days that
might make it difficult for a person to feel happy, the
mitzvah to rejoice requires him to overcome all obstacles to
joy.

The Torah's position is that joy is not simply a
spontaneous feeling that accompanies pleasant experiences. Joy requires work: meditation on why a person who
is privileged to serve God should rejoice. Joy can be
achieved even under adverse circumstances. This is something which is expected not only of great *tzaddikim*, but
also of every Jew.

On Succos we must make the necessary effort to be in
constant joy throughout the entire festival, and we should
learn therefrom how to generate joy all year round.

NOTES

Today I shall . . .

. . . try to find ways to bring more joy into my life, and
strive to achieve joy even when circumstances are not
conducive thereto.

בַּיּוֹם הַשְּׁמִינִי עֲצֶרֶת תִּהְיֶה לָכֶם *From the*

O n the eighth day there shall be an *Scriptures*
assembly for you *(Numbers* 29:35).

TISHREI

תשרי

Shemini Atzeres
*[Yizkor — in the
Land of Israel
this day is also
celebrated as
Simchas Torah.]*

Oct. 19, 1992
Oct. 7, 1993
Sept. 27, 1994
Oct. 16, 1995
Oct. 5, 1996
Oct. 23, 1997

Shemini Atzeres marks the close of the holiday season of the month of Tishrei. (Simchas Torah is merely an extension of Shemini Atzeres observed in the diaspora. In Israel, Simchas Torah is celebrated as Shemini Atzeres.)

The literal meaning of *atzeres* is "restraint," and various interpretations have been given for the use of this term to designate the eighth day of the festival.

Perhaps the idea of restraint in this context refers to holding on to the spiritual joy and holiness experienced during this month, beginning with the repentance of the awesome days of Rosh Hashanah and culminating in the joy and love of Torah and *mitzvos* manifested during Succos. There is a great risk that once the holidays are behind us and we return to the daily life of work and business transactions, we may become so absorbed in those activities that we may dissipate all the spiritual wealth we had acquired during the month of festivals.

Just as one tightly seals a bottle of fine wine so that it does not lose its bouquet, so we should make this last day of the festival an *atzeres*, a tight seal that will retain all that we have harvested during Tishrei. Just as it is foolish to earn and not to conserve, so it would be foolish to achieve spirituality and not retain it.

NOTES

Today I shall . . .

. . . concentrate on how I can continue the self-improve-ment of the Days of Awe and the joy of the festive days throughout the entire year.

TISHREI

23

תשרי

Simchas Torah
Oct. 20, 1992
Oct. 8, 1993
Sept. 28, 1994
Oct. 17, 1995
Oct. 6, 1996
Oct. 24, 1997

From the Scriptures

וּלְכֹל הַיָּד הַחֲזָקָה וּלְכֹל הַמּוֹרָא הַגָּדוֹל אֲשֶׁר עָשָׂה מֹשֶׁה לְעֵינֵי כָּל יִשְׂרָאֵל . . . בְּרֵאשִׁית בָּרָא אֱלֹקִים אֵת הַשָּׁמַיִם וְאֵת הָאָרֶץ

And for all the mighty hand and all the great awe that Moses did before the eyes of all Israel (*Deuteronomy* 34:12) . . . In the beginning God created the heaven and the earth (*Genesis* 1:1).

On Simchas Torah we conclude the reading of the Torah in *Deuteronomy* and immediately begin another cycle with the first portion of *Genesis*. This symbolizes that the Torah, like a circle, is without end; its beginning and end are forever intertwined.

By reading the last portion and the first portion of the Torah contiguously, we connect the miraculous wonders performed by Moses to Creation. In other words, all the marvelous happenings in Egypt and the Wilderness were to impress upon the Israelites that there is a Creator Who rules the universe and conducts it as He wishes.

Without an ultimate goal, life is futile, and there can hardly be an ultimate goal in a universe that happened to come about through the accidental interaction of impersonal, mechanical forces. Furthermore, there can be no joy in a life that is futile, and indeed, people who feel that life is futile are apt to seek to escape from it rather than live it to its fullest.

The joy of the Succos festival reaches its zenith on Simchas Torah, and our celebration of this joyous day is based on the awareness that our lives are purposeful and meaningful. The teachings and miracles of Moses, which instilled within us the faith that God created heaven and earth, are thus the key not only to the joy of the day, but to that of the entire year.

NOTES

_____
_____
_____
_____
_____
_____
_____
_____
_____
_____

Today I shall . . .

. . . try to realize that what gives meaning to life is that it is purposeful, and to the degree that I am convinced that God created the universe, to that degree can I achieve joy in living.

אִסְרוּ חַג בַּעֲבֹתִים עַד קַרְנוֹת הַמִּזְבֵּחַ *From the*
Restrain the festival by bonds to the *Scriptures*
corners of the altar (*Psalms* 118:27).

Oct. 21, 1992
Oct. 9, 1993
Sept. 29, 1994
Oct. 18, 1995
Oct. 7, 1996
Oct. 25, 1997

The Talmud states that if a person celebrates the day after the holiday with a festive meal, it is considered as though he had built an altar and had brought sacrificial offerings upon it (*Succah* 45b).

Rashi states that the reason for the eighth day, Shemini Atzeres, can be explained with the parable of a king who invited his children for several days of feasting. When the time came for them to leave, the king said, "Your departure is so difficult for me. Please stay with me for yet one more day" (*Rashi, Leviticus* 23:36). Similarly, after seven days of Succos, in His great love for Israel, God asks us to stay with Him for yet one more day before returning to our mundane activities, which so often distract us from Him.

To indicate that we cherish our closeness to God just as He does, we add a day of festivity *after* the last day of the holiday, to extend even further the intimate companionship with God. This testimony, that we value our intimacy with Him and that we leave the Sanctuary only because we must tend to our obligations, is held equivalent to building an altar and bringing votive offerings.

Indeed, God wants us to engage in work — *Six days shall you work* (*Exodus* 20:9) — but our attitude toward the workweek should be that of a person who is away from home on an assigned duty, and who longs to return home to his loved ones. The importance of our closeness to God should be manifest not only on the day following the festival but all year round as well.

NOTES

Today I shall ...

... try to maintain the closeness with God, that I achieved during the festival, even when I am involved with the activities of everyday life.

Oct. 22, 1992
Oct. 10, 1993
Sept. 30, 1994
Oct. 19, 1995
Oct. 8, 1996
Oct. 26, 1997

From the **H**e [Hillel] was accustomed to say, "If I *Sages* am not for myself, then who will be for me?" (*Ethics of the Fathers* 1:14).

הוּא הָיָה אוֹמֵר: אִם אֵין אֲנִי לִי מִי לִי

This phrase is sometimes misinterpreted to mean that one must primarily look out for oneself, as though Hillel was advocating selfishness as a desirable trait.

What Hillel really meant can be better understood with a statement by the Rabbi of Kotzk, who said, "If I am I because I am I, and you are you because you are you, then I am and you are. But if I am I because you are you, and you are you because I am I, then I am not and you are not."

Every person must have an identity, and that identity should not depend on what others think of him or what someone else wants him to be. A person who allows himself to be molded and manipulated by others does not have an identity or even an existence of his own, because he will always become whatever others want him to be, and he is essentially an extension of others, rather than an individual in his own right.

People, who allow others to determine who they are and what they are to do, generally do not assume full responsibility for their behavior. Their attitude is often, "He made me do it."

Both Hillel and the Rabbi of Kotzk demand that a person be fully responsible for his actions, and that he decide what he expects of himself and what he sees as his purpose in life.

NOTES

_____
_____
_____
_____
_____
_____

Today I shall . . .

. . . try to achieve my own identity. Whereas I will listen to the advice of those who are wiser than me, I will nonetheless never hold others responsible for what I do.

שַׁוְעָתֵנוּ קַבֵּל וּשְׁמַע צַעֲקָתֵנוּ יוֹדֵעַ תַּעֲלֻמוֹת *From*
May He Who knows what is hidden *our*
accept our call for help and listen to *Prayers*
our cry (*Siddur*).

Oct. 23, 1992
Oct. 11, 1993
Oct. 1, 1994
Oct. 20, 1995
Oct. 9, 1996
Oct. 27, 1997

The Talmud states that a person may be coerced to perform a *mitzvah* even if it is required that the *mitzvah* be done of one's own volition (*Rosh Hashanah* 6a).

But are not coercion and volition mutually exclusive? Not necessarily, explains *Rambam*. Inasmuch as the soul of the Jew intrinsically wishes to do the Divine will, and it is only the physical self — which is subject to temptation — that may be resistive, the coercion inflicted upon the person overcomes that external resistance. Thus, when one performs the *mitzvah*, it is with the full volition of the inner self, the *true* self, for at his core, every Jew wishes to comply with the mandates of the Torah.

There is a hidden part of us, to which we may have limited access, yet we know it is there. When we pray for our needs, said Rabbi Uri of Strelisk, we generally ask only for that which we feel ourselves to be lacking. However, we must also recognize that our soul has spiritual needs, and that we may not be aware of its cravings.

We therefore pray, said Rabbi Uri, that God should listen not only to the requests that we verbalize, but also to our hidden needs that are very important to us — but which He knows much better than we.

NOTES

Today I shall . . .

. . . try to realize that there is a part of me of which I am only vaguely aware. I must try to get to know that part of myself, because it is my very essence.

Oct. 24, 1992
Oct. 12, 1993
Oct. 2, 1994
Oct. 21, 1995
Oct. 10, 1996
Oct. 28, 1997

From the Scriptures

יִשְׂמַח לֵב מְבַקְשֵׁי ה'. דִּרְשׁוּ ה' וְעֻזּוֹ בַּקְּשׁוּ פָנָיו תָּמִיד

The heart of those that seek God shall rejoice. Seek God and His might, constantly seek His countenance (*Psalms* 105:3-4).

One might ask, "Why should I try to seek God? He is infinitely great, and so totally beyond human grasp that the search to understand Him is all in vain. Is it not senseless to exhaust oneself in an effort that is doomed to failure from its very outset?"

Rabbi Simcha Zissel of Kelm states that the above verses are the Psalmist's reply to this question. Spiritual quests are qualitatively different from physical ones. In worldly matters, a quest is futile if one finds nothing, and the disappointment is frustrating. Not so in one's search for God, wherein the search itself brings joy, for the very inquiry elevates the searcher.

Indeed, the Psalmist urges us never to cease the search, because the promise of joy in searching is contingent upon its continuity. One cannot stop midway, abandon the effort, and retire with one's winnings. Abandoning the search for God at any point brings a person back to square one. To achieve the joy in searching, it must be בַּקְּשׁוּ פָנָיו תָּמִיד, *constantly seek His countenance.*

This thought was also expressed by the Rabbi of Kotzk, on the verse, *And from there you shall seek your God, and you shall find Him, if you seek Him with all your heart and soul (Deuteronomy* 4:29). The Kotzker interpreted the verse to mean that the seeking *is* the finding; "you shall find Him *if* you seek . . ." — but only if it is a lifelong quest, with all one's heart and soul.

NOTES

Today I shall . . .

. . . try to find God everywhere in the universe. I will study Torah literature to help me in this search.

הִנֵּה זֶה עוֹמֵד אַחַר כָּתְלֵנוּ מַשְׁגִּיחַ מִן *From the*
הַחַלּוֹנוֹת מֵצִיץ מִן הַחֲרַכִּים *Scriptures*

Behold, He stands behind our walls, looking through the windows, and peering through the lattices (*Song of Songs* 2:9).

Oct. 25, 1992
Oct. 13, 1993
Oct. 3, 1994
Oct. 22, 1995
Oct. 11, 1996
Oct. 29, 1997

"Whether God watches through the windows or through the lattices," said Rabbi Yisrael of Salant, "God watches over us. The difference is that sometimes it is through a window, and then we can see Him just as He sees us. At other times, it is through a crack in the partition, where He can see us, but we do not see Him."

Both in the history of the nation and in our personal lives, there have been times when Divine intervention was manifest. There have also been times when we were in great distress and felt abandoned, but even then, though God seemed to be absent, He was watching over us. The Torah foretold that there would be times of anguish when we would feel that God is not among us. At such times we must strengthen our faith and declare, "Behold, the Keeper of Israel does not sleep nor slumber."

Commenting on the verse, *He does great marvels alone* (*Psalms* 136:4), our Sages tell us that "alone" means that only God is aware of some of the miracles He performs for us, because we are unable to recognize them as such. Those who failed to see the protective hand of God when the Iraqis rained scuds on Israel were morally and psychologically blind; anyone should have been aware of God's protection. But even when His intervention is less evident, we must know that He watches over us, albeit "through cracks in the lattices."

NOTES

Today I shall . . .

. . . try to reinforce my faith in the everpresent watchfulness of God over Israel as a whole, and over me as an individual.

*Erev Rosh
Chodesh*
*[Eve of the
New Month]*
Oct. 26, 1992
Oct. 14, 1993
Oct. 4, 1994
Oct. 23, 1995
Oct. 12, 1996
Oct. 30, 1997

*From
our
Prayers*

הַשְׁכִּיבֵנוּ ה' אֱלֹקֵינוּ לְשָׁלוֹם וְהַעֲמִידֵנוּ מַלְכֵּנוּ לְחַיִּים וּלְשָׁלוֹם

Cause us to lie down, HASHEM, our God, in peace, and cause us to rise up again to life and peace (*Siddur*).

I once asked a recovered alcoholic with many years of sobriety to share his experiences with a newcomer who was unable to understand how, after so many years of dependence on alcohol, someone under stress could avoid recourse to drink.

"It's simple," the veteran said. "Every morning when I get up, I ask God to help me stay sober one more day. Every night when I retire, I thank Him for having given me another day of sobriety, and hope that He will do the same for me tomorrow."

The novice listened in partial disbelief. "How do you know it was God that gave you the day of sobriety?" he asked.

The old-timer responded, "How stupid can you get? I hadn't asked anyone else!"

It is amazing how we sometimes complicate things that are quite simple.

Each night we entrust our weary soul to God, and each morning He not only returns it to us, but gives it to us in a refreshed state. Indeed, if we ask Him sincerely to cleanse it for us by removing the sins that stained it during the day, we can be assured that this request too will be granted, as long as it is sincere — because an honest request constitutes *teshuvah*, and the combination of repentance and faith is certain to earn us forgiveness.

NOTES

Today I shall . . .

. . . try to realize that each day of life is a Divine gift, and that I have the means of starting each day with a soul cleansed by God.

כָּל הַנְּגָעִים אָדָם רוֹאֶה חוּץ מִנְּגְעֵי עַצְמוֹ *From*

A person can see all lesions, except for *the* his own (*Negaim* 2:5). *Sages*

First day of
Rosh Chodesh
Cheshvan

Oct. 27, 1992
Oct. 15, 1993
Oct. 5, 1994
Oct. 24, 1995
Oct. 13, 1996
Oct. 31, 1997

The above Talmudic law refers to the particular kinds of lesions that must be examined by a *Kohen* (priest) to determine whether they are ritually clean or contaminated. The Talmud states that a *Kohen* is not eligible to pass judgment on lesions affecting his own person, since he cannot have the necessary objectivity where he is involved.

This statement has been interpreted homiletically to mean that a person is capable of recognizing all defects except his own; a person will tend to deny his *own* faults, although he will easily recognize similar flaws in others.

The Baal Shem Tov gave this statement yet another profound interpretation simply by moving the comma ahead by one word. In his formulation, the statement reads, "A person can see all defects on the *outside*, [if they are like] his own." We see in others only the sort of defects that exist in ourselves. The Baal Shem Tov taught that whenever we find fault with another person, we should analyze *ourselves* carefully to discover where that same fault exists within ourselves. We will deny it vehemently, and project it onto others.

The Talmudic commentaries anticipated modern psychological discoveries by many centuries. "Denial" and "projection" go hand in hand to focus on others and prevent us from making the necessary improvements in our character.

NOTES

Today I shall . . .

. . . try to do a personal inventory, to seek out where I might have those faults that I identify in others, and make an effort to correct them.

**Second Day of
Rosh Chodesh
Cheshvan**

Oct. 28, 1992
Oct. 16, 1993
Oct. 6, 1994
Oct. 25, 1995
Oct. 14, 1996
Nov. 1, 1997

*From the
Scriptures*

וַיֹּאמֶר ה' לְנֹחַ בֹּא . . . אֶל הַתֵּבָה

God said to Noah, "Enter . . . into the ark" (*Genesis* 7:1).

The Hebrew word for ark, *teivah*, has two meanings: it can mean "an ark," and it can also mean "a word." In the above verse, the latter meaning tells us that God instructed Noah to "enter into the word." Rabbi Moshe of Kobrin expounded on this theme, explaining that when we pray, we should "enter into the words," i.e. totally immerse ourselves into each word of prayer, as though the word is encompassing us.

A listener once asked him: "How can a big human being possibly enter into a little word?" Rabbi Moshe answered, "People who consider themselves bigger than the word are not the kind of person we are talking about."

The Talmud states that people's prayers are not accepted unless they efface themselves before God (*Sotah* 5a). God abhors those who are egotistical, and therefore the prayers of a vain person are not likely to be received favorably.

People preoccupied with their egos remain external to their prayers. The truly humble person feels small enough to "enter" even the tiniest word.

NOTES

Today I shall . . .

. . . try to throw myself entirely into my prayers by setting aside those thoughts and feelings that would inflate my ego.

לֹא תַגּוּרוּ . . . לֹא תַכִּירוּ פָנִים בַּמִּשְׁפָּט *From the*
מִפְּנֵי אִישׁ *Scriptures*

Do not show favoritism in judgment
... fear no person (*Deuteronomy*
1:17).

Oct. 29, 1992
Oct. 17, 1993
Oct. 7, 1994
Oct. 26, 1995
Oct. 15, 1996
Nov. 2, 1997

Rabbi Yaakov of Lisa summoned one of his town's wealthiest citizens, a pillar of the community, to appear before him in a rabbinic court. When the man ignored the summons for the third time, Rabbi Yaakov notified him that unless he complied at once, he would feel the full wrath of the court.

The man came to the rabbi and sharply rebuked him. "You should be aware, Rabbi," he said, "that I was the one who was instrumental in your getting the position as rabbi of this community. This is not how I expected to be repaid."

Without a word, Rabbi Yaakov left his study, packed his and his family's belongings, and they all left town. Rabbi Yaakov later explained that the man had not intimidated him, but he may have caused him to be unconsciously biased and he might not be completely objective in his case. Furthermore, if his judgment would have been in this man's favor, he might have been suspected of favoritism.

When we bring a dispute before a judge, we should value truth sufficiently to avoid using personal influence which might undermine a just decision.

NOTES

Today I shall ...

... try to keep myself rigorously honest by avoiding the urge to tilt the truth to my interests.

Oct. 30, 1992
Oct. 18, 1993
Oct. 8, 1994
Oct. 27, 1995
Oct. 16, 1996
Nov. 3, 1997

*From the
Scriptures*

אַל תִּלְחַם אֶת לֶחֶם רַע עָיִן

Do not partake of the bread of one who is miserly (*Proverbs* 23:6).

Yankel was known for his extreme miserliness. When he came to *shul* one day and announced that his wife had given birth to a son, his face was less than glowing with happiness. When asked why, he admitted: "Well, a baby boy requires a *bris,* and a *bris* requires refreshments, and those cost money."

"You say 'refreshments,' Yankel?" his friend, Boruch, said. "Why, Yankel, for a *bris* you must serve a whole feast! And I'll tell you something, Yankel. You will have to provide even more food than someone else, because it's a known fact that when the host does not *fargin* (i.e. he is stingy), the guests eat twice as much!"

Poor Yankel had no choice but to comply with custom. He reluctantly prepared a meal for the *bris.* During the meal, painfully watching everyone eat with much gusto, he ran to Boruch and said, "Help. Boruch, help! I'm *farginning* (not being stingy), but they're still eating twice as much anyway!"

We must be cautious not to let our emotions deceive us. If we have undesirable feelings, we should not make believe that they do not exist, but we should try to correct them. Self-deception can result only in absurd contradictions, such as Yankel's assertion that he really was being generous.

NOTES

Today I shall . . .

. . . try to examine my feelings and perhaps ask someone else to help me evaluate them, lest I deceive myself.

וִיהְיוּ דְבָרַי אֵלֶּה אֲשֶׁר הִתְחַנַּנְתִּי לִפְנֵי ה' קְרֹבִים אֶל ה' אֱלֹקֵינוּ יוֹמָם וָלָיְלָה לַעֲשׂוֹת מִשְׁפַּט עַבְדּוֹ וּמִשְׁפַּט עַמּוֹ יִשְׂרָאֵל דְּבַר יוֹם בְּיוֹמוֹ

From our Prayers

May these words that I have prayed before God be close to God day and night, that He may do justice for His servant and for His people Israel, the needs of each day on that day (*Siddur*).

Oct. 31, 1992
Oct. 19, 1993
Oct. 9, 1994
Oct. 28, 1995
Oct. 17, 1996
Nov. 4, 1997

When people lift heavy loads, they are likely to develop severe back pain. When they realize that they are overtaxing their bodies, they discontinue this practice and from then on will lift only as much as their bodies can safely bear.

While we can easily determine our body's stress capacity, our psychological and emotional stress tolerance is not so readily measurable. Yet, if we exceed that stress level, symptoms of discomfort and dysfunction are just as apt to occur as when the body's level is exceeded. How is one to determine one's safe emotional and psychological stress level?

What could be simpler than following the instruction book provided by the Manufacturer?

During the Israelites' sojourn in the desert, the manna was provided in portions just sufficient for one day, and any excess rotted away.

As for what they would eat the next day, the Israelites had been assured that there would be fresh manna the following day. Our appropriate stress tolerance is to be concerned for just one day — twenty-four hours. If we take on more than that, we may be overburdening the system. In our economy, lacking the miraculous manna and having the ability to save for the future, there may be justification for putting something aside for a rainy day. However, we often take on worries far in advance, about things that we are powerless to alter or to prepare for today. Such futile worry is harmful to a person.

NOTES

Today I shall . . .

. . . try to concentrate on my present needs and avoid worrying about things that are not within my capacity to change.

Nov. 1, 1992
Oct. 20, 1993
Oct. 10, 1994
Oct. 29, 1995
Oct. 18, 1996
Nov. 5, 1997

From the Scriptures

בֶּן שָׁנָה שָׁאוּל בְּמָלְכוֹ

hen Saul was king for one year . . .
(*I Samuel* 13:1).

The literal translation of this verse is, "Saul was one year old when he became king." The Talmud explains that Scripture uses this wording to convey that when Saul assumed the throne, he was as free of sin as a one-year-old child.

People grow wiser as they mature, but some features of childhood should not be abandoned. Rabbi Shlomo Luria stated that when he recited the *Shema*, he could have meditated upon the profound hidden meanings and esoteric combinations of the Divine Name. He instead concentrated on the simplest meanings of the words, just as a small child would who knows only the literal translation, "Hear, O Israel, our God is Lord, our God is One."

God created man simple, but man made complex calculations (*Ecclesiastes* 7:29). The problems of life need not be anywhere near as complicated as we make them. In matters of faith and in following instructions, we would benefit greatly if we used childlike simplicity, trusting in the superior wisdom of our Father and doing what we are told instead of trying to analyze everything.

NOTES

_____
_____
_____
_____
_____
_____
_____
_____
_____
_____

Today I shall . . .

. . . try to keep things as simple as possible, and allow myself to be taught and guided by those wiser than myself.

וַיֵּרָא ה' אֶל אַבְרָם וַיֹּאמֶר אֵלָיו אֲנִי קֵל *From the*
שַׁקַּי הִתְהַלֵּךְ לְפָנַי וֶהְיֵה תָמִים *Scriptures*

God appeared to Abram and said to him, "I am Almighty God. Walk before Me and be perfect" (*Genesis* 17:1).

Nov. 2, 1992
Oct. 21, 1993
Oct. 11, 1994
Oct. 30, 1995
Oct. 19, 1996
Nov. 6, 1997

If a human being cannot be perfect, why did God demand perfection of Abraham?

The entire context of the verse indicates both the definition of this perfection and the way in which it can be achieved. It is obvious that no human being can aspire to equal God's degree of perfection. What man *can* achieve is to live according to God's teachings and thereby live up to his own *human* potential; more than man's personal maximum is not possible or expected. Thus, God did not say simply, "Be perfect"; He said, "Walk before Me — and *thereby* you will be perfect." When a person tries to live according to the Divine teachings, that constitutes human perfection, although one is technically never perfect.

Rabbi Samson Raphael Hirsch notes that the Hebrew word for "walk" in the above verse is not תֵּלֵךְ, but הִתְהַלֵּךְ, which implies, "Go your way in spite of opposition, not making your progress dependent on external circumstances, but being led from within yourself: Let your movement proceed from your own free-willed decisions."

The picture is now complete; human perfection can be achieved by making a free-willed choice to live according to the Divine teaching.

NOTES

Today I shall . . .

. . . try to realize that although I cannot be absolutely without flaw, I can be perfect if I make free-will decisions to obey the Divine will.

Nov. 3, 1992
Oct. 22, 1993
Oct. 12, 1994
Oct. 31, 1995
Oct. 20, 1996
Nov. 7, 1997

*From the
Scriptures*

וְאָהַבְתָּ אֵת ה' אֱלֹקֶיךָ . . .
וְאָהַבְתָּ לְרֵעֲךָ כָּמוֹךָ . . .

And you shall love Hashem your God
. . . (*Deuteronomy* 6:5)

And you shall love your neighbor as
yourself. . . (*Leviticus* 19:18).

Both of these statements are positive commandments. We might ask: How can a commandment demand that we *feel* something? Since love is an emotion, it is either there or it is not there.

The Torah does not hold that love is something spontaneous. On the contrary, it teaches that we can and should cultivate love. No one has the liberty to say: "There are some people whom I just do not like," nor even, "I cannot possibly like that person because he did this and that to me."

We have within us innate attractions to God and to other people. If we do not feel love for either of them, it is because we have permitted barriers to develop that interfere with this natural attraction, much as insulation can block a magnet's inherent attraction for iron. If we remove the barriers, the love will be forthcoming.

The barriers inside us come from defects in our character. When we improve ourselves, our bad character traits fall away, and as they fall away, we begin to sense that natural love which we have for others and for God.

NOTES

Today I shall . . .

. . . try to improve my *midos* (character traits), so that I will be able to feel love for God and for my fellow man.

בַּמָּרוֹם יְלַמְּדוּ עֲלֵיהֶם וְעָלֵינוּ זְכוּת . . . וְנִמְצָא
חֵן וְשֵׂכֶל טוֹב בְּעֵינֵי אֱלֹקִים וְאָדָם

From our Prayers

From on high may they plead merit for them (our hosts) and for us . . . and may we find favor and understanding in the eyes of God and man (*Grace After Meals*).

Nov. 4, 1992
Oct. 23, 1993
Oct. 13, 1994
Nov. 1, 1995
Oct. 21, 1996
Nov. 8, 1997

We all wish to be liked and appreciated. What is the best road to popularity?

Some people are "people pleasers." They do things for others to earn their favor and affection. While it is certainly commendable to do things for others, "buying" their affection should not be the motivation. Furthermore, there are times when we are not able to fulfill a particular request that someone may make of us. If we force ourselves because we are afraid that our refusal may result in losing the other person's friendship, we may resent what we do. This process is counterproductive; doing acts of kindness should not result in resentment.

All we need to be liked and appreciated is to have a sincere attitude of caring for others. A benevolent attitude will translate itself into benevolent deeds. This "intangible" will be felt by other people, even when we are unable to do anything for them.

In the above prayer, we ask God to bless our hosts and to consider them meritorious. Showing this benevolent attitude is sufficient for us to find favor in the eyes of both God and others.

NOTES

_____
_____
_____
_____
_____
_____
_____

Today I shall . . .

. . . try to cultivate feelings of sincere concern for others, and pray for their well-being just as I pray for my own.

Nov. 5, 1992
Oct. 24, 1993
Oct. 14, 1994
Nov. 2, 1995
Oct. 22, 1996
Nov. 9, 1997

From our Prayers

אֲנִי מַאֲמִין בֶּאֱמוּנָה שְׁלֵמָה . . .

I believe with perfect faith that . . . (*Siddur*).

There are Thirteen Principles of Faith whose absolute certainty we declare after the morning services. These are the *only* principles of absolute certainty. Everything else is subject to doubt. If there were anything else of absolute certainty, there would be fourteen principles.

Rabbi Issachar of Wolborz told his followers that the soul of a departed person had once come to him and stated that he was destitute and needed money for his daughter's wedding.

"But you are no longer alive," the Rabbi said to the soul, "and you have no need for money." The soul refused to believe him.

"How pathetic," the Rabbi said. "There are souls who are not privileged to enter *Gehinnom* (perdition) to undergo the cleansing process that will qualify them for *Gan Eden* (paradise). These lost souls may wander for years in a fantasy world, believing they are still alive."*

One follower asked, "How can we be sure that we are indeed living? Perhaps we too are in this fantasy world now, but are under the delusion that we are still alive."

The Rabbi answered, "People who consider it a possibility that they *may be* delusional are *not* delusional. Psychotics do not think for a single moment that they may be hallucinating."

The Thirteen Principles of Faith are axioms. With the exception of these, we should always be ready to examine our convictions, regardless of how strongly we may feel about them. It is when we are absolutely certain that we are right and have no doubt whatever about the validity of our opinions that we are most likely to be in error.

NOTES

* In Kabbalah there is a concept of a "world of emptiness" where souls may dwell until they are cleansed.

Today I shall . . .

. . . try to keep an open mind and be willing to listen to opinions other than my own.

הַחַיִּים וְהַמָּוֶת נָתַתִּי לְפָנֶיךָ . . . וּבָחַרְתָּ *From the*
בַּחַיִּים *Scriptures*

I have placed before you life and
death. . .and you shall choose life
(*Deuteronomy* 30:19).

Nov. 6, 1992
Oct. 25, 1993
Oct. 15, 1994
Nov.3, 1995
Oct. 23, 1996
Nov. 10, 1997

How can a lobster grow? After all, its shell is rigid and cannot expand.

When the lobster feels itself compressed within its shell, it retreats to a crevice in one of the underwater rock formations, sheds its shell, and grows a new one. When it outgrows this shell, it repeats the process and continues doing so until it reaches its maximum size.

During the stage when it is without its shell, the lobster is in great danger. A predatory fish may eat it, or a strong current may dash it against a rock. In order to grow, the lobster must risk its very life.

It is impossible to achieve success without risking failure; sometimes life can only be lived by risking death. Since life consists of growth and progress, we must learn to live with risk.

People for whom failure is devastating may never try anything. They will never grow.

The greatest failure of all is the failure to grow and to maximize one's potential. This passive failure is even more serious than active failure.

We must develop sufficient courage and self-confidence to not retreat from taking risks (though reasonable ones) in order to progress.

NOTES

Today I shall . . .

. . . try to increase my feelings of self-worth so that I may be able to accept new challenges without the fear that any failure would destroy me.

GROWING EACH DAY / **41**

Nov. 7, 1992
Oct. 26, 1993
Oct. 16, 1994
Nov. 4, 1995
Oct. 24, 1996
Nov. 11, 1997

From the Scriptures

הַלְלוּ אֶת ה' מִן הַשָּׁמַיִם . . . הַלְלוּ אֶת ה'
מִן הָאָרֶץ

Let the praises of God come from the heavens . . . let the praises of God come from the earth (*Psalms* 148:1,7).

The Scriptures have many references to seeing the presence of God in everything in the world. Psalm 104, for example, is a beautiful song of nature, which recounts God's presence in all His works. As we are swept along by the exquisite poetry of the psalm, we can actually sense how this realization culminated in David's declaration, *How many are Your works, O God. You have fashioned them all with wisdom* (104:24).

Today, more than ever, people have been privileged to see the marvels of Divine wisdom. Thanks to the marvels of electronic technology, we can see the Divine engineering in the structure of a blade of grass, in the function of a cell of protoplasm, in the complex structure of the atom, and in the awesome composition of super galaxies.

It is wrong to live in a world that testifies to the omnipresence of God and not acknowledge it. This is one reason we have not only daily prayers, but also blessings for so many things. Everything with which we come in contact is a testimony to God as Creator.

NOTES

_____
_____
_____
_____
_____
_____
_____
_____
_____

Today I shall . . .

. . . try to be more aware of the omnipresence of God, and to be attentive to the marvels of nature that testify to His infinite wisdom.

אַשְׁרֵי אִישׁ יָרֵא אֶת ה' בְּמִצְוֹתָיו חָפֵץ מְאֹד *From the*
Fortunate is the person who fears *Scriptures*
God, and has a great desire for His
mitzvos (*Psalms* 112:1).

Nov. 8, 1992
Oct. 27, 1993
Oct. 17, 1994
Nov. 5, 1995
Oct. 25, 1996
Nov. 12, 1997

We think of fear as a negative emotion, so we try to
eliminate it. We therefore lose sight of the fact that fear can
also be constructive. Fear motivates us to drive cautiously
even when in a great hurry, and fear makes a diabetic
adhere to his diet and take his insulin daily.

Religion has often been criticized for advocating the fear
of God. This criticism may be justified if we were
conditioned to think of Him as an all-powerful Being
holding a huge club, ready to beat a sinner to a pulp for
doing something wrong. All ethical works discourage the
use of this type of fear as motivation. Rather, fear of God
should be understood to mean the fear of the harmful
consequences that are inherent in violating His instructions. The Psalmist says that wickedness itself destroys the
wicked person (see *Psalms* 34:22).

"Fortunate is the person who fears God," in the sense
that "he has great desire for His *mitzvos*" (*Psalms* 112:1). It
is only natural for one to desire the very best, and the
realization that observing the *mitzvos* is indeed in one's
best interest should constitute the "fear" that should deter
someone from transgressing the Divine will.

NOTES

Today I shall . . .

. . . try to realize that observance of the *mitzvos* is in my
best interest, and that I should fear transgressing the
mitzvos in the same way I fear any injurious act.

Nov. 9, 1992
Oct. 28, 1993
Oct. 18, 1994
Nov. 6, 1995
Oct. 26, 1996
Nov. 13, 1997

From the
Scriptures

ה' מִי יָגוּר בְּאָהֳלֶךְ מִי יִשְׁכֹּן בְּהַר קָדְשֶׁךְ
. . . דֹּבֵר אֱמֶת בִּלְבָבוֹ . . . נִשְׁבַּע לְהָרַע
וְלֹא יָמֵר

O, God, who will dwell in Your tabernacle, who will rest on Your holy mountain? . . . One who speaks the truth in his heart . . . who swears to his own hurt but will not retract (*Psalms* 15:1-4).

In their mind's eye, people believe that they are acting as truthfully as possible. We all know, however, how easily we can deceive ourselves. Since truth may be elusive, how then can we know that we have the truth?

There is a useful litmus test. We can know that we have the truth when we have the courage to feel the pain of accepting the truth. People lie because they think the lie will be less painful or costly for them than the truth.

People often fail to grow because they are reluctant to face the painful truth that they have done wrong. We have an innate tendency to avoid pain, and therefore we are apt to conjure up rationalizations that justify our behavior. These rationalizations are nothing but lies — sometimes clever and convincing, but lies nonetheless. Facing the truth and accepting the pain that comes with it requires courage.

People who "speak the truth in their heart," says the Psalmist, do not retract their word even if it is to their own hurt. On the other hand, those who constantly seek to change everything to conform to their maximum comfort are only lying to themselves.

NOTES

Today I shall . . .

. . . try to be courageous and not automatically withdraw from everything that is painful. I shall try to examine my actions to make sure I am not sacrificing truth for comfort.

שְׁלֹשָׁה חַיֵּיהֶן אֵינָם חַיִּים. הָרַחְמָנִין *From the*
וְהַרַתְחָנִין וַאֲנִינֵי הַדַּעַת *Scriptures*

Three types of people live an unlivable life: those who are overly compassionate, overly irritable, or overly
sensitive (*Pesachim* 113b).

Nov. 10, 1992
Oct. 29, 1993
Oct. 19, 1994
Nov. 7, 1995
Oct. 27, 1996
Nov. 14, 1997

Why is being overly sensitive so unlivable? If we sustain
a severe sunburn, we avoid contact with other people,
because what would normally be a friendly pat on the back
or a gentle caress can cause exquisite pain.

Our emotions can become as overly sensitive as our
skin, and things which would otherwise be neutral, if not
pleasant, may be very painful. To avoid being hurt, we may
withdraw from human contact or set up other barriers to
communication.

The ego is the source for this touchiness. When people's
egos become inflated, they feel superior to others and
imagine that they deserve more recognition. No amount of
recognition is sufficient, however, and other people's
innocent comments or actions are misinterpreted as insults
or slights.

Unlike sunburnt skin, ego-burnt emotions are not easily
recognized. This lack of awareness may then cause these
poor people to think that others intend to harm them. Such
misinterpretations will make their lives unlivable.

NOTES

Today I shall . . .

. . . try to avoid reacting reflexively to painful experiences,
and try to understand that my discomfort may be due to my
sensitivity rather than to others' behavior.

Nov. 11, 1992
Oct. 30, 1993
Oct. 20, 1994
Nov. 8, 1995
Oct. 28, 1996
Nov. 15, 1997

From the Scriptures

דְּאָגָה בְלֶב אִישׁ יַשְׁחֶנָּה: יְשִׂיחֶנָּה לַאֲחֵרִים

If a person has a worry in his heart, let him relate it to others (*Proverbs* 12:25, *Yoma* 75a).

Many people are hesitant to share their painful feelings with others. They may not wish to burden others with their problems, or they may be too ashamed to reveal their thoughts and feelings. The Scriptures and Talmud advocate the value of ventilating problems.

Rabbi Elimelech of Lizensk stated: "One should regularly relate to one's mentor or to a trusted friend all the improper thoughts and feelings one has experienced . . . and this is an incomparable technique (for proper conduct)."

The value of sharing our troublesome thoughts, feelings, and actions with another person is inestimable. First, by not repressing our true feelings, we become more honest with ourselves. Second, by elucidating our problems with someone else, we may gain greater insight into them and even discover their solutions. Third, by considering our problem from a non-biased perspective, the listener can give an opinion far more objective than we could ever formulate on our own.

Rabbi Elimelech recommends that such sharing be done *regularly*. Troublesome thoughts and feelings should not be allowed to accumulate. Not only can they add up to become overwhelming, they can also fester, become even more serious, and therefore be more difficult to eliminate.

NOTES

Today I shall . . .

. . . find someone whom I can trust with my most private thoughts and feelings, and relieve myself of the burdensome baggage I have been carrying.

חַסְדֵי ה׳ כִּי לֹא תָמְנוּ כִּי לֹא כָלוּ רַחֲמָיו *From the*
It is a Divine kindness that His mer- *Scriptures*
cies are endless (*Lamentations* 3:22).

Another way to translate this verse is, "It is a Divine kindness that *we* are never finished."

The Maggid of Koznitz was extremely frail and sickly as a child. It was not thought that he would survive to adulthood. Much of his life was spent sick in bed, and he was so weak that he was often unable to sit up to meet visitors. Still, he lived to an advanced age.

Nov. 12, 1992
Oct. 31, 1993
Oct. 21, 1994
Nov. 9, 1995
Oct. 29, 1996
Nov. 16, 1997

The Maggid once revealed the secret of his longevity. "I never allowed myself to be without an assignment or a task to perform," he said. "People are taken from this world only when their missions here are completed. Whenever I was just about to finish one task, I would start another; hence, I could not be removed from this world if my assignment was not completed."

Even from a purely physiological aspect, the Maggid's concept is valid. Some think that the healthiest thing for us is rest and relaxation. Not so. In reality, unused muscles tend to atrophy, while muscles that are exercised and stimulated are strengthened.

The same principle applies to the entire person. If we constantly stimulate ourselves to achieve new goals, we avoid the apathy that leads to atrophy.

NOTES

Today I shall . . .

. . . try to take on a new spiritual goal, and stimulate myself to greater achievement in serving God and being of help to other people.

Nov. 13, 1992
Nov. 1, 1993
Oct. 22, 1994
Nov. 10, 1995
Oct. 30, 1996
Nov. 17, 1997

From our Prayers

הָרַחֲמָן הוּא יִשְׁבּוֹר עֻלֵּנוּ מֵעַל צַוָּארֵנוּ וְהוּא קוֹמְמִיּוּת לְאַרְצֵנוּ

May the Merciful One lift the yoke of exile from our necks and lead us upright to our land (*Grace After Meals*).

Rabbi Naftali of Ropschitz related that a Russian czar was inspecting his troops on the front lines, when one enemy soldier took aim at him. A brave Russian soldier threw himself at the czar, pushed him out of the line of fire, and thereby saved his life. The grateful czar told the soldier that he would reward him by granting any request he made. The soldier complained that his sergeant was very cruel to him, and asked the czar to order the sergeant to treat him more kindly.

"You fool!" the czar responded. "You should have asked to be made a senior officer, and then the sergeant would have to take orders from *you!*"

Rabbi Naftali commented that we come before God with a variety of petty requests, forgetting that the single request we should be making is to be returned to our homeland and to the glory of old, and then all our other requests would be fulfilled.

As we thank God for our food and ask Him to continue to provide for us, we are reminded not to be as foolish as the soldier, but rather to make the most important request of all — that we be returned to the position of favor in the eyes of God.

NOTES

Today I shall . . .

. . . try to remember that our greatest need is that we be what which we were chosen to be — a kingdom of priests and a sacred nation.

מִפְּנֵי שֵׂיבָה תָּקוּם וְהָדַרְתָּ פְּנֵי זָקֵן *From the* **A**rise before an aged person, and give *Scriptures* honor to one mature in wisdom (*Leviticus* 19:32).

Nov. 14, 1992
Nov. 2, 1993
Oct. 23, 1994
Nov. 11, 1995
Oct. 31, 1996
Nov. 18, 1997

Although they are basically God-fearing and wish to do what is right, many people have not succeeded in the struggle to overcome their temptations. In judging their shortcomings, however, it is important to evaluate their underlying attitude — do they truly respect the proper course of action and those who are more successful than they in having it?

Rabbi Levi Yitzchok of Berdichev told of a general who lost an important battle. His king replaced him as commander. Now that the deposed general was vulnerable, his enemies accused him of treason, claiming that he had intentionally lost the battle. When the new commander, who subsequently was victorious, was honored for his triumph, the first general genuinely rejoiced at his successor's celebration. The king then dismissed the treason charges. "Had he been disloyal, he would not have celebrated his successor's victory. That he did so proves that his defeat was simply due to his lack of ability, and not to treason."

Similarly, said Rabbi Levi Yitzchok, even if one is lax in full observance of the *mitzvos*, the fact that one honors those who *do* observe the *mitzvos* indicates that one's intentions are good, but that one has just not been strong enough to resist temptation. The desire to do good, however, is likely to predominate ultimately."

By honoring *talmidei chachamim* (Torah scholars), one indicates the desire to do the will of God.

NOTES

Today I shall . . .

. . . show my respect for those who are more learned and more committed to Torah observance than I am.

Nov. 15, 1992
Nov. 3, 1993
Oct. 24, 1994
Nov. 12, 1995
Nov. 1, 1996
Nov. 19, 1997

*From the
Scriptures*

הוֹכֵחַ תּוֹכִיחַ אֶת עֲמִיתֶךָ

Y̶ou shall rebuke your friend (*Leviticus* 19:17).

A famous *maggid* (preacher) once visited Rabbi Chaim of Sanz. Rabbi Chaim complained to him that since he was a Rebbe, a leader, no one ever rebuked him for anything. He asked the *maggid* to please tell him where he could improve himself.

The *maggid* remarked that he was surprised that Rabbi Chaim's house did not have the requisite square cubit of unfinished wall space that one is to leave as a reminder of the ruin of the Temple. Rabbi Chaim promptly arose and scraped the paint off an area of the wall, deeply thanking the *maggid* for calling his attention to this delinquency.

We are often unable to see our own faults. Still, most people dislike rebuke. Even if they are not frankly offended by someone else pointing out their imperfections, they are rarely grateful for being reprimanded. Knowing that we might react defensively, people who note our mistakes and are in a position to rebuke us will be reluctant to provoke us. We should actively encourage them, as Rabbi Chaim did, for we can learn from their observations, eliminate our character defects, and thereby better ourselves.

NOTES

Today I shall . . .

. . . try to encourage others to tell me what I might be doing that they consider wrong, and be sincerely grateful to anyone who provides constructive criticism.

מִי הָאִישׁ הֶחָפֵץ חַיִּים אֹהֵב יָמִים לִרְאוֹת *From the* טוֹב. נְצֹר לְשׁוֹנְךָ מֵרָע וּשְׂפָתֶיךָ מִדַּבֵּר *Scriptures* מִרְמָה

Who is the person who desires life and loves days to see good? Guard your tongue from evil and your lips from deceitful speech (*Psalms* 34:13-14).

Nov. 16, 1992
Nov. 4, 1993
Oct. 25, 1994
Nov. 13, 1995
Nov. 2, 1996
Nov. 20, 1997

Who would be so foolish as not to desire life and days to see good? Yet, we may forfeit something so desirable and precious by abusing the gift of speech, by speaking gossip or slander, or by lying.

Resolving to not lie or speak evil is not enough; we must always be on constant guard. In this case, the best guard is a fence. We put fences around our homes and properties because we wish to protect them from damage that may come from unsuspected sources. Likewise, to avoid gossip, slander, or lies, we must set up protective "fences" to avoid such an occurrence, as for example, avoiding associating with gossipers, and pausing to think before we talk about another person.

Lashon hara is not only a grievous sin, but actually defiles our speech, thus devaluating the words we utter in prayer and Torah study. Just think how revolting it would be if someone served you the finest delicacies in filthy utensils! The precious words of Torah study and prayer that we bring before God should not be contaminated by delivering them through a vehicle of speech that has been soiled by *lashon hara*.

NOTES

Today I shall . . .

. . . try to be on the alert not to speak an untruth, not to gossip or tattletale, and not to speak disparagingly about another person.

Nov. 17, 1992
Nov. 5, 1993
Oct. 26, 1994
Nov. 14, 1995
Nov. 3, 1996
Nov. 21, 1997

From the Scriptures

שִׁוִּיתִי ה' לְנֶגְדִּי תָמִיד

I have set God always before me (*Psalms* 16:8).

Late one night, Rabbi Naftali of Ropschitz took a walk in the outskirts of town, where he met a night watchman and struck up a conversation with him. The watchman assumed that Rabbi Naftali was also a guard and, not recognizing him as one of the regular group, asked him, "For whom are you on duty?"

Rabbi Naftali was taken aback. He realized that while he was engaged in light conversation, his thoughts had momentarily deviated from the awareness of the presence of God and the need to concentrate always on serving Him. In the watchman's question "For whom are you on duty?", the Rabbi detected a reminder that he should get back on track. *Tzaddikim* consider themselves constantly duty bound, like a sentry charged with protecting the lives of comrades. Even a brief lapse of alertness constitutes gross negligence.

Many people think that God is served only during prayer and Torah study, or while performing *mitzvos*. The very first paragraph of the *Shulchan Aruch* contains the verse cited above and explains that a person's behavior should be regulated by the awareness that one is always in God's presence and under Divine vigilance. Such constant awareness will assure that every action, great or small, will conform to the Divine will.

NOTES

Today I shall . . .

. . . try to maintain a constant awareness that I am in the presence of God, and that I may not, at any time, do something that would displease Him.

שֶׁקֶר שָׂנֵאתִי וָאֲתַעֵבָה תּוֹרָתְךָ אָהָבְתִּי *From the*
I despise falsehood and I abhor it; it is *Scriptures*
Your Torah that I love (*Psalms*
119:163).

Nov. 18, 1992
Nov. 6, 1993
Oct. 27, 1994
Nov. 15, 1995
Nov. 4, 1996
Nov. 22, 1997

Although we may condemn falsehood and champion truth, many of us are not beyond stretching the truth a bit when circumstances appear to warrant it. It is after all very easy to rationalize and to justify a white lie. On the other hand, some things are so repulsive and disgusting that we instinctively avoid them. We feel revolted by the very thought of coming into contact with something grossly polluted, and no amount of cajoling from anyone would help us overcome this revulsion.

True love of truth requires that we not only avoid evil, but that we despise it. *Those who love God should despise evil*, says the Psalmist (97:10), and in the verse cited above, King David goes one step further. The hatred of falsehood and evil should be so intense and profound that the very thought of them is abhorrent; we should instinctively reject them in the same manner that we shun something so foul that it contaminates anyone who touches it.

We may think that we possess true love of truth, but the litmus test is how much we despise falsehood. Unless falsehood automatically repels us, we have not yet achieved true love of Torah.

Today I shall . . .

. . . try to intensify my dislike for anything false, to the point that lying and deceit become physical impossibilities for me.

NOTES

Nov. 19, 1992
Nov. 7, 1993
Oct. 28, 1994
Nov. 16, 1995
Nov. 5, 1996
Nov. 23, 1997

From the Scriptures כִּי קָרוֹב אֵלֶיךָ הַדָּבָר מְאֹד בְּפִיךָ וּבִלְבָבְךָ לַעֲשֹׂתוֹ

For this thing (observance of the mitzvos) is extremely close to you, in your mouth and in your heart to do it (*Deuteronomy* 30:14).

Given the 365 restrictions and prohibitions of the Torah and the demand for performance of 248 *mitzvos*, how can Moses say that it is not only easy to observe, but that it is *extremely* close to you; i.e. extremely easy to do?

The answer lies in one simple word that is repeated no less than fourteen times in this short (forty-verse) portion of the Torah: "Today." Moreover, the word appears superfluous; every verse could read just as well without it. The Torah must be telling us that if we concentrate on today's challenges and leave tomorrow's for tomorrow, then this challenge is extremely easy to accomplish.

I have seen this message in my own work. When people who have abused alcohol for decades come for treatment of their alcoholism, they can be extremely frightened by the prospect that they will never again be able to take a drink. Giving up alcohol for life appears to be virtually impossible. The method that works best in overcoming alcoholism is that advocated by Alcoholics Anonymous: since you can do nothing today about tomorrow's sobriety, don't worry today about how you will stay sober tomorrow. You will have ample opportunity to concern yourself tomorrow about tomorrow's challenge. Today, just take care of today.

NOTES

_____
_____
_____
_____
_____
_____
_____
_____
_____

Today I shall . . .

. . . try to concentrate on those things that are within my capacity to do today, and avoid worrying about challenges that are not within today's range of action.

יוֹתֵר מִמָּה שֶׁבַּעַל הַבַּיִת עוֹשֶׂה עִם הֶעָנִי, הֶעָנִי *From*
עוֹשֶׂה עִם בַּעַל הַבַּיִת *the*

What the recipient of alms does for the *Sages*
donor is greater than what the donor
does for the recipient (*Vayikra Rabbah* 34:8).

Nov. 20, 1992
Nov. 8, 1993
Oct. 29, 1994
Nov. 17, 1995
Nov. 6, 1996
Nov. 24, 1997

Rabbi Yitzchok of Zidachov said, "Life consists of give
and take. Everyone must be a giver and a receiver. Those
who are not both are as a barren tree."

There is a charming Jewish custom: on *Erev* Yom Kippur
or on Hoshana Rabbah, people ask or "beg" for cake from
friends. The rationale is that just in case it was Divinely
decreed for someone to be a beggar, the begging for cake
will fulfill this decree, and so one would be free from such
a fate.

Another important reason for this custom could be that
giving is easy, because we can then feel magnanimous.
Still, it is crucial that we also empathize with the person
who needs assistance and realize how painful and degrading it is to beg and to depend on others. Only then will we
be able to take into consideration the feelings of those who
must ask for help and express our feelings by providing
words of comfort and encouragement along with the
material help. Lack of empathy when giving charity can lead
to arrogance.

We must realize that in some ways we are all takers, for
even in the very act of giving charity we take more than we
give.

NOTES

Today I shall . . .

. . . try to identify with people who ask for help and avoid
considering myself superior to those whom I offer help or
give charity.

CHESHVAN

25

חשון

Nov. 21, 1992
Nov. 9, 1993
Oct. 30, 1994
Nov. 18, 1995
Nov. 7, 1996
Nov. 25, 1997

From our Prayers

חַיִּים שֶׁיִּמָּלְאוּ מִשְׁאֲלוֹת לִבֵּנוּ לְטוֹבָה

May we have life in which God fulfills our hearts' desires for good (*Siddur*).

The followers of Rabbi Uri of Strelisk were all poor. When another Chassidic master visited him, he asked Rabbi Uri why he did not pray that his congregants become more prosperous.

Rabbi Uri called in a follower whose shabby clothing attested to his poverty. He said to him, "Now is a special moment of grace, and you will be granted anything your heart desires. Ask for whatever you wish."

Without a moment's hesitancy, the man said, "I wish to be able to say *Baruch She'amar* (the opening prayer of the morning service) with the same fervor as the Rabbi does."

Rabbi Uri turned to his friend. "You see now for yourself!" he said. "They do not want riches. Why should I intercede to get them something they do not want?"

We ask God for many things, but most importantly, we should pray that He enlighten us what it is that we should pray for, lest we waste our prayers by asking for things that are not to our ultimate advantage and fail to ask for what is really essential.

NOTES

_____
_____
_____
_____
_____
_____
_____
_____
_____

Today I shall . . .

. . . try to think about what it is that I really need and that is in my best interest, instead of focusing on things that may seem desirable but are really inconsequential.

וְאִם בָּטַלְתָּ מִן הַתּוֹרָה יֶשׁ לָךְ בְּטֵלִים הַרְבֵּה כְּנֶגְדֶּךְ *From the Sages*

If you should neglect [the study] of Torah, you will find many excuses to neglect it
(*Ethics of the Fathers* 4:12).

Rabbi Mendel of Kotzk once met a disciple of Rabbi Moshe of Kobrin.

"What was most important to your Rabbi?" he asked.

The disciple replied, "Whatever he happened to be doing at the moment."

Time should be precious to us. It is irreplaceable; unlike money, a moment that is lost can never be regained. Still, we protect our money far more than our time.

Absolute idleness consists of doing nothing. But there is also a relative idleness, when we occupy ourselves with things of lesser value.

If what we are doing at any given time is not the most important thing at that moment, something else must be even more important. If that is so, why are we neglecting what is more important and spending our time on what is less important? Would we be so foolish to spend our time earning less money when we could just as well be earning more?

Nov. 22, 1992
Nov. 10, 1993
Oct. 31, 1994
Nov. 19, 1995
Nov. 8, 1996
Nov. 26, 1997

NOTES

Today I shall . . .

. . . try to realize the value of time, and make every moment count.

CHESHVAN

חשון

Nov. 23, 1992
Nov. 11, 1993
Nov. 1, 1994
Nov. 20, 1995
Nov. 9, 1996
Nov. 27, 1997

From the Sages

וְהַבֵּינוֹנִי תּוֹלִין אוֹתוֹ עַד יוֹם הַכִּפּוּרִים אִם עָשָׂה תְשׁוּבָה נֶחְתָּם לְחַיִּים וְאִם לָאו נֶחְתָּם לְמִיתָה

If a person has an equal number of mitzvos and sins, he is given the opportunity to repent until Yom Kippur. If he repents, he is inscribed for life; but if not, he is inscribed for death (*Maimonides, Teshuvah* 3:3).

Why should people be condemned if, by Yom Kippur, their *mitzvos* still equal their sins? If the two exactly balance each other, should they not be judged with mercy?

Rabbi Yisrael of Salant said that the answer is obvious. If people are given the opportunity to repent for their sins, yet still fail to do so, their negligence is a sin so terrible that it outweighs all the *mitzvos*.

While people cannot justify their sins, they can say that the intensity of temptation was overwhelming. As one Chassidic master pleaded, "Almighty God, if You had placed the terrors of *Gehinnom* before people's eyes and had concealed temptation in books, I swear to You that no one would sin. But You put temptation right before people's eyes and relegated the terrors of *Gehinnom* to the books, where it exists as an abstraction! Is it any wonder that people sin?"

Still, once the sin has been committed and the temptation assuaged, what justification can there be for not regretting that one has done wrong? Hence, said Rabbi Yisrael of Salant, the seriousness of a failure to repent. Sin may stem from an inherent weakness; neglect to rectify past wrongs constitutes an act of defiance and an attitude of unforgivable, arrogant self-righteousness which cannot be forgiven.

NOTES

Today I shall . . .

. . . make a reckoning of things I have done, and have the courage to recognize and admit what I have done wrong.

וַאֲפִילוּ כָּל הָעוֹלָם כּוּלוּ אוֹמְרִים לְךָ צַדִּיק אַתָּה *From*
הֱיֵה בְּעֵינֶיךָ כְּרָשָׁע *the*

Even if the entire world considers you a *Sages*
tzaddik (pious and righteous), you
should nevertheless think of yourself as if
you were sinful (*Niddah* 30b).

Nov. 24, 1992
Nov. 12, 1993
Nov. 2, 1994
Nov. 21, 1995
Nov. 10, 1996
Nov. 28, 1997

In 1965, I visited the Steipler Gaon, a sage whom people often consulted for medical advice. Since he had heard that I was a psychiatrist, he wanted to find out new developments in medications for mental illnesses. I related to the Gaon whatever I knew about the most recent advances.

"Is anything available that can cure someone from delusions?" he asked. I told the Gaon that delusions were very resistant to treatment, and that while antipsychotic medications could subdue overt psychotic behavior, the delusional thinking itself was difficult to eradicate.

"But what if someone has the delusion that he is the greatest *tzaddik* in the generation?" the Gaon asked. I could not restrain myself and laughingly replied, "No medication can cure that."

The Gaon shook his head sadly. "Too bad," he said. "That malady is so widespread."

Delusions of any kind are a sign of mental illness. How sick a person must be to consider oneself a *tzaddik*, and how wise the Talmud was to caution us against developing such delusions!

NOTES

Today I shall . . .

. . . try to be honest with myself, and even if my behavior is such that people may think I am a *tzaddik*, I must not allow myself to be deluded.

*Erev Rosh
Codesh
[Eve of the
New Month]*
Nov. 25, 1992
Nov. 13, 1993
Nov. 3, 1994
Nov. 22, 1995
Nov. 11, 1996
Nov. 29, 1997

*From
the
Sages*

הַחֲלוֹנוֹת בֵּין מִלְמַעְלָן בֵּין מִלְמַטָּן בֵּין כְּנֶגְדָן
אַרְבַּע אַמּוֹת

If one builds a wall adjacent to a neigh-bor's windows, it must be built far enough that he not intrude on his neigh-bor's privacy (*Bava Basra* 22a, free translation).

In Jewish law, privacy is a right. As the above excerpt from the Talmud shows, a court can protect an individual's privacy.

Physical privacy is but one dimension of one's right; we also have the right to keep knowledge of our affairs away from the public eye. Not only can discussing or disclosing another person's affairs cause great damage, but in addition, it can intrude upon the other person's privacy. People have a right to their own thoughts and feelings, and this right to privacy must be respected, even among friends and family members.

Some people get offended when they discover that someone withheld personal information that they felt they had a right to know. Of course, while a person entering a partnership (whether business or personal) has a right to know certain things (such as the other party's past record of honesty), the other party certainly has the right to keep other things private.

Intimacy is a bridge between two separate people; only if we respect another person's right to a "self," a sense of privacy, can we expect intimacy to exist.

NOTES

_____
_____
_____
_____
_____
_____
_____
_____
_____

Today I shall . . .

. . . try to remember that other people have rights to their own thoughts and feelings, and avoid intruding on other people's privacy.

From the Scriptures

לֹא תִקֹּם וְלֹא תִטֹּר אֶת בְּנֵי עַמֶּךָ וְאָהַבְתָּ
לְרֵעֲךָ כָּמוֹךָ אֲנִי ה׳

Do not take revenge nor bear grudge among your people, and you should love your neighbor as yourself, I am God (*Leviticus* 19:18).

This verse may well be the Torah's most difficult demand. The Talmud gives an example of revenge: someone refuses to give you a loan; then, when he or she asks you for one, you say, "I will not lend you money because you turned me down when I was in need." Bearing a grudge comes when you do give the person the loan, but say, "I want you to see that I am more decent than you. I am willing to lend you the money, even though you did not give me that consideration." The Torah forbids both reactions; we must loan in silence.

R' Moshe Chaim Luzzato says that revenge is one of the sweetest sensations a person can have, and that the Torah's demand that we suppress this impulse is asking us to virtually be akin to angels (*Path of the Just,* Chap. 11). Still, the fact that we are required to do so tells us that this level of control is within our grasp. The key to this is contained in the end of the verse cited above.

The Torah wishes us to consider the other person as we would ourselves. For example, if a person stubbed his toe and felt a sharp pain, he would hardly hit his foot as punishment for having hurt him. Just as we would neither take revenge nor bear a grudge on a part of our own body, we should not do so toward another person.

First Day of Rosh Chodesh Kislev
[Most years, Cheshvan has only 29 days and Kislev has only one day of Rosh Chodesh.]
Nov. 14, 1993
Nov. 23, 1995

NOTES

_____
_____
_____
_____
_____
_____
_____
_____

Today I shall . . .

. . . try to think of other people as extensions of myself, and avoid responding with hostility when I am offended.

**Second day of
Rosh Chodesh**

*Nov. 26, 1992
Nov. 15, 1993
Nov. 4, 1994
Nov. 24, 1995
Nov. 12, 1996
Nov. 30, 1997*

NOTES

*From the
Scriptures* I am but dust and ashes (*Genesis* 18:27).

וְאָנֹכִי עָפָר וָאֵפֶר

*From
the
Sages* Everyone must say, "The world was created for my sake" (*Sanhedrin* 37a).

כָּל אֶחָד וְאֶחָד חַיָּיב לוֹמַר בִּשְׁבִילִי נִבְרָא הָעוֹלָם

Rabbi Bunim of Pshis'cha said that everyone should have two pockets; one to contain, "I am but dust and ashes," and the other to contain, "The world was created for my sake." At certain times, we must reach into one pocket; at other times, into the other. The secret of correct living comes from knowing when to reach into which.

Humility is the finest of all virtues and is the source of all admirable character traits. Yet, if a person considers himself to be utterly insignificant, he may not care about his actions. He may think, "What is so important about what I do? It makes no difference, so long as I do not harm anyone." Such feelings of insignificance can cause immoral behavior.

When a person does not feel that his actions are significant, he either allows impulses to dominate his behavior or slouches into inactivity. At such a time, he must reach into the pocket of personal grandeur and read: "I am specially created by God. He has a mission that only I can achieve. Since this is a Divine mission, the entire universe was created solely to enable me to accomplish this particular assignment."

When presidents and premiers delegate missions to their officials, those officials feel a profound sense of responsibility to carry out the mission in the best possible manner. How much more so when we are commissioned by God!

Today I shall . . .

. . . keep in mind both the humbleness and the grandeur of the human being.

בְּמַקְהֵלִים אֲבָרֵךְ ה׳ *From the*
I shall praise God among a multitude *Scriptures*
(*Psalms* 26:12).

KISLEV

2

כסלו

Nov. 27, 1992
Nov. 16, 1993
Nov. 5, 1994
Nov. 25, 1995
Nov. 13, 1996
Dec. 1, 1997

While the prayer and performance of a *mitzvah* are always praiseworthy, it is especially meritorious when an entire community participates in it, as the Sages teach, *The prayer of a multitude is never turned away* (*Devarim Rabbah* 2).

Nothing is more pleasing to God than to see His children bound together in friendship and placing the common welfare above personal ambitions. Indeed, the Talmud states that when Jews are united, God is willing to overlook even serious transgressions.

As for ourselves, nothing is more important than realizing that no one is an island, and that we are all interdependent. The idea of complete self-sufficiency is an illusion and probably a desperate attempt at ego-building by someone who is plagued by feelings of inferiority and inadequacy.

When we do things together, we both give and receive. Others are strengthened in their resolve and actions by our participation, and we are stimulated and encouraged by theirs.

Another added benefit: Commenting on the verse, *Five of you will pursue one hundred enemies and one hundred will pursue ten thousand* (*Leviticus* 26:8), the Midrash states that when a multitude observes the Torah, their strength is not merely additive, but increases exponentially.

In working with alcoholics, I have observed the enormous power that can come from a group effort. As one recovering person said to the group, "There is nothing I could do without you, and there is nothing I cannot do when I have you."

NOTES

Today I shall . . .

. . . try to pool my strength by joining others in prayer, Torah study, and the performance of *mitzvos*.

Nov. 28, 1992
Nov. 17, 1993
Nov. 6, 1994
Nov. 26, 1995
Nov. 14, 1996
Dec. 2, 1997

From the Scriptures **G**od is your shadow at your right hand (*Psalms* 121:5).

ה' צִלְּךָ עַל יַד יְמִינֶךָ

The Baal Shem Tov taught that God acts toward individuals accordingly as they act toward other people. Thus, if people are willing to forgive those who have offended them, God will similarly overlook their misdeeds. If a person is very judgmental and reacts with anger to any offense, God will be equally strict. The meaning of, *God is your shadow*, is that a person's shadow mimics his or her every action.

At a therapy session for family members of recovering alcoholics, one woman told the group that she had experienced frustration from many years of infertility and tremendous joy when she finally conceived. Her many expectations were shattered, however, when the child was born with Down's syndrome.

"I came to love that child dearly," she said, "but the greatest thing that child has done for me is to make me realize that if I can love him so in spite of his imperfections, then God can love me in spite of my many imperfections."

If we wish to know how God will relate to us, the answer is simple: exactly in the same way we relate to others. If we demand perfection from others, He will demand it of us. If we can love others even though they do not measure up to our standards and expectations, then He will love us in spite of our shortcomings.

NOTES

Today I shall . . .

. . . try to relate to people in the same manner I would wish God to relate to me.

KISLEV

כסלו

Nov. 29, 1992
Nov. 18, 1993
Nov. 7, 1994
Nov. 27, 1995
Nov. 15, 1996
Dec. 3, 1997

קוֹל ה' בַּכֹּחַ *From the*
The voice of God is in the force *Scriptures*
(*Psalms* 29:4).

The Midrash on this verse comments, "It does not say that 'the voice of God is in *His* force,' but in *the* force; it 'is in the force of every individual.'" What God demands of every individual never exceeds the capacities He gave that person. Similarly, the Midrash notes that when the first of the Ten Commandments states: אָנֹכִי ה' אֱלֹקֶיךָ, *I am Hashem, your God,* it uses the singular possessive form, because every Israelite felt that God was addressing him or her individually.

The stresses of life may be extremely trying, and the burden some people must carry may appear to be excessive. Yet, we must never despair. Rather, we must believe that regardless of how great our burdens may be, we have the strength to bear it. This faith should give us the courage to struggle with and master our struggle.

Sometimes circumstances become so taxing that we believe we are at our breaking point. This is when a righteous person will be sustained by the faith that although his or her burden may be heavy, it is never *too* heavy.

Today I shall . . .

. . . try to remember that God has given me enough strength to withstand the stresses to which I am subject.

NOTES

Nov. 30, 1992
Nov. 19, 1993
Nov. 8, 1994
Nov. 28, 1995
Nov. 16, 1996
Dec. 4, 1997

From the Scriptures

וְאָמַרְתָּ בִּלְבָבֶךָ כֹּחִי וְעֹצֶם יָדִי עָשָׂה לִי אֶת הַחַיִל הַזֶּה

You might say to yourself, "My might and the power of my hand have gained me this wealth" *(Deuteronomy* 8:17).

Moses warned the Israelites that upon entering Canaan and inheriting a prosperous and fertile land "flowing with milk and honey," they should not think that their own prowess had made them wealthy. Rather, they should be aware that Israel was a Divine gift.

For that generation, the challenge was not too difficult, because as Moses had pointed out to them earlier, they had personally experienced forty years of miraculous survival in the desert wilderness, fed by the daily manna and watered by a spring which accompanied them on their journeys. With such overt manifestations of Divine wonders, they would not be likely to ascribe any future success to their own strength and cunning.

Today, however, we stand many centuries away from the Biblical times. We may think that the world operates purely by natural law; that we can completely determine our own fate and fortune, and in which success or failure are due to our shrewdness in business or how much effort we exert.

Thus, Moses' message was intended for us even more than for his generation. Surely we are required to engage in work for the Torah itself states that *God will bless the work of "your hands"* *(Deuteronomy* 14:29)], but we should not lose sight of the fact that the Divine blessing, not brains or brawn, ultimately determines our fortune. The only difference between today and Moses' time is that there, God's hand was manifest everywhere, but today it is concealed.

NOTES

Today I shall . . .

. . . try to remember that even though I work hard, the results of my efforts are determined by Divine blessing.

כִּי יְדַעְתִּיו לְמַעַן אֲשֶׁר יְצַוֶּה אֶת בָּנָיו וְאֶת *From the* בֵּיתוֹ אַחֲרָיו וְשָׁמְרוּ דֶּרֶךְ ה' *Scriptures*

For I have loved him [Abraham], because he commands his children and household after him to observe the way of God (*Genesis* 18:19).

Dec. 1, 1992
Nov. 20, 1993
Nov. 9, 1994
Nov. 29, 1995
Nov. 17, 1996
Dec. 5, 1997

God knew that Abraham would be able to convey the Divine teachings to future generations, because He knew Abraham to be capable of overcoming his intense love and apply stern discipline when it was needed.

In my work with addicted individuals, one of the most difficult tasks I have is to convince their family members, especially the parents, of the importance of "tough love"; that condoning destructive behavior actually encourages it, and enables it to continue and worsen. Although Abraham loved his son Ishmael, he did not allow these feelings to deter him from the necessary discipline (Genesis 21:9-14).

Love is an admirable feeling, but it can be destructive if it is misdirected. Sometimes we must rein in our love and apply strict measures. While doing so will cause us great distress, our failure to do so will ultimately cause even greater distress to all concerned. Loving parents submit their infants to immunization which may be painful. "Tough love" is not cruelty, but, like some life-saving medicines that taste bitter, it is helpful albeit unpleasant.

NOTES

Today I shall . . .

. . . try to direct my love where it is appropriate and constructive, and be able to apply discipline when it is necessary.

Dec 2, 1992
Nov. 21, 1993
Nov. 10, 1994
Nov. 30, 1995
Nov. 18, 1996
Dec. 6, 1997

From the Sages

מְאֹד מְאֹד הֱוֵי שְׁפַל רוּחַ

Be very, very humble (*Ethics of the Fathers* 4:4).

Rabbi Raphael of Bershed complained bitterly to his teacher, Rabbi Pinchas of Koretz, that he was unable to eradicate feelings of vanity. Rabbi Pinchas tried to help him by suggesting different methods, but Rabbi Raphael replied that he had already tried every one without success. He then pleaded with his mentor to do something to extirpate these egotistical feelings.

Rabbi Pinchas then rebuked his disciple. "What is it with you, Raphael, that you expect instant perfection? Character development does not come overnight, regardless of how much effort you exert. Eradication of stubborn character traits takes time as well as effort. Today you achieve a little, and tomorrow you will achieve a bit more.

"You are frustrated and disappointed because you have not achieved character perfection as quickly as you had wished.

"Continue to work on yourself. Pray to God to help you with your character perfection. It will come in due time, but you must be patient."

The Talmud states, "Be very, very humble," to indicate that true self-betterment is a gradual process. We achieve a bit today, and a little more tomorrow.

NOTES

Today I shall . . .

. . . try to be patient with myself. While I will do my utmost to rid myself of undesirable character traits, I will not become frustrated if I do not achieve instant perfection.

עֲבֵירוֹת שֶׁבֵּין אָדָם לַחֲבֵירוֹ אֵין יוֹם הַכִּיפּוּרִים *From*
מְכַפֵּר עַד שֶׁיְרַצֶּה אֶת חֲבֵירוֹ *the*

Sins that are between a man and his *Sages*
fellow man are not forgiven on Yom
Kippur unless he has appeased him (*Yoma*
85b).

One Sabbath day, the aged Steipler Gaon insisted on
going to a particular synagogue some distance away. His
family tried to dissuade him because the long walk would
be too taxing, but he insisted and in fact made the difficult
walk.

Dec. 3, 1992
Nov. 22, 1993
Nov. 11, 1994
Dec. 1, 1995
Nov. 19, 1996
Dec. 7, 1997

The Gaon later explained that some time earlier, he had
reprimanded a young boy for putting a volume of the
Talmud into the bookcase upside down, which is considered to be disrespectful handling of a sacred book. The boy
then showed the Gaon that the volume was bound
incorrectly; the cover was upside down, but the book itself
was put away upright. The Gaon then apologized to the
young boy.

"But because this young boy was not yet *bar mitzvah*,"
the Gaon explained, "he was a minor who was unable
(according to Jewish law) to grant forgiveness. When I
heard that he was to become *bar mitzvah* this Sabbath, I
had to avail myself of the opportunity to obtain proper
forgiveness."

Everyone at some point says or does something that
offends another person. Too often, we dismiss the incident
without giving it a second thought and so are unlikely to
remember it so that we will apologize when the opportunity arises. The above incident should help us realize the
seriousness of offending a child, and the importance of
obtaining proper forgiveness.

NOTES

_____
_____
_____
_____

Today I shall . . .

. . . try to make amends to anyone whom I have offended,
and make certain that I do more than lip service in
apologizing.

_____
_____
_____

Dec 4, 1992
Nov. 23, 1993
Nov. 12, 1994
Dec. 2, 1995
Nov. 20, 1996
Dec. 8, 1997

From the Sages תְּפַשְׂתָּ מְרוּבֶּה לֹא תָּפַשְׂתָּ, תָּפַשְׂתָּ מוּעָט תָּפַשְׂתָּ

If you seize too much, you are left with nothing. If you take less, you may retain it (*Rosh Hashanah* 4b).

Sometimes our appetites are insatiable; more accurately, we act as though they were insatiable. The Midrash states that a person may never be satisfied. "If he has one hundred, he wants two hundred. If he gets two hundred, he wants four hundred" (*Koheles Rabbah* 1:34). How often have we seen people whose insatiable desire for material wealth resulted in their losing everything, much like the gambler whose constant urge to win results in total loss.

People's bodies are finite, and their actual needs are limited. The endless pursuit for more wealth than they can use is nothing more than an elusive belief that they can live forever (*Psalms* 49:10).

The one part of us which is indeed infinite is our *neshamah* (soul), which, being of Divine origin, can crave and achieve infinity and eternity, and such craving is characteristic of spiritual growth.

How strange that we tend to give the body much more than it can possibly handle, and the *neshamah* so much less than it needs!

NOTES

Today I shall . . .

. . . try to avoid striving for material excesses, and increase my efforts to provide my *neshamah* with spiritual nourishment.

חֲנֹךְ לַנַּעַר עַל פִּי דַרְכּוֹ גַּם כִּי יַזְקִין לֹא יָסוּר מִמֶּנָּה *From the Scriptures*

Train a young lad according to his method, so that when he grows older he will not deviate from it (*Proverbs* 22:6).

Dec. 5, 1992
Nov. 24, 1993
Nov. 13, 1994
Dec. 3, 1995
Nov. 21, 1996
Dec. 9, 1997

He shall not deviate from it — the child will not deviate from the *method* with which he was taught. That method refers to the way we are taught to adapt to life's many hurdles, struggles, and tests.

Education consists of more than just imparting knowledge; it also means training and preparation in how to deal with life. Knowledge is certainly important, but is by no means the sum total of education.

"A person does not properly grasp a Torah principle unless he errs in it" (*Gittin* 43b). People usually do not really grasp *anything* unless they first do it wrong. In fact, the hard way is *the* way to learn. Children learn to walk by stumbling and picking themselves up; young people learn to adjust to life by stumbling and picking themselves up.

Parents and teachers have ample opportunities to serve as role models for their children and students, to demonstrate how to adapt to mistakes and failures. If we show our children and students only our successes, but conceal our failures from them, we deprive them of their most valuable learning opportunities.

We should not allow our egos to interfere with our roles as educators. Parents and teachers fulfill their obligations when they become role models for real life.

NOTES

Today I shall . . .

. . . try to share with others, especially with younger people, how I have overcome and survived my mistakes.

Dec. 6, 1992
Nov. 25, 1993
Nov. 14, 1994
Dec. 4, 1995
Nov. 22, 1996
Dec. 10, 1997

From the Scriptures

וְהַמִּכְתָּב מִכְתַּב אֱלֹקִים הוּא חָרוּת עַל הַלֻּחֹת

The writing was the writing of God, inscribed on the tablets (*Exodus* 32:16).

The Talmud states that the word חָרוּת (inscribed) can also be read phonetically as חֵרוּת (liberty). The verse is thus telling us that Divine law which stresses using our minds to control ourselves provides true liberty and freedom.

In working with alcoholics and addicts, I have come to realize that the most absolute slavery does not come from enslavement by another person, but from enslavement by one's own drives. No slavemaster has ever dominated anyone the way alcohol, heroin, and cocaine dominate the addict, who must lie, steal, and even kill to obey the demands of the addiction.

Such domination is not unique to addiction. We may not realize that passion of any kind may totally control us and ruthlessly terrorize us. We may rationalize and justify behavior that we would otherwise have considered as totally alien to us, but when our passion demands it, we are helpless to resist.

Many people think they are free, yet they are really pawns in the hands of their drives. Like the addict, they are not at all in control, and do not have the fundamental feature of humanity: freedom.

Our only defense is to become masters over our desires rather than their slaves. We must direct our minds to rule over the passions of our hearts.

NOTES

_____

Today I shall . . .

. . . try to achieve true freedom, which means doing what I know is the best thing to do, instead of what I feel like doing.

יִשְׁמַע חָכָם וְיוֹסֶף לֶקַח *From the*

The wise person will listen (to repri- *Scriptures*
mand) and add to his wisdom
(Proverbs 1:5).

Dec. 7, 1992
Nov. 26, 1993
Nov. 15, 1994
Dec. 5, 1995
Nov. 23, 1996
Dec. 11, 1997

One night, when Yehudah Aryeh, the future author of the *Sfas Emes,* was a young boy, he studied Torah the entire night and did not get to bed until shortly before dawn. Although he slept only a short while, he arose later than usual, and his grandfather, Rabbi Yitzchak Meir of Gur, sharply reprimanded him for not arising early to study. The young Yehudah Aryeh absorbed the rebuke in silence.

A friend who knew the real reason asked him: "Why didn't you explain to your grandfather why you awoke late?"

"What!" said the young Yehudah Aryeh. "And miss the opportunity to hear *mussar* (reprimand) from my grandfather?"

At a tender age, Yehudah Aryeh understood the profound wisdom of King Solomon, who repeatedly stresses that the wise actively pursue *mussar* while fools avoid it.

Mussar is to our character what water is to a plant. Abundant *mussar* promotes growth of character, just as water promotes the growth of a plant. Yehudah Aryeh realized that he could easily have justified his late arising, and perhaps might have even received commendation from his grandfather for his diligence. He knew, however, that while praise may be pleasant, it is not as conducive to growth as is reprimand, even though the latter may be unpleasant.

NOTES

Today I shall . . .

. . . try to realize that accepting constructive criticism will help me grow, and that reprimand can be helpful even when there is no actual grounds for rebuke.

Dec. 8, 1992
Nov. 27, 1993
Nov. 16, 1994
Dec. 6, 1995
Nov. 24, 1996
Dec. 12, 1997

From the Sages בְּדֶרֶךְ שֶׁאָדָם רוֹצֶה לֵילַךְ בָּהּ מוֹלִיכִין אוֹתוֹ

In whatever way a person chooses, therein is he led *(Makkos* 10b).

We tend to disown those thoughts, feelings, and actions that we dislike. Something we saw, read, or heard upset us, we like to think, and caused us to think, feel, or act in a certain way. We forget that we have considerable say in what we choose to see or or hear.

Psychiatry and psychology have contributed to this abdication of responsibility. Their emphasis on the impact of early-life events on our emotions has been taken to mean that these factors determine our psyche, and that we are but helpless victims of our past.

We forget that if someone puts trash on our doorstep, we do not have to take it in; even if it was put into the house and filled it with an odor, we have the option to throw it out and clean up. Similarly, even if early-life experiences have an impact, the effects are not cast in stone; we can take steps to overcome them.

A man once complained to his rabbi that alien thoughts were interfering with his prayer and meditation. The rabbi shrugged his shoulders. "I don't know why you refer to them as alien," he said. "They are your own."

If we stop disowning feelings and actions, we may be able to do something about them.

NOTES

_____
_____
_____
_____
_____
_____
_____
_____
_____

Today I shall . . .

. . . try to avoid exposing myself to those influences that are likely to stimulate feelings and behavior that I think are wrong.

וְאִם לֹא עַכְשָׁו אֵימָתָי *From the Sages*

And if not now, then when? *(Ethics of the Fathers 1:14).*

KISLEV

14

כסלו

Dec. 9, 1992
Nov. 28, 1993
Nov. 17, 1994
Dec. 7, 1995
Nov. 25, 1996
Dec. 13, 1997

Hillel's famous statement is a bit enigmatic. The simple answer is, "Later." Why can't we take care of whatever it is some other time? Granted that procrastination is not a virtue, why does Hillel imply that if not now, then it will never be?

The Rabbi of Gur explained that if I do something later, it may indeed get done, but I will have missed the current "now." The present "now" has but a momentary existence, and whether used or not, it will never return. Later will be a different "now."

King Solomon dedicates seven famous verses of *Ecclesiastes* to his principle that everything has its specific time. His point comes across clearly: I can put off doing a good deed for someone until tomorrow, but will that deed, done exactly as I would have done it today, carry the same impact?

The wisdom that I learn at this moment belongs to this moment. The good deed that I do at this moment belongs to this moment. Of course I can do them later, but they will belong to the later moments. What I can do that belongs to *this* moment is only that which I do *now*.

NOTES

Today I shall . . .

. . . try to value each moment. I must realize that my mission is not only to get something done, but to get things done in their proper time, and the proper time may be now.

Dec. 10, 1992
Nov. 29, 1993
Nov. 18, 1994
Dec. 8, 1995
Nov. 26, 1996
Dec. 14, 1997

From our **E**nlighten our eyes in Your Torah *(Siddur).*
Prayers

וְהָאֵר עֵינֵינוּ בְּתוֹרָתֶךָ

This prayer is not only for an understanding of Torah, but also that Torah may help us perceive the truth in everything.

The Torah tells the story of Hagar and Ishmael, who were stranded in the desert without water. Hagar abandoned her son and fled, saying that she could not bear to see him die of thirst. *God opened her eyes, and she saw a well of water* (*Genesis* 21:19). God did not create a well where none had existed, but "opened her eyes" so that she could see an already-existing well, which she had not seen because of her state of panic.

Many opportunities may be right before our eyes, but if we become desperate and panicky, we may fail to see them, and the result may be a misfortune that could have been averted. Hagar almost lost Ishmael, not because there was no water, but because she could not see it. What was necessary was not a miracle, but just a correct perception of reality.

Torah teachings can provide guidance that can assist in avoiding distortions of reality.

NOTES

Today I shall . . .

. . . try to avoid panic and any other emotion that clouds my ability to see what is truly before me.

A smooth mouth makes for a slippery וּפֶה חָלָק יַעֲשֶׂה מִדְחֶה *From the* course *(Proverbs 26:28).* *Scriptures*

Dec. 11, 1992
Nov. 30, 1993
Nov. 19, 1994
Dec. 9, 1995
Nov. 27, 1996
Dec. 15, 1997

The ethical Torah writings such as the Book of *Proverbs* vehemently condemn flattering people to obtain their favor. When we do so, we may not care whether the object of our praise deserves it. Praising people who do not merit it has at least two harmful effects. First, it reinforces that person's behavior. Second, it delivers a dangerous message, particularly to young people who like to emulate recipients of honor.

We should instead rebuke wrongdoers, and if we cannot reprimand them, we can at least refrain from praising them.

The key is to avoid becoming dependent on those whom we do not respect. We should not seek any prestige they can offer, nor place our livelihood in their hands. Flattery may cause us to compromise ourselves, reinforce wrong behavior, and teach our children that we respect wrongdoing.

Furthermore, we gain nothing from our sycophancy. The Sages observed that those who flatter to obtain favors may end up disgraced (*Avos De'R' Nosson* 29:4).

NOTES

_____

_____

_____

_____

_____

_____

_____

Today I shall . . .

_____

_____

. . . try to avoid giving false praise to those who do not deserve it. I will not allow ulterior motives to compromise my principles.

_____

Dec. 12, 1992
Dec. 1, 1993
Nov. 20, 1994
Dec. 10, 1995
Nov. 28, 1996
Dec. 16, 1997

From the Scriptures

מִכָּל מְלַמְּדַי הִשְׂכַּלְתִּי

From all those who have taught me I have gained wisdom *(Psalms* 119:99).

The Psalmist is telling us that he learned from everyone, that everyone was his teacher. From some, he learned what to do; from others, what not to do.

If we learn from others' mistakes, we need not make our own.

Just as we can learn from every person, we can learn from every event. Positive experiences are obvious sources of learning, because each positive act we do adds to our character and prepares us to better face the next challenge in life. Negative experiences can be valuable, too, but only if we are sufficiently alert to learn from them.

The list of lessons that we have learned the hard way may be long, but each one has taught us what *not* to do and thereby it becomes a positive experience. Indeed, the Talmud states that when people sincerely regret their mistakes and change themselves for the better, the wrongs that they did become actual merits *(Yoma* 86b). Only when we fail to learn from our mistakes and, rationalizing and justifying, obstinately insist that we were right, do our misdeeds remain defects.

We have the capacity to make life itself a tremendous learning and growth experience.

NOTES

_____
_____
_____
_____
_____
_____
_____
_____
_____
_____

Today I shall . . .

. . . try to look for lessons from everyone and everything, whether my teacher is positive or negative.

In those days there was no king in Israel; each man did that which was proper in his own eyes *(Judges* 21:25).

At first glance, this verse appears to describe a chaotic state of affairs — anarchy itself — where in absence of a central authority everyone did as they pleased.

The Rabbi of Satmar said that this interpretation is incorrect. Everyone has common sense, which can reliably guide him to do right and avoid wrong. He derives his proof from the verse: וְעָשִׂיתָ הַיָּשָׁר וְהַטּוֹב, *Do that which is proper and good (Deuteronomy* 6:18). How do we know what is proper and good if the Torah does not specify it? It must be that we have an innate common sense.

If so, why does the world seem so unjust? One reason might be that people do not act according to their *own* common sense, but rather according to what they think *others* might think of them. If people did *what was good in their own eyes,* we might have less injustice.

The driving force behind the lusts for power, fame, and wealth — which themselves lead to corrupt behavior— may not necessarily be what people want for *themselves* as much as their desire to impress *others* . If we stop behaving according to what we wish others to think, we might give our common sense a fighting chance.

Dec. 13, 1992
Dec. 2, 1993
Nov. 21, 1994
Dec. 11, 1995
Nov. 29, 1996
Dec. 17, 1997

NOTES
_____
_____
_____
_____
_____
_____
_____
_____
_____
_____

Today I shall . . .

. . . try to stop impressing others. Instead, I will try to reason for myself what is right and wrong.

Dec. 14, 1992
Dec. 3, 1993
Nov. 22, 1994
Dec. 12, 1995
Nov. 30, 1996
Dec. 18, 1997

From the Scriptures

בַּיָּמִים הָהֵם אֵין מֶלֶךְ בְּיִשְׂרָאֵל אִישׁ הַיָּשָׁר בְּעֵינָיו יַעֲשֶׂה

In those days there was no king in Israel; each man did that which was proper in his own eyes (*Judges* 21:25).

While people have common sense which can lead them to do right and avoid wrong, they also face another obstacle (see yesterday) that could cause them to stray from the correct path — the drive for immediate gratification.

How powerful is this force? Imagine a car being driven along a highway, which is pulled off its course by a powerful magnet. The "magnet" affecting our behavior is the craving for gratification.

The force of seeking immediate gratification can mislead us. We may yield to it because its lure blinds our perception of justice. In reality, we have been bribed, and the Torah accurately states that *a bribe will blind the eyes of even the wise* (*Deuteronomy* 16:19). Thus, we only do what is proper when our "eyes" function well.

The Rabbi of Rhizin gave an antidote for the distorting forces of temptation. He stated that we should go through life the way tightrope walkers maintain their delicate balance: when they feel a tug on one side, they lean toward the opposite side. When we feel tempted to do something, our first reaction should be to steer ourselves away from it. Only then can we apply our common sense and decide what to do.

Summing up, once we recognize and control our desire to impress others and our drive for immediate gratification, we will be able to exercise proper judgment.

NOTES

Today I shall . . .

. . . try to be on guard against temptations that may affect my sense of propriety and justice.

הִסְתַּכֵּל בִּשְׁלֹשָׁה דְבָרִים וְאֵין אַתָּה בָא לִידֵי *From*
עֲבֵרָה: דַּע מֵאַיִן בָּאתָ וּלְאָן אַתָּה הוֹלֵךְ וְלִפְנֵי מִי *the*
אַתָּה עָתִיד לִתֵּן דִּין וְחֶשְׁבּוֹן *Sages*

Consider three things, and you will not
approach sin. Know whence you came,
whereto you are going, and before Whom
you are destined to give an accounting
(*Ethics of the Fathers* 3:1).

Dec. 15, 1992
Dec. 4, 1993
Nov. 23, 1994
Dec. 13, 1995
Dec. 1, 1996
Dec. 19, 1997

If we thought about our humble origin on the one hand,
and the greatness we can achieve on the other, we would
come to only one logical conclusion: the potential for such
greatness could not possibly reside in the microscopic
germ-cell from which we originated. This capacity for
greatness can reside only in the *neshamah* (soul), the spirit
which God instills within man.

What an extraordinary stretching of the imagination it
must take to think that a single cell can develop into the
grandeur which a human being can achieve! People have
the power to contemplate and reflect upon infinity and
eternity, concepts which are totally beyond the realm of the
physical world. How could something purely finite even
conceive of infinity?

Our humble origins are the greatest testimony to the
presence of a Divine component within man. Once we
realize this truth, we are unlikely to contaminate ourselves
by behavior beneath our dignity. We have an innate
resistance to ruining what we recognize to be precious and
beautiful. We must realize that this is indeed what we are.

NOTES

Today I shall . . .

. . . try to make my behavior conform to that which I
recognize to be the essence of my being: the spirit that
gives me the potential for greatness.

Dec. 16, 1992
Dec. 5, 1993
Nov. 24, 1994
Dec. 14, 1995
Dec. 2, 1996
Dec. 20, 1997

*From the
Scriptures*

וַיְדַבֵּר ה' אֶל מֹשֶׁה פָּנִים אֶל פָּנִים כַּאֲשֶׁר
יְדַבֵּר אִישׁ אֶל רֵעֵהוּ

And God spoke to Moses face to face, just as a person would speak to a friend (*Exodus* 33:11).

Moses was the only prophet to whom God spoke directly, just as a person would converse with a friend. However, this uniqueness went only one way; every single human being has the ability to speak to God directly, "as a person would speak to a friend." Indeed, we should do so.

In this way, we can fully express our innermost feelings. True, we address God as the King of the Universe, which He is. We also plead with Him as a child does with a parent, which He is. But we certainly would never tell a king everything about ourselves, and we all have things which we would never want our parents to know. With a friend, however, we have fewer restrictions and less resistance. We can reveal everything to a friend, even things that we would be too embarrassed or otherwise reluctant to tell anyone else.

The Torah refers to God as "a friend" (e.g. *Proverbs* 27:10), because it wishes us to have this relationship with God, as well as that of subject to sovereign and child to father.

One might ask, "Since God knows our thoughts, why should we reveal them to Him verbally in prayer?" The answer is that by doing so, we reinforce our relationship to Him as a friend.

When you complete your formal prayers, add some of your own composition, and speak to God as a friend.

NOTES

Today I shall . . .

. . . try to enhance the quality of my prayer by revealing to God everything that is on my mind, just as I would with a trusted friend.

שְׁמַע יִשְׂרָאֵל ה׳ אֱלֹקֵינוּ ה׳ אֶחָד *From the*
Hear, O Israel, Hashem is our God, *Scriptures*
Hashem the One and Only (*Deuteronomy* 6:4).

Dec. 17, 1992
Dec. 6, 1993
Nov. 25, 1994
Dec. 15, 1995
Dec. 3, 1996
Dec. 21, 1997

When reciting the declaration of the unity of God, we are required to commit ourselves to this belief, that in the event we were coerced to deny Him, we would surrender our lives rather than do so. This concept is called *mesiras nefesh*, and in addition to our belief in God, there are only two other instances where we are to choose martyrdom rather than transgression: murder and adultery.

While the thought of surrendering one's life is frightening, it has unfortunately characterized much of Jewish history. However, since the urge for survival is innate and most intense and generally overrides all other considerations, how can so many Jews have risen to the challenge of *mesiras nefesh*?

The answer is quite simple. Just think of what life would be like if nothing was worth dying for: no ideals, no principles, no loyalty, no sacredness, no ultimate value. Under duress, everything would go. Could thinking people who pride themselves in living on a plane of life higher than that of brute beasts see any value in this kind of life?

There are things that are dearer than life that give life its great value.

NOTES

Today I shall . . .

. . . try to appreciate the full value of life, and realize that there are absolute values that make life precious.

Dec. 18, 1992
Dec. 7, 1993
Nov. 26, 1994
Dec. 16, 1995
Dec. 4, 1996
Dec. 22, 1997

From the Sages

לְעוֹלָם יַעֲסוֹק אָדָם בְּתוֹרָה וּמִצְוֹת אַף עַל פִּי שֶׁלֹא לִשְׁמָה. שֶׁמִּתוֹךְ שֶׁלֹא לִשְׁמָה בָּא לִשְׁמָה

One should study Torah and do mitzvos even if not for their own sake, for doing so will eventually result in study and performance for their own sake (*Pesachim* 50b).

This Talmudic statement has given rise to questions by the commentaries. Why is the Talmud condoning study of Torah for ulterior motives? What happens to the emphasis on sincerity in observance of Torah and *mitzvos*?

Acting "as if" can be constructive. If a person who suffers from a headache goes on with his or her activities "as if" the headache did not exist, that headache is more likely to disappear than if he or she interrupts activities to nurse the headache. "Rewarding" the headache by taking a break only prolongs it.

Study of Torah and performance of *mitzvos* require effort, may be restrictive, and may interfere with other things one would rather do. Under such circumstances, there may not be great enthusiasm for Torah and *mitzvos*. However, if one nevertheless engages in Torah and *mitzvos* "as if" one really wanted to, the resistance is likely to dissipate. The reasoning is that since one is determined to do so anyway, there is no gain in being reluctant, and true enthusiasm may then develop. On the other hand, if one were to delay engaging in Torah and *mitzvos* until one had the "true spirit," that spirit might never appear.

It is not only permissible but also desirable to develop constructive habits by doing things "as if" one really wanted to.

NOTES

Today I shall. . .

. . . try to practice good habits, and do those things that I know to be right even though I may not like doing them.

He [the God-fearing person] will not מִשְּׁמוּעָה רָעָה לֹא יִירָא נָכוֹן לִבּוֹ בָּטֻחַ בַּה' *From the Scriptures*
fear evil tidings, his heart being
firm in his trust in God (*Psalms* 112:7).

Is a person supposed to take steps to provide for oneself, or should one rely completely on God to take care of everything?

If relying on God is taken to mean doing nothing for oneself, this is certainly not the Divine will. The Torah says that *God will bless you in all that you do* (*Deuteronomy* 15:18), which obviously means that God expects us to do for ourselves.

But one's trust in God is all important. Some people have the capacity to do things for themselves, but are unable to put their capabilities into action because of intense anxiety. For example, some students who know their material thoroughly report that their minds go blank when they take an exam. They may fail the course not because they lack the requisite knowledge, but because they panic and are unable to use the knowledge they have. A person who has firm faith and trusts in God is much less likely to become a victim of such paralyzing anxiety.

While there are such things as panic or anxiety attacks that are medical problems and require treatment, there is also a variety of anxiety that is due to feelings of insecurity and apprehension. This kind of anxiety is greatly mitigated by a firm trust in God.

Erev Chanukah
[Eve of Chanukah]
Dec. 19, 1992
Dec. 8, 1993
Nov. 27, 1994
Dec. 17, 1995
Dec. 5, 1996
Dec. 23, 1997
[The first candle is lit tonight.]

NOTES

_____
_____
_____
_____
_____
_____
_____
_____

Today I shall . . .

. . . try to develop a firm trust in God, that nothing terrible will happen to me, and then go on to use my God-given abilities.

KISLEV

25

כסלו

Chanukah

Dec. 20, 1992
Dec. 9, 1993
Nov. 28, 1994
Dec. 18, 1995
Dec. 6, 1996
Dec. 24, 1997

*[The second
candle is
lit tonight.]*

NOTES

_____
_____
_____
_____
_____
_____
_____
_____
_____

*From
our
Prayers*

וְקָבְעוּ שְׁמוֹנַת יְמֵי חֲנֻכָּה אֵלוּ לְהוֹדוֹת וּלְהַלֵּל לְשִׁמְךָ הַגָּדוֹל

They established these eight days of Chanukah to give thanks and praise to Your great Name (*Siddur*).

Jewish history is replete with miracles that transcend the miracle of the Menorah. Why is the latter so prominently celebrated while the others are relegated to relative obscurity?

Perhaps the reason is that most other miracles were Divinely initiated; i.e. God intervened to suspend the laws of nature in order to save His people from calamity.

The miracle of the Menorah was something different. Having defeated the Seleucid Greek invaders, the triumphant Jews entered the Sanctuary. There they found that they could light the Menorah for only one day, due to a lack of undefiled oil. Further, they had no chance of replenishing the supply for eight days. They did light the Menorah anyway, reasoning that it was best to do what was within their ability to do and to postpone worrying about the next day until such worry was appropriate. This decision elicited a Divine response and the Menorah stayed lit for that day and for seven more.

This miracle was thus initiated by the Jews themselves, and the incident was set down as a teaching for all future generations: concentrate your efforts on what you can do, and *do it!* Leave the rest to God.

While even our best and most sincere efforts do not necessarily bring about miracles, the teaching is nevertheless valid. Even the likelihood of failure in the future should not discourage us from any constructive action that we can take now.

_____

Today I shall . . .

_____

. . . focus my attention on what it is that I can do now, and do it to the best of my ability.

אַף עַל פִּי שֶׁשִּׁעוּרָם בִּרְבִיעִית יוֹסִיף לִיטוֹל *From*
בְּשֶׁפַע *the*
Sages

Although the acceptable amount [of water for ritual washing of the hands before meals] is a fourth of a log, one should use abundant water in washing (*Orach Chaim* 158:10).

Chanukah
Dec. 21, 1992
Dec. 10, 1993
Nov. 29, 1994
Dec. 19, 1995
Dec. 7, 1996
Dec. 25, 1997
[The third candle is lit tonight.]

The Talmud states that Rabbi Chisda attributed his good fortune to his practice of using abundant water in the ritual washing.

Rabbi Yisroel of Salant was at an inn, and when he washed his hands for the meal, he was careful to use the minimum amount of water required. When his students wondered why he did not follow the recommendations of the *Shulchan Aruch* (Code of Law), Rabbi Yisroel replied, "Perhaps you did not notice that a servant fetched the water from a well. If I used water lavishly, it would be at her expense."

Many times the *Shulchan Aruch* states the letter of the law, then adds that it is commendable to go beyond it in stricter observance. However, such extra observance is only done for oneself. For instance, when rabbis are asked about the permissibility of any given practice, they must render their decision according to the letter of the law and may add that stricter observance is commendable but not mandatory. Rabbis are not permitted to require from others more than the law dictates, even if their personal standards of observance are more demanding.

NOTES

Today I shall . . .

. . . try to increase my expectations of myself, but not at the expense of others.

Chanukah

Dec. 22, 1992
Dec. 11, 1993
Nov. 30, 1994
Dec. 20, 1995
Dec. 8, 1996
Dec. 26, 1997

[The fourth candle is lit tonight.]

From the Sages

כָּל יָמַי גָּדַלְתִּי בֵּין הַחֲכָמִים וְלֹא מָצָאתִי לַגּוּף טוֹב אֶלָּא שְׁתִיקָה

All my days I grew up among the wise, and I have not found what is good for the body other than silence (*Ethics of the Fathers* 1:17).

In his famous instructions on the "golden mean of virtue," Maimonides states that a person should avoid either extreme of any character trait.

If we were to place unbridled talk at one extreme and total silence at the other, the mean of virtue would not be at the midpoint between the two, but much closer to silence. While sometimes we refrain from saying something we should have said, more often do we say something we should not have said.

We can choose one of two paths of conversation: We either keep quiet unless we are certain that we should speak, or we assume that we should speak unless we are certain that we should hold our peace. Since the mean of virtue is closer to silence, the first option is preferable.

People who were forbidden to talk for medical reasons and therefore had to communicate by writing have told me that they realized how much of an average person's conversation is non-essential. Unfortunately, non-essential talk is likely to contain much that is not simply "neutral," but actually destructive, such as lies, gossip, insults, and boasting.

NOTES

_____
_____
_____
_____
_____
_____
_____
_____

Today I shall . . .

. . . try to measure my words very carefully. If there is no real need for saying something, I should reflect on why I wish to say it.

מִצְוָתָה מִשֶּׁתִּשְׁקַע הַחַמָּה *From*
The mitzvah of kindling the Chanukah *the*
lights begins with sunset (Shabbos 21b). *Sages*

Chanukah
Dec. 23, 1992
Dec. 12, 1993
Dec. 1, 1994
Dec. 21, 1995
Dec. 9, 1996
Dec. 27, 1997
[The fifth
candle is
lit tonight.]

Chanukah commemorates both physical and spiritual triumphs. Israel had been politically, that is physically, under the domination of the Greek-Syrians, and the Hellenist culture was jeopardizing the spirituality of Judaism. The miracle of Chanukah, which occurred at one of the darkest moments in Jewish history, should remind us that no matter how bleak life may appear, whether in a physical or spiritual sense, we should never abandon hope. Hence, we commemorate Chanukah in the evening, when it is just beginning to get dark.

We might ask, "Why light the candles at dusk? Why not wait until it is completely dark, when the candles will shine their brightest and banish the total darkness?"

In my work with alcoholics, I often hear that "one does not recover until one hits rock bottom." However, the changes that may occur on the way to rock bottom are often so irreversible and catastrophic that rehabilitation programs put in much effort and ingenuity to intervene at an earlier stage.

We light the Chanukah candles when the sky is just beginning to get dark, instead of waiting for complete darkness. Our action teaches us when we should combat moral and spiritual deterioration — at the very first indication that it is occurring. Delaying action until the latter has occurred may be too costly.

NOTES

Today I shall. . .

. . . try to identify the very earliest signs of weakening and make an effort to avoid deterioration.

Chanukah —
Erev Rosh
Chodesh
Dec. 24, 1992
Dec. 13, 1993
Dec. 2, 1994
Dec. 22, 1995
Dec. 10, 1996
Dec. 28, 1997

[The sixth
candle is
lit tonight.]

From אִם הַדְלֵיקָה בִּמְקוֹם הָרוּחַ וְכָבְתָה זָקוּק לָהּ
the לַחֲזוֹר וּלְהַדְלִיקָה
Sages If the Chanukah lights were extinguished because they were lit in a place where a wind could be expected, one is obliged to relight them *(Mishnah Berurah 673:25).*

Although we are not obligated to relight the Chanukah candles if they are accidentally extinguished, this rule does not apply if the condition could have been foreseen.

In civil law, a person may be held liable for failure to take proper precautions that would prevent a mishap. This concept also holds for spiritual and moral issues as well. While parents may not be able to control the behavior of their children and cannot be held responsible for whatever decisions the children make in their lives, they can and must provide their children with the education and guidance that will enable them to choose wisely and properly.

Many parents who failed to provide their children with a sound Torah education have expressed deep regret for this omission when their children intermarried. Although they may not have been observant, they nevertheless wished their grandchildren to have a Jewish identity, and they realized too late that the most effective way to discourage intermarriage is to practice the *mitzvos*. We have had many variations of, ''If we had to do it over again, we would observe kosher, if not because of our own convictions, then to maintain our children within the Jewish fold.''

We cannot cut down on intermarriage by hoping that our children will not wish to disappoint us, but by creating a life-style for ourselves and for our children that makes intermarriage inconceivable. If we are lax in foresight, we cannot shirk the responsibility for the consequences.

NOTES

_____
_____
_____
_____
_____
_____

Today I shall . . .

_____
_____ ... try to consider the long-term consequences of my behavior, and try to foresee the problems that may occur if I simply do what is most convenient for me now.

מוֹסֵף וְהוֹלֵךְ א' בְּכָל לַיְלָה *From*
One should add an additional light each *the*
night (of Chanukah) (*Orach Chaim* *Sages*
671:2).

Chanukah —
First Day of
Rosh Chodesh
Teves

Although frequently translated as "dedication," Chanukah also means "renewal." The way that we celebrate Chanukah teaches us that renewal requires something more than returning to a former state, even if that state itself had been satisfactory. Renewal requires advancing beyond the previous state.

[Some years Kislev
has only 29 days
and Teves has
only one day of
Rosh Chodesh.

I once heard a recovered alcoholic, twenty years sober, say, "The man that I *was* drank, and the man that I *was* will drink again." If people who emerge from a deteriorated state go back to the state prior to the deterioration, nothing has been accomplished, because history will repeat itself. To avoid the deterioration from recurring, they must change themselves into new beings.

During those years
the 7th and 8th
candles are lit on
the nights
following 1 and 2
Teves, and the last
day of Chanukah
is 3 Teves.]

To achieve a renewal, we must progress. Adding a Chanukah candle every night symbolizes this concept in a spiritual way.

Dec. 14, 1993
Dec. 3, 1994
Dec. 23, 1995
Dec. 29, 1997

Remaining at a plateau is hardly desirable for anyone, but it is utterly unacceptable for people who seek renewal. For them, progress is not only essential for growth, but for survival.

[The seventh
candle is
lit tonight.]

NOTES

_____
_____
_____
_____
_____
_____

Today I shall . . .

. . . try to add to my life by intensifying and increasing those practices that are conducive to growth.

Chanukah —
[Second Day of]
Rosh Chodesh
Teves
Dec. 25, 1992
Dec. 15, 1993
Dec. 4, 1994
Dec. 24, 1995
Dec. 11, 1996
Dec. 30, 1997
[The eighth (in
some years the
seventh) candle
is lit tonight.]

From the
Scriptures

וַיַּעֲמֹד פִּינְחָס וַיְפַלֵּל וַתֵּעָצַר הַמַּגֵּפָה

Pinchas arose and wrought judgment,
and so the plague was checked
(*Psalms* 106:30).

The word *tefillah,* or "prayer," has its origin in the word *pallel,* which means "to seek justice." Prayer should therefore be an activity whereby one seeks justice. The first recorded prayer in Jewish history is that of the Patriarch Abraham. He sought justice for the people of Sodom and pleaded with God to spare them (*Genesis* 18:23-33). Thus, when we pray, whether for ourselves or for others, it should be with the understanding that we are seeking justice.

How, then, can we ask of God to grant our various requests? Are we deserving of this? Do we deserve them? Are they within the realm of justice?

Two answers come to mind. If, as part of our prayers, we admit the wrongs we have done, sincerely regret them, and commit ourselves not to repeat them, then we may indeed be deserving. We therefore do not make our requests on the basis of what we are, but on the basis of what we will be. Second, if we extend ourselves by forgiving people who have offended us and acting with kindness toward them, then God's acting accordingly toward us can in itself be considered justice.

Thus, *teshuvah* (the process of regret and return) and *gemilas chasadim* (acts of kindness) are the foundations of prayer.

NOTES

Today I shall . . .

. . . try to do *teshuvah,* and to act toward others in a way that I wish God to act toward me.

אָנֹכִי הֹלֵךְ בְּדֶרֶךְ כָּל הָאָרֶץ וְחָזַקְתָּ וְהָיִיתָ לְאִישׁ *From the Scriptures*

I am going in the way of all the land (all mankind), and you shall strengthen yourself and be a man (*I Kings* 2:2).

TEVES

טבת

Chanukah
Dec. 26, 1992
Dec. 16, 1993
Dec. 5, 1994
Dec. 25, 1995
Dec. 12, 1996
Dec. 31, 1997
[In some years, the eighth candle is lit tonight.]

These were the last words of King David to his son and successor, Solomon. David is essentially saying, "I am no longer able to struggle. My strength is failing, and I must now go in the way of all humans. But you are young and vigorous. You must be strong and be a man." Implied in this message is that Solomon was to be strong enough *not* to go in the way of all men, but to be his own man.

Being a non-conformist is not virtuous in itself. Behaving in a manner similar to others in our environment is not wrong, as long as we know that our behavior is right and proper. In this case, we are acting according to our conscience. What is wrong is when we abdicate our right to think, judge, and decide for ourselves. It is easy for us to allow ourselves to be dragged along by the opinions and decisions of others, and thereby fail to act according to our conscience.

The expression "I am going in the way of all mankind" does more than euphemize death; it actually defines spiritual death. It states that true life exists only when we actively determine our behavior. A totally passive existence, in which the body is active but the mind is not, may be considered life in a physical sense, but in a spiritual sense it is closer to death.

No wonder the Talmud states that "wrongdoers are considered dead even during their lifetime" (*Berachos* 18b). Failure to exercise our spiritual capacities and instead relegating the mind to a state of passivity, allowing our physical and social impulses to dominate our lives, is in reality death.

NOTES

Today I shall . . .

. . . try to engage my mind to reflect on what I do, and think things through for myself rather than submitting to a herd mentality.

[Last day of Chanukah in some years.]
Dec. 27, 1992
Dec. 17, 1993
Dec. 6, 1994
Dec. 26, 1995
Dec. 13, 1996
Jan. 1, 1998

From the **R**age deprives one of one's senses (*Pesikta Zuta Va'eira* 6:9).

הַכַּעַס מְסַלֵּק אֶת הַדַּעַת

Sages

Anger can be a constructive emotion (e.g. if we see an injustice and our anger helps bring us to correct it). We can compare it to an electric generator, which we constructively harness. Rage, however, has no use. It is like an erupting volcano, which benefits no one and only causes widespread destruction.

Unlike a volcanic eruption, rage is controllable. However, the time to act is before the outburst begins, because once it is in motion, we lack the good judgment necessary for control.

Preventive action consists of training ourselves to react with restraint when a provocative event occurs, even if we feel we are right. We can practice restraint by responding in a soft voice, by keeping silent, or by walking away from the situation and allowing for a "cooling off" period.

Rage feeds upon itself, and if we can stifle rage at its very onset, when it is still controllable, it is akin to smothering a small fire by depriving it of oxygen. Failure to do so may result in a destructive, unmanageable conflagration, and so it is with rage.

NOTES

_____
_____
_____
_____
_____
_____
_____
_____
_____
_____

Today I shall . . .

. . . try to practice restraint in responding to all provocations.

כָּל דַּרְכֵי אִישׁ זַךְ בְּעֵינָיו *From the* *Scriptures*

All the ways of a person are pure in one's eyes *(Proverbs* 16:2).

Dec. 28, 1992
Dec. 18, 1993
Dec. 7, 1994
Dec. 27, 1995
Dec. 14, 1996
Jan. 2, 1998

As a rule, people do not do anything that they believe to be wrong. Those who do wrong have somehow convinced themselves that what they are doing is in fact right. They justify themselves with ingenious rationalizations.

If we are so susceptible to our minds playing tricks on us and deluding us that what is wrong is right, what can we do to prevent improper behavior? Solomon provides the answer: *Direct your actions toward God, and your thoughts will be right (Proverbs* 16:3).

The distortion is greatest when the motivation is, "What do I want?" If we remove ourselves from the picture and instead ask, "What does God want?" the possibility of distortion shrinks.

While there is less distortion in the latter case, we cannot say that distortion is completely absent. Some people have strange ideas about what God wants. However, if we take ourselves out of the picture and are motivated to do what God wants, there is greater likelihood that we might consult someone in a position to give us an authoritative opinion as to the will of God. While this is not foolproof, there is at least a chance of escaping the distortions of rationalization that are dominant when one seeks to satisfy primarily oneself.

NOTES

_____

_____

_____

_____

_____

_____

_____

_____

_____

Today I shall . . .

. . . try to dedicate myself to doing the will of God, and try to learn what His will is by studying the Torah and accepting guidance from Torah authorities.

Dec. 29, 1992
Dec. 19, 1993
Dec. 8, 1994
Dec. 28, 1995
Dec. 15, 1996
Jan. 3, 1998

From the Sages

אֶחָד הַמַּרְבֶּה וְאֶחָד הַמַּמְעִיט וּבִלְבַד שֶׁיְּכַוֵּין לִבּוֹ לַשָּׁמָיִם

If one person does more and another does less, they are both equal before God if they have sincerely dedicated themselves to Him (*Berachos* 5b).

All that can be asked of people is to do whatever is within their means. No one is expected to do more than one can, but by the same token, anyone who does less than that is derelict. For example, people of meager means who give a small amount of money are considered to have performed that *mitzvah* satisfactorily if they have given whatever they can, whereas wealthy people who give a thousand times that much but could have given more are considered derelict in their performance of this *mitzvah*.

The key to proper fulfillment of a *mitzvah* is dedication. One who performs a *mitzvah* perfunctorily may seek to get away with the bare minimum required for its fulfillment, whereas someone who is dedicated will invest himself in the *mitzvah* to the very maximum.

This dedication must be to God. While it is praiseworthy to dedicate oneself to the community or to friends, the recipients of one's benevolent actions may be so grateful to the benefactor that the latter may get carried away by this outpouring of gratitude, and believe that one has done enough. The only true judge of how much one can and should do is God; hence, it is only a sincere dedication to God that can lead one to perform *mitzvos* to the fullest of one's capacities.

NOTES

Today I shall . . .

. . . try to sincerely fulfill my obligations toward God and toward my fellow man by doing the utmost within my means.

כִּי פְשָׁעַי אֲנִי אֵדָע וְחַטָּאתִי נֶגְדִּי תָמִיד *From the*

My transgressions are known to me *Scriptures*
and my sin is ever before me
(*Psalms* 51:5).

הֵן בְּעָווֹן חוֹלָלְתִּי וּבְחֵטְא יֶחֱמַתְנִי אִמִּי

Lo, I was begotten in sin, and my
mother conceived me in iniquity
(ibid. 7).

TEVES

6

טבת

Dec. 30, 1992
Dec. 20, 1993
Dec. 9, 1994
Dec. 29, 1995
Dec. 16, 1996
Jan. 4, 1998

In this heart-rending psalm, David begs for forgiveness for his relationship with Bath-Sheba.

While David does state that he was "begotten in sin," or in other words, that he may have been born with the character trait of intense passion, he does not cite it to free himself of guilt. In verse 5, he owns up to his transgression and does not try to absolve himself. David accepts full responsibility for his behavior, even if it comes from an inherited trait.

How refreshing is this thought! How different it is from the teachings of modern psychology, which so often scapegoat parents and excuse even the grossest misbehavior by arguing that the person was a victim of early-life experiences or influences that distorted his or her values, and hence should not be held responsible for subsequent misdeeds.

In this exquisite psalm of *teshuvah* (repentance), David rejects this position. He says that we must assume responsibility for our behavior, regardless of factors from our past.

NOTES

Today I shall . . .

. . . try to avoid projecting blame onto others, and accept full responsibility for whatever I do.

TEVES

7

טבת

Dec. 31, 1992
Dec. 21, 1993
Dec. 10, 1994
Dec. 30, 1995
Dec. 17, 1996
Jan. 5, 1998

From the Sages אֵיזוֹ הִיא דֶרֶךְ יְשָׁרָה שֶׁיָּבֹר לוֹ הָאָדָם? כֹּל שֶׁהִיא תִפְאֶרֶת לְעֹשֶׂהָ וְתִפְאֶרֶת לוֹ מִן הָאָדָם

Which is the proper path that one should choose for oneself? That which is honorable to the one who adopts it and also merits the admiration of others** (*Ethics of the Fathers* 2:1).

At first glance, this statement is bothersome. Right and wrong are, we know, absolute and not subject to public opinion. "The admiration of others" should have no place in determining morality.

The statement is not referring here to what is right versus what is wrong. Rather, it is discussing the mode of conduct *within* the realm of what is right.

The Midrash relates that Rabbi Shimon ben Shatach bought a mule from an Arab, and when his students discovered a precious gem in the saddlepack, they congratulated him on his good fortune. Rabbi Shimon responded, "I bought a mule, not a precious gem." He sought out the Arab and he returned the gem to him. The Arab said, "Blessed be the God of Rabbi Shimon ben Shatach."

Ethical behavior elicits admiration and serves as an example for others.

NOTES

Today I shall . . .

. . . try to behave in a manner that goes beyond right and wrong, and make my "right" into a "true right."

אֲנִי ה' אֱלֹקֵיכֶם אֲשֶׁר הוֹצֵאתִי אֶתְכֶם *From the*
מֵאֶרֶץ מִצְרָיִם *Scriptures*

I am your God Who has delivered you from the land of Egypt (*Shema, Numbers* 15:41).

Jan. 1, 1993
Dec. 22, 1993
Dec. 11, 1994
Dec. 31, 1995
Dec. 18, 1996
Jan. 6, 1998

This verse is recited twice daily, because the deliverance from Egypt was more than a historic event. It was a deliverance from a state of enslavement, and this deliverance should repeat itself daily in everyone's life.

No enslavement and no tyranny are as ruthless and as demanding as slavery to physical desires and passions. Someone who is unable to resist a craving, and who must, like a brute beast, do whatever the body demands, is more profoundly enslaved than someone subject to a human tyrant. Addicted people are an extreme example of those who have become slaves to their bodies.

Dignity comes from freedom, in the capacity to make free choices, and hence, in our ability to refuse to submit to physical desires when our judgment indicates that doing so is wrong. Freedom from domination by the body is the first step toward spiritual growth.

NOTES

Today I shall . . .

. . . declare my freedom from the tyranny of my body.

Jan. 2, 1993
Dec. 23, 1993
Dec. 12, 1994
Jan. 1, 1996
Dec. 19, 1996
Jan. 7, 1998

From the **A** *Sages*

הַמִּדּוֹת הֵן לְפִי עֶרֶךְ הַשֵּׂכֶל

person's drives are related to the degree of one's intellect (*Tanya*, Chapter 6).

The *Tanya* explains that children have strong desires for things that are important to them. They may passionately desire a simple toy, perhaps only a small colorful block of wood, and may become very angry and enraged if they do not get it. To adults, this item has no value, but to children it may be very important.

As we grow older and hopefully wiser, we can see that things that had at one time great importance are in retrospect of no greater importance than that toy. At that time, it seemed important to us because we could use only the intellect we had at that particular moment; we could not apply wisdom that would come with greater maturity.

Is it not strange, however, that we do not apply the lessons of the past? When we are absolutely certain that something we want is most vital, why do we not stop and think that we are feeling precisely the way we had felt in the past about something which we now realize is trivial? Why don't we learn from our experiences and not become frustrated and enraged when we are denied something we strongly desire?

Although we cannot have tomorrow's wisdom today, we can utilize the wisdom of our elders and others who have been in the situation which now confronts us. They may help us ascribe more realistic values to our desires.

NOTES

Today I shall . . .

. . . try to realize that tomorrow I might think myself foolish for having become so enraged about something that frustrated me today.

אֱלֹקִים בָּאוּ גוֹיִם בְּנַחֲלָתֶךָ טִמְּאוּ אֶת הֵיכַל קָדְשֶׁךָ *From the Scriptures*

TEVES

10

טבת

*Fast of
Asarah B'Teves*

Jan. 3, 1993
Dec. 24, 1993
Dec. 13, 1994
Jan. 2, 1996
Dec. 20, 1996
Jan. 8, 1998

O, God, alien nations have come into Your inheritance and have defiled Your Sanctuary (*Psalms* 79:1).

The tenth day of Teves is a fast day, on which we remember the beginning of the siege of Jerusalem that led to the destruction of the Temple. By depriving ourselves of food and drink, we experience the discomfort of hunger and thirst, and in this way we share in the national distress.

No other nation has anything similar to a fast day for an event that occurred thousands of years ago. Most historic events are remembered by historians interested in the subject. The average person is untouched by such ancient events.

Not so with Jews, for whom spirituality and closeness to God are a vital part of life. The loss of intimacy with God that occurred with the destruction of the Temple is something from which we have never recovered, and is a source of grief today. The fast of the tenth day of Teves is not merely a commemoration of a historic event, but an expression of the grief we experience today in being deprived of the close presence of God in the Temple.

We have been promised that the Temple will be restored with the ultimate Redemption of Israel, and we will again have the *kedushah* which is the breath of spiritual life. To achieve this Redemption we must merit it, by committing ourselves to total observance of Torah and *mitzvos*.

NOTES

_____
_____
_____
_____
_____
_____
_____
_____
_____
_____
_____

Today I shall . . .

. . . try to understand how the loss of the Sanctuary thousands of years ago is a personal loss to me, and what I can do to restore that *kedushah*.

Jan. 4, 1993
Dec. 25, 1993
Dec. 14, 1994
Jan. 3, 1996
Dec. 21, 1996
Jan. 9, 1998

From the O*ne who responds "Amen" after a bless-*
Sages ing surpasses the one who recites the
blessing (*Berachos* 53b).

גָּדוֹל הָעוֹנֶה אָמֵן יוֹתֵר מִן הַמְבָרֵךְ

"Amen" is an expression of confirmation, whereby we attest that what the other person has said is indeed true. Thus, when someone recites a blessing expressing gratitude to God or asserting that God has commanded the performance of a particular *mitzvah,* one is making a declaration of one's faith. When we respond by saying "Amen," we are essentially stating, "What you have said is indeed true," and thereby we are not only concurring with what was said and expressing our own faith, but also reinforcing the other person's statement and strengthening the other person's faith.

There are things that one can do that will strengthen other people's faith in God, and things that will weaken it. In Torah there is a concept of *arvus* — mutual responsibility — by virtue of which one is obligated to try to strengthen other people's belief and trust in God. Although every person has free will, and God does not intervene to deter someone from committing a wrong, people who have suffered because of someone's misdeeds often feel that God has abandoned them. Thus, if we deal unfairly with others, we may not only cause them to be angry at us, but also bring them to doubt God for allowing an injustice to happen. While such reasoning is faulty, the one who caused it is nevertheless responsible for causing the victim to feel that way. On the other hand, when we behave in the manner which God wishes, the result is *kvod shamayim* — bringing glory and honor to God, and strengthening people's faith. Our actions can and do affect how other people will think and act.

NOTES

Today I shall . . .

. . . try to behave in a way that will result in people having greater respect for and trust in God.

TEVES

12

טבת

Jan. 5, 1993
Dec. 26, 1993
Dec. 15, 1994
Jan. 4, 1996
Dec. 22, 1996
Jan. 10, 1998

וּבֹצֵעַ בֵּרֵךְ נִאֵץ ה' *From the*

When a thief recites a blessing, he *Scriptures* **angers God** (*Psalms* 10:3).

The Talmud explains this verse as referring to someone who stole wheat, ground it into flour, and kneaded it into dough, then took off the required tithe for the *Kohen* (priest) and recited the blessing for the tithe. Far from being pleased with this prayer, God becomes angry, for not only did this person sin by stealing, but he or she had the audacity to pronounce God's Name over something acquired dishonestly (*Bava Kama* 94a).

Much of Torah law deals with business. Indeed, the greatest piety is achieved when people observe the laws regulating commercial transactions and property rights, and thereby respect other's belongings and rights (*Bava Kama* 30a). Doing a *mitzvah* with something not acquired honestly is the grossest of all distortions.

In a highly competitive society, we may think that all is fair, especially if we can find a way to make dishonest actions appear legitimate. The Torah condemns such thinking.

NOTES

_____
_____
_____
_____
_____
_____
_____
_____
_____
_____

Today I shall . . .

. . . try to maintain rigorous honesty in all that I do, so that all my *mitzvos* will be welcomed by God.

Jan. 6, 1993
Dec. 27, 1993
Dec. 16, 1994
Jan. 5, 1996
Dec. 23, 1996
Jan. 11, 1998

From the מְעַט שֵׁנוֹת מְעַט תְּנוּמוֹת מְעַט חִבֻּק יָדַיִם
Scriptures לִשְׁכָּב וּבָא כִמְהַלֵּךְ רֵאשֶׁךָ

A bit more sleep, a little slumber, a little folding of the hands to rest, and like a wanderer, your poverty will come (*Proverbs* 6:10-11).

No one sets out in life with the goal of being a failure, and if people would only recognize the consequences of bad habits, they would avoid them.

From my work with alcoholics, I can attest that no one sets themselves a goal of becoming alcoholic, but what may have started out as safe social drinking advances very surreptitiously to become dependence and addiction. Future addicts find they need gradually increasing amounts of alcohol to put themselves at ease, until the quantity they consume becomes toxic and results in disaster.

So it is with laziness. What harm can there be in just a bit more sleep or a little more rest? Indolence, however, can stealthily creep up on people, catch them, and suck out their vigor and diligence.

Suddenly, as if out of nowhere, like a "wanderer" who appears on the scene unexpectedly, one finds oneself in poverty. Indolence has taken its toll.

Breaking bad habits does not come easily, and even some people who arise early and who may feel they are not indolent might discover that they are fond of procrastination, which is just another variety of indolence.

A proper amount of sleep and rest is essential for good health. Diligent people schedule their rest and relaxation so that they do not inadvertently become victims of the seductive character of indolence.

NOTES

Today I shall . . .

. . . try to do that which needs to be done without delay, and schedule my periods of sleep, rest, and relaxation.

הַיְינוּ דְּאָמְרֵי אֱינָשֵׁי אוֹ חַבְרוּתָא אוֹ מִיתוּתָא *From*
This is why people say, "Either compan- *the*
ionship or death" (*Taanis* 23a). *Sages*

The Talmud quotes this aphorism after relating the story of Choni, who awoke after a sleep of seventy years, and, because everyone whom he had known had died, was totally without friends. When he found that no one of the new generation appreciated him, he prayed for death as an escape from an intolerable existence.

One does not have to sleep for seventy years to be alone. Many people are "loners," deprived of the comfort of sharing their lives with others. Much of their loneliness may be self-inflicted.

Withdrawal from human contact is invariably caused by a negative self-image. People who think poorly of themselves assume that others will not welcome them and in fact that they will reject them. To avoid the pain of possible rejection, they simply withdraw from human contact and retreat behind a wall of isolation that they erect to keep people away. Unfortunately, such a wall is not only a barrier; it becomes a prison.

I dealt with this subject in my book *Let Us Make Man* (C.I.S. Publishing 1987). There are ways that we can overcome the negative self-image, but before we can implement such techniques, we must be aware of the problem: we have indeed isolated ourselves due to faulty self-perception.

Jan. 7, 1993
Dec. 28, 1993
Dec. 17, 1994
Jan. 6, 1996
Dec. 24, 1996
Jan 12, 1998

NOTES

Today I shall . . .

. . . try to analyze whether I have as many friends as I would like, and if not, whether this may not be due to my withdrawal.

Jan. 8, 1993
Dec. 29, 1993
Dec. 18, 1994
Jan. 7, 1996
Dec. 25, 1996
Jan. 13, 1998

From the **F**ortunate **are we that our youth has not caused us embarrassment in later life** *Sages* (*Succah* 53a).

אַשְׁרֵי יַלְדוּתֵנוּ שֶׁלֹּא בִּיְּישָׁה אֶת זִקְנוּתֵנוּ

Many people gain wisdom in their later years. When they look back on their youth, they regret having squandered so much time. Some people's "golden years" are unfortunately marred with regret over the time they lost.

Young people can learn from their elders. People who reflect on the past during their last days often say, "My greatest regret is that I did not spend more time with my family." Has anyone ever said, "My greatest regret is that I did not spend more time at the office"?

While experience teaches most efficiently, some things are simply too costly to be learned by experience, because the opportunity to apply these lessons may never arise. Our learning too late that we have spent time foolishly is a prime example.

Ask your father and he will tell you; your elders and they will say it to you (*Deuteronomy* 32:7). In his last words, Moses gives us this most important teaching: "Why learn the hard way when you can benefit from the experience of others who have been there?" We should regularly ask: "How pleased will I be in the future about what I am doing now?"

NOTES

_____
_____
_____
_____
_____
_____
_____
_____
_____
_____

Today I shall . . .

. . . try to examine my actions with the consideration of how I will look back at them in the future.

הֱוֵו זְהִירִין בָּרָשׁוּת שֶׁאֵין מְקָרְבִין לוֹ לְאָדָם *From*
אֶלָּא לְצֹרֶךְ עַצְמָן *the*

Be cautious in associating with the ruling *Sages*
powers, because they seek people's
closeness only for their own purposes
(*Ethics of the Fathers* 2:3).

Jan. 9, 1993
Dec. 30, 1993
Dec. 19, 1994
Jan. 8, 1996
Dec. 26, 1996
Jan. 14, 1998

Time has not changed some things. Even several thousand years ago government figures were known to be fair-weather friends who exploited their friendship for personal advantage.

While this is as true now as it was then, why is it written in a volume on ethics?

Some people lust for power. Those who lack their own authority try to associate themselves with the powers-that-be in order to share in their power. Just as actual power can corrupt, so also can the desire for power, since we may then do whatever is necessary to ingratiate ourselves with the authorities, including compromising on our principles.

The Talmud discourages such associations by pointing out that they are likely to be exercises in futility. Like so many other lusts, the lust for power holds out a promise of bliss, and inevitably results in bitter disappointment.

NOTES

Today I shall . . .

. . . try to avoid seeking authority and dominion over others, and rather seek mastery over myself.

Jan. 10, 1993
Dec. 31, 1993
Dec. 20, 1994
Jan. 9, 1996
Dec. 27, 1996
Jan. 15, 1998

From the Scriptures

רַק הִשָּׁמֶר לְךָ וּשְׁמֹר נַפְשְׁךָ מְאֹד פֶּן תִּשְׁכַּח אֶת הַדְּבָרִים אֲשֶׁר רָאוּ עֵינֶיךָ

Beware and guard yourself lest you forget the words that your eyes witnessed [at Sinai] (*Deuteronomy* 4:9).

While forgetting is a spontaneous occurrence, it is nevertheless perfectly appropriate to instruct someone not to forget. Personal experience is that if we have something extremely important to do and we are afraid we might forget it, we leave ourselves various reminders to make certain that we remember.

Except when it is due to an aberration in the brain, forgetting something is an indication that it was of relatively little importance. How do you feel when someone who you expected would remember you does not know your name? Also, do you not feel awkward upon meeting someone and having to admit you do not remember his/her name? These feelings are due to the awareness that forgetting something indicates that it was not all that important.

The revelation at Sinai at which we received the Torah was not only the most important event in the history of the Jewish nation, but also the event that should be the fulcrum of the life of every individual Jew. It is the Divine origin of the Torah that makes its values permanent and unalterable, rendering it beyond human manipulation. If we forget the Divine origin of Torah, we are likely to tamper with it and adapt it to comply with our own wishes. When this occurs, all values become relative, and this may result in the behavior of the individual and the group being determined by expedience, hardly a standard of ethics that dignifies a human being.

NOTES

Today I shall . . .

. . . try to remember that there are fundamental and unalterable values that should guide me, and that these are the will of God as revealed in the Torah.

אָמְרוּ עָלָיו עַל רַבָּן יוֹחָנָן בֶּן זַכַּאי שֶׁלֹּא הִקְדִּימוֹ *From*
אָדָם שָׁלוֹם מֵעוֹלָם וַאֲפִילוּ נָכְרִי בַּשּׁוּק *the*

No one ever anticipated (Rabbi Yochanan *Sages*
ben Zakai) with a greeting in the public
place *(Berachos 17a).*

Jan. 11, 1993
Jan. 1, 1994
Dec. 21, 1994
Jan. 10, 1996
Dec. 28, 1996
Jan. 16, 1998

The Talmud states that when Rabbi Yochanan ben Zakai met someone in the street, he always initiated the greeting, and that never, in his entire lifetime, did he ever wait to be greeted first.

Rabbi Yochanan ben Zakai is one of the most outstanding personalities in Jewish history. After Jerusalem fell to the Romans, in 70 C.E., he served as both the political and religious leader of the Jewish nation for forty years. He is singlehandedly responsible for the survival of Israel during that difficult era.

When this great leader walked down the street, he undoubtedly engaged in important conversation with his colleagues and disciples on the vital issues of the day. We certainly could understand that he could not interrupt such weighty discussions to respond to people who greeted him, let alone to initiate greetings to others.

Still, the Talmud states that regardless of his preoccupation with the leadership of Israel, this great personality never waited to be greeted first, and not even the importance of his position could cause him to expect recognition from others.

The great Hillel prophesied about Rabbi Yochanan that he would be "a father of wisdom and a father to many generations." Rabbi Yochanan was a leader who followed in the footsteps of Moses, whose humility also paralleled his greatness.

NOTES

Today I shall . . .

. . . try to consider every person as being worthy of recognition, and avoid the false pride of expecting to be acknowledged first.

Jan. 12, 1993
Jan. 2, 1994
Dec. 22, 1994
Jan. 11, 1996
Dec. 29, 1996
Jan. 17, 1998

From the Scriptures וּלְךָ אֲדֹנָי חָסֶד כִּי אַתָּה תְשַׁלֵּם לְאִישׁ כְּמַעֲשֵׂהוּ

For kindness is Yours, O God, when You compensate each person according to his actions (*Psalms* 62:13).

In our productivity-oriented society, we tend to place value on the product rather than on the process. Success is praised and failure is condemned, and we have little interest in the circumstances under which others function.

This attitude might be justified in the marketplace, since commerce lives by the bottom line. Still, our preoccupation with commerce should not influence us to think that people's successes and failures should be the yardsticks for how we value them.

God does not judge according to outcome. God knows that people have control only over what they do, not over the results. Virtue or sin are determined not by what materializes, but by what we do and why.

Since the Torah calls on us to "walk in His ways," to emulate God as best we can, we would do well to have a value system so that we judge people by their actions, not their results. This system should be applied to ourselves as well. We must try to do our utmost according to the best ethical and moral guidance we can obtain. When we do so, our behavior is commendable, regardless of the results of our actions.

NOTES

Today I shall . . .

. . . try to be considerate of others and of myself as well, and realize that none of us is in control of the outcome of our actions, only of their nature.

From בָּרוּךְ אַתָּה ה' . . . שֶׁעָשָׂה לִי כָּל צָרְכִּי

Blessed are You, O God ... Who has *our* provided me my every needs *(Siddur).* **Prayers**

Jan. 13, 1993
Jan. 3, 1994
Dec. 23, 1994
Jan. 12, 1996
Dec. 30, 1996
Jan. 18, 1998

One of the great *tzaddikim* lived in abject poverty, yet always had a happy disposition. He was asked how he managed to maintain so pleasant an attitude in the face of such adverse conditions.

"Each day I pray to God to provide all my needs," he said. "If I am poor, that means that one of my needs is poverty. Why should I be unhappy if I have whatever I need?"

Tzaddikim are great people and we are little people who may not always be able to achieve the intensity of trust in God that would allow us to accept adversity with joy. But even if we cannot attain it to the highest degree, we should be able to develop some sincere trust.

When our children are little, we as parents know what they need. They might prefer a diet of sweets, but we give them nourishing foods. They certainly despise receiving painful injections that immunize them against dreadful diseases, but we forcibly subject them to these procedures because we know what is good for them.

Some people do not believe in God. But to those that do, why not realize that He knows our needs better than we do, and that even some very unpleasant experiences are actually for our own betterment?

Today I shall . . .

. . . try to bear adversity with less anger and resentment, remembering that God is a compassionate Father, and that He gives me that which He knows, far better than I, that I truly need.

NOTES

_____
_____
_____
_____
_____
_____
_____
_____
_____

Jan. 14, 1993
Jan. 4, 1994
Dec. 24, 1994
Jan. 13, 1996
Dec. 31, 1996
Jan. 19, 1998

From the Scriptures רֵאשִׁית חָכְמָה יִרְאַת ה'

The beginning of wisdom is the fear of God (*Psalms* 111:10).

Would it not have been more appropriate to refer to the fear of God as the beginning of piety rather than wisdom?

One of the Chassidic masters interpreted the above verse most uniquely. "The fear of God," he said, "refers not to man's fear of God, but to God's fear." It might seem strange to speak of God as having fear, but his explanation quells this objection.

God has decreed that people have free will. Although everything else in the universe is under Divine control, God wishes our moral choice to be free, and He therefore does not intervene to influence our moral decisions. Since God wishes us to be just and virtuous, He thus has a fear that we will harm ourselves by sin. This fear is similar to that of parents who fear that their young children may harm themselves by doing things that they do not recognize as dangerous.

If we would realize that everything else in the universe is controlled by God, and that only our moral choice is not under Divine control, we would then concentrate on moral choices and leave everything else up to God. It would be wise, therefore, if we had the fear that God has for us; namely, that we might sin. We show wisdom, not just piety, if we devote our attention to what is not under Divine control.

NOTES

Today I shall . . .

. . . try to turn my attention and efforts to my moral choices, since these are really the only things that are decided by my choice.

לֹא יֶאֱהַב לֵץ הוֹכֵחַ לוֹ *From the* A scoffer does not like to be repri- *Scriptures* manded (*Proverbs* 15:12).

Jan. 15, 1993
Jan. 5, 1994
Dec. 25, 1994
Jan. 14, 1996
Jan. 1, 1997
Jan. 20, 1998

Hardly anyone is as thoroughly condemned and treated as contemptuously as the scoffer, who behaves with scorn and ridicule. King Solomon does not condemn a *rasha* —a sinner — as much as he does a scoffer. The *rasha* of *Proverbs* sins by indulgence — by submitting to temptation — and thus is tolerated, though criticized. The scoffer, who acts with derision, is totally rejected, much like the "wicked son" mentioned in the Passover *Haggadah*.

Those who sin because of temptation are redeemable. Someday they may realize the folly and futility of a life of self-indulgence, and then they will do *teshuvah* and turn themselves toward spirituality. Not so scoffers, whose attitude of mocking everything puts them beyond redemption. As R' Moshe Chaim Luzzato says, "The scoffer can be compared to a shield coated with grease, which causes oncoming arrows to slip off. Likewise, scoffers are immune to reprimand and direction, not because of any lack of intelligence, but because of their attitude of derision, which destroys every ethical concept" (*Path of the Just*:5).

Criticism may not be pleasant, and not all criticism must be accepted. Sometimes, the reproof we receive may be incorrect, and we are actually right. But we must always listen to criticism and then make a proper decision. Frank rejection of reproof without giving it serious consideration renders us beyond help.

Today I shall . . .

. . . try to keep my ears and mind open to criticism, and avoid reflexively dismissing anything I do not like to hear.

NOTES

Jan. 16, 1993
Jan. 6, 1994
Dec. 26, 1994
Jan. 15, 1996
Jan. 2, 1997
Jan. 21, 1998

*From the
Scriptures* **W**here were you when I established the earth? (*Job* 38:4).

אֵיפֹה הָיִיתָ בְּיָסְדִי אָרֶץ

One who reads the book of *Job* cannot but have compassion for just and pious Job, who appears to be unfairly subjected to suffering. All the rational arguments that his friends offer to account for his innocent suffering appear hollow, and the only acceptable answer is God's remark to Job, "Where were you when I established the earth?"

In other words, a human being can see only a tiny fragment of the universe, an infinitesimally small bit of time and space. Our vantage point is much like a single piece of a huge jigsaw puzzle, a tiny fragment of the whole picture, which makes no sense on its own. Only when the entire puzzle is assembled do we realize how this odd-shaped piece fits properly. Since no human being can have a view of the totality of the universe in both time and space, we cannot possibly grasp the meaning of one tiny fragment of it.

This explanation does not tell us why the innocent may suffer, but only why there cannot be a satisfactory explanation. Acceptance of suffering therefore requires faith in a Creator who designed the universe with a master plan in which everything that happens has a valid reason. This belief may not comfort a sufferer nor prevent the sufferer from becoming angry at the Designer of the universe. The Torah does not in fact condemn the anger of the sufferer (*Bava Basra* 16b), but does require that he accept adversity with trust that God is just (*Deuteronomy* 32:4).

Acceptance does not mean approval, but it does allow us to avoid the paralyzing rage of righteous rage, and to go on with the business of living.

NOTES

Today I shall . . .

. . . try to realize that nothing ever happens that is purposeless, and that I must go on living even when I disapprove of the way the world operates.

אָסְיָא דְּמָגָּן בְּמָגָּן מָגָּן שָׁוֶה *From*
A doctor who treats for nothing is worth *the*
nothing (*Bava Kama* 85a). *Sages*

Jan. 17, 1993
Jan. 7, 1994
Dec. 27, 1994
Jan. 16, 1996
Jan. 3, 1997
Jan. 22, 1998

The Talmud teaches that "there is no free lunch." Anything of value comes with a price tag, and if something is given away free, we should suspect that it may be worthless.

People are reluctant to accept some things as true. Today, a millennium and a half after the Talmud was written down, we still yearn to get things for free, and if not completely free, then at the least possible cost.

Nothing is wrong with bargain hunting. At the end of a season, some leftover merchandise of good quality may be put on sale, or discontinued models may be available at a fraction of their original price. Still, we must be cautious that we do not extend this penchant for bargains to areas where it can be destructive, such as relationships or other things of spiritual value.

Valuable relationships can be costly. If we are not willing to sacrifice our comfort for a relationship, but look only for friends or spouses that will demand nothing of us, the Talmud teaches that this relationship will be worth exactly what we invest in it: nothing. Likewise, if we seek spiritual goals that will come easily to us without any effort or deprivation on our part, we will achieve goals that are worth nothing.

The Talmud uses the example of free medical care to teach us that for things that are truly important, such as our health, we must be willing to bear the cost. We should apply this lesson to other items of value.

NOTES

Today I shall . . .

. . . try to avoid bargain hunting for those things that are truly important to me.

TEVES

טבת

Jan. 18, 1993
Jan. 8, 1994
Dec. 28, 1994
Jan. 17, 1996
Jan. 4, 1997
Jan. 23, 1998

From the Sages

„קוֹל ה' בַּכֹּחַ" בְּכֹחוֹ לֹא נֶאֱמַר אֶלָּא בַּכֹּחַ
בְּכֹחוֹ שֶׁל כָּל אֶחָד וְאֶחָד

The voice of God is within might (*Psalms* 29:4). **The verse does not read "within His might"; it therefore means [that God communicates] with each person according to that person's might or capacity** (*Shemos Rabbah* 5:9).

A young couple who began to observe Torah and *mitzvos* suffered severe adversity after becoming observant. They were not only deeply affected by their misfortune, but were also very confused. "Why is God doing this to us *now?* Before we became Torah observant, everything went smoothly for us. Now we have all this happening. Is this God's way of rejecting us, telling us that He does not welcome our observance?"

No one knows why certain people suffer in certain ways. However, this much is certain: for whatever reason that suffering does occur, God does not burden people with more than they can bear. No one can explain why adversity visited this young couple, but for whatever reason that it happened, they had already achieved enough strength to bear it.

Can we then say that people would be better off being less spiritual so that they would not be subjected to as much suffering? No, for if we carry this argument to its logical extreme, we would be still better off being cows in the pasture and not suffering at all.

Solomon said, *As one increases wisdom, so one increases suffering* (*Ecclesiastes* 1:18). The Rabbi of Kotzk commented, "Maybe so, but let me suffer and be wise rather than be tranquil and a fool."

NOTES

Today I shall . . .

. . . try to have the faith that God will give me no greater burden than I can bear (see 26 Teves).

עֲשָׂרָה נִסְיוֹנוֹת נִתְנַסָּה אַבְרָהָם אָבִינוּ וְעָמַד *From* בְּכֻלָּם לְהוֹדִיעַ כַּמָּה חִבָּתוֹ שֶׁל אַבְרָהָם אָבִינוּ *the*

The Patriarch Abraham was tested (by *Sages* God) ten times and withstood them all. This proves Abraham's great love for God (*Ethics of the Fathers* 5:3).

Jan. 19, 1993
Jan. 9, 1994
Dec. 29, 1994
Jan. 18, 1996
Jan. 5, 1997
Jan. 24, 1998

Abraham was tested with ten trials of progressively increasing severity, ultimately culminating in the test of sacrificing his beloved son Isaac if God so willed.

Abraham successfully passed all the tests. Still, while he did demonstrate his intense loyalty and devotion to God, how did it prove his love for God?

In yesterday's message we learned that God does not challenge people beyond their capacities. It follows, then, that as they advance in spiritual growth and strength, they actually render themselves vulnerable to trials of greater intensity. In the course of his many trials, Abraham detected this pattern. He could have logically decided to avoid any further spiritual progression, because it might subject him to even greater ordeals than those he had already sustained.

Abraham decided otherwise. He desired so much to come closer to God that he was willing to pay any price. Thus, when he was put to the ultimate task — to sacrifice Isaac — Abraham was not taken aback. He had fully anticipated such an eventuality.

We are not of the mettle of Abraham, and we pray every day, "Do not put us to test." While we indeed wish to advance spiritually, we ask to be spared the distress of trial. Yet, should we experience adversity in life, we would do well to realize that this may be a testimony to our spiritual strength.

Today I shall . . .

. . . try to advance myself spiritually. Although I pray to be spared from distress, I will try not to recoil if adversity does occur.

NOTES

Jan. 20, 1993
Jan. 10, 1994
Dec. 30, 1994
Jan. 19, 1996
Jan. 6, 1997
Jan. 25, 1998

From the Sages

הָאוֹהֵב אֶת אִשְׁתּוֹ כְּגוּפוֹ וְהַמְכַבְּדָהּ יוֹתֵר מִגּוּפוֹ . . . עָלָיו הַכָּתוּב אוֹמֵר,,וְיָדַעְתָּ כִּי שָׁלוֹם אָהֳלֶךְ"

He who loves his wife as he loves himself and who respects her even more than himself . . . it is of him that the Scripture says, "You will know there is peace in your dwelling" (*Yevamos* 62b).

The secret of peace in the home is the awareness that husband and wife are not two distinct individuals living in a contractual relationship, but are one unit. If they love each other, they are also loving themselves, and if they respect each other, they are also respecting themselves.

I heard a man say, "I used to argue with my wife. Then one day I realized that I did not like to lose an argument because I did not want to be a loser. On the other hand, if I won the argument, then my wife would have lost, and I did not want to be married to a loser. The only solution was to stop arguing."

In marriage, there is no winner *and* loser. In any given situation, both spouses either win or lose.

The Torah emphasizes the concept of unity in describing the marriage relationship: *Man shall cling unto his wife and they shall be one* (*Genesis* 2:24). Anything less than that, any situation where one considers him or herself superior to the other or triumphant over the other, falls short of this concept of marriage.

NOTES

_____
_____
_____
_____
_____
_____
_____
_____
_____

_____

Today I shall . . .

_____

. . . try to realize that marriage is a fusion, a unit rather than a union, and that whatever I do to my spouse I am doing to myself as well.

וַיְהִי הָאָדָם לְנֶפֶשׁ חַיָּה *From the*
Man became a living soul (*Genesis Scriptures*
2:7).

Rabbi Leib, the son of the Chassidic master Rabbi Mordechai of Nesh'chiz, related that he remembered being a small child sitting on his father's lap. His father told him, "The Targum (Aramaic translation of the Torah) interprets *living soul* as a *speaking spirit*. In other words, people acquire the capacity to speak by virtue of the Divine soul that is instilled within them. Inasmuch as God is truth, the Divine soul, which is part of God, is also truth. Since people's souls are linked with this ability to speak, speech can only be truth. That is why," the Rabbi continued, "if someone lies, that is not speech, only meaningless noise."

"Ever since then," Rabbi Leib said, "whenever someone lies to me, all I hear is undistinguishable sounds, just noise. I cannot make out words, and I cannot understand what the person is saying."

How wonderful it would be if we too could so refine our hearing that our ears could perceive only truth, and that untruths would be just scrambled sounds! Still, if we cannot rise to the spiritual heights of Rabbi Leib, we may nevertheless understand that if we lie, we are not really speaking, but only making noise. To lie is to distort the God-given gift of speech into meaningless sounds that cannot possibly achieve anything truly beneficial to us.

Think of yourself as a concert pianist who, instead of playing melodious music, bangs indiscriminately on the keys, producing an annoying cacophony. When you are not speaking the truth, you are making the same noise.

Jan. 21, 1993
Jan. 11, 1994
Dec. 31, 1994
Jan. 20, 1996
Jan. 7, 1997
Jan. 26, 1998

Today I shall . . .

. . . try to realize that speech is not only a special gift of God, but is in itself Divine, and I shall not demean it by lying.

NOTES

Erev
Rosh Chodesh
[Eve of the
New Month]
Jan. 22, 1993
Jan. 12, 1994
Jan. 1, 1995
Jan. 21, 1996
Jan. 8, 1997
Jan. 27, 1998

From רַבִּי אֱלִיעֶזֶר אוֹמֵר . . . וְשׁוּב יוֹם אֶחָד לִפְנֵי
the מִיתָתְךָ
Sages Rabbi Eliezer said . . . do teshuvah (repentance) one day before your death
(*Ethics of the Fathers* 2:15).

Rabbi Eliezer's disciples asked him, "How can we know on what day we will die?" He answered, "That is precisely the point. Since we do not know when we will die, we should live every day as though it were our last" (*Shabbos* 153a).

While Judaism is life oriented, and we all pray to live one hundred and twenty years, the fact is that life does come to an end, and sometimes unexpectedly so. If we were to think, "How would I like to spend my last day on earth?" and live each day as though it were that last, we would undoubtedly establish a different set of values.

If we knew that we had only twenty-four hours of life left, we certainly would not idle away these precious moments. We would not go to a movie that day. Rather, we would wish to spend every moment with the people we love, telling them how much we love them and apologizing for any possible offense done to them. We would do the same with our friends, both giving and asking for forgiveness. We might spend some time in sincere and dedicated prayer, not mumbling a word.

What a day that would be!

NOTES

Today I shall . . .

. . . pray for long life, but behave as though today is my last day on earth.

הָבִינוּ פְתָאיִם עָרְמָה וּכְסִילִים הָבִינוּ לֵב. *From the*
שִׁמְעוּ כִּי נְגִידִים אֲדַבֵּר *Scriptures*

You simpletons, understand cleverness; you fools, understand with
the heart. Listen, for my words merit
serious attention (*Proverbs* 8:5-6).

Rosh Chodesh
Jan. 23, 1993
Jan. 13, 1994
Jan. 2, 1995
Jan. 22, 1996
Jan. 9, 1997
Jan. 28, 1998

The simpletons and fools to whom Solomon refers repeatedly in *Proverbs* are not people born without intellect. Why would he demand understanding from those who cannot understand? Solomon is calling out to people who do have the capacity for wisdom, but who choose to behave foolishly.

People who have a limited amount of money, yet squander it on unnecessary incidentals and leave themselves without the means to buy food and clothing, are not necessarily feeble-minded. Rather, they place the pleasures of the moment above the more important things in life. These people allow themselves to be dominated by their desires rather than using their judgment. They do not lack the ability to make a proper judgment, but are lax in applying that ability.

Solomon is speaking to everyone. Few people are as wise as they can be. How often have we regretted doing something, yet we fail to learn from the experience and end up repeating the regrettable behavior?

We would be deeply insulted if someone called us fools or simpletons. We should have sufficient pride not to insult ourselves by behaving in a manner that would warrant such epithets.

NOTES

Today I shall . . .

. . . take pride in my intelligence, and be cautious not to do anything that would classify me as a fool or as a simpleton.

Jan. 24, 1993
Jan. 14, 1994
Jan. 3, 1995
Jan. 23, 1996
Jan. 10, 1997
Jan. 29, 1998

From the **A**cts of benevolence are greater than *Sages* giving charity (*Succah* 49b).

גְּדוֹלָה גְּמִילוּת חֲסָדִים יוֹתֵר מִן הַצְּדָקָה

The Talmud explains that charity consists of the giving of our possessions, whereas by performing acts of benevolence, we give of ourselves as well.

This teaching is of special importance in an era where everything is done by agencies. Agencies care for the needy, for the homeless, for abused and neglected children, and for almost any other cause we can imagine. Few people become involved in providing direct care. Most discharge their obligations by contributing to a community fund which supports these various agencies.

The problem with this arrangement is that such agencies are often grossly understaffed. They therefore cannot provide more than a fraction of the needed services. However, having made a contribution to the community fund, people generally feel that they have thereby discharged their obligations. Since those in need of help rarely confront us directly, we may not be aware that their needs remain largely unmet. One check to the community fund has placated our consciences, and we can sleep peacefully.

The Torah calls for a different attitude. While giving charity is indeed very great, becoming personally involved in helping those in need is even greater. Only in this way can we avoid deceiving ourselves that the job has been satisfactorily accomplished by the agencies that we fund.

It is, of course, easier to donate to an agency than to become personally involved, but the easy way is not necessarily the right way.

NOTES

Today I shall . . .

. . . try to familiarize myself with the actual needs that exist in my community, and take a personal interest to see that they are satisfactorily met.

זוּ קְצָרָה וַאֲרוּכָּה וְזוּ אֲרוּכָה וּקְצָרָה *From the Sages*

This path is short and long, and the other is long and short (*Eruvin* 53b).

The Talmud relates that these were the directions a young child gave to Rabbi Yehoshua when he asked the way to the city. Rabbi Yehoshua first took the short way. Although he soon found himself in the city's outskirts, fenced-in orchards blocked the entrance, and he had to retrace his steps and take the longer route, which eventually brought him to his destination.

Jan. 25, 1993
Jan. 15, 1994
Jan. 4, 1995
Jan. 24, 1996
Jan. 11, 1997
Jan. 30, 1998

In our haste, we often look for shortcuts. Who hasn't driven to an unfamiliar area, found what looked like a shortcut on the map and taken it, only to discover that it really was a very slow route, and that taking the highway might have indeed been a few miles longer, but it would have brought them to their destination much sooner? As someone said, "A shortcut is often the fastest way to get to somewhere you don't want to be."

Two men were put into a maze, and one soon found his way out. He stated that whenever he came to a dead end, he retraced his steps and marked the entrance to that path, so that he would know which one *not* to take.

If this principle is true with road travel, how much more so it is with the paths through life, where the apparent easier way is so often misleading. Some paths in life lead nowhere. We can either discover them ourselves, or we can ask our elders and profit by their experience. They may have marked off those paths that they found led nowhere.

NOTES

Today I shall . . .

. . . ask for guidance from older and wiser people who have had experience in life, so that I may avoid mistakes that they have made.

Jan. 26, 1993
Jan. 16, 1994
Jan. 5, 1995
Jan. 25, 1996
Jan. 12, 1997
Jan. 31, 1998

From the Scriptures

וַיִּקְרָא ה' אֱלֹקִים אֶל הָאָדָם וַיֹּאמֶר לוֹ
אַיֶּכָּה

God called unto man [Adam] and said to him, "Where are you?" (*Genesis* 3:9).

We read in *Genesis* that after Adam sinned, he tried to hide in the Garden of Eden. Was Adam so foolish to think that he could hide from God? Certainly not! He was hiding from himself, because it was himself that he could no longer confront. God's question to him was very pertinent: "I am here. I am always here, but where are *you*?"

Adam's answer to God describes man's most common defense: "I was afraid because I was exposed, and I therefore tried to hide" (*Genesis* 3:10). Since people cannot possibly conceal themselves from God, they try to hide from themselves. This effort results in a multitude of problems, some of which I described in *Let Us Make Man* (CIS, 1987).

We hear a great deal about people's search for God, and much has been written about ways that we can "find" God. The above verse throws a different light on the subject. It is not necessary for people to find God, because He was never lost, but has been there all the time, everywhere. We are the ones who may be lost.

When an infant closes its eyes, it thinks that because it cannot see others, they cannot see it either. Adults may indulge in the same infantile notion — if they hide from themselves, they think they are hiding from God as well. If we find ourselves by getting to know who we are, we will have little difficulty in finding God, and in letting Him find us.

NOTES

_____
_____
_____
_____
_____
_____
_____
_____
_____
_____

Today I shall . . .

. . . try to establish a closer relationship with God by coming out of hiding from myself.

בִּנְפֹל אוֹיִבְךָ אַל תִּשְׂמָח *From the* **When your enemy falls, do not re-** *Scriptures* **joice** *(Proverbs* 24:17).

The Torah explicitly forbids taking revenge, or when doing a favor to someone who had denied your request, to say, "You see, I am not like you. I am doing you a favor even though you refused me when I needed your help."

Solomon goes one step further. He states that passive revenge is also wrong. Even if your enemies have come to grief without your contributing to it in any way, you should not enjoy their downfall.

Solomon's father David was the victim of a ruthless rebellion led by another son, Avshalom, who drove him from the land. As David was in the process of quelling the rebellion, Avshalom was killed. Although the son had been his father's mortal enemy, David grieved bitterly for him, going so far as to say, "Would that I had died instead of you" *(II Samuel* 19:1). He was of course, feeling the paternal love which can prevail over all other emotions.

While it is not realistic to expect anyone to grieve over an enemy's misfortune as a father might grieve over the misfortune of a defiant son, we can have enough compassion for other human beings to at least not rejoice in their downfall, even if they were our enemies.

Jan. 27, 1993
Jan. 17, 1994
Jan. 6, 1995
Jan. 26, 1996
Jan. 13, 1997
Feb. 1, 1998

NOTES

Today I shall . . .

. . . try to overcome any natural tendency to passive revenge, and have enough compassion even toward my enemies to avoid rejoicing in their downfall.

Jan. 28, 1993
Jan. 18, 1994
Jan. 7, 1995
Jan. 27, 1996
Jan. 14, 1997
Feb. 2, 1998

From the Scriptures

כִּי יָשׁוּב ה' לָשׂוּשׂ עָלֶיךָ לְטוֹב כַּאֲשֶׁר שָׂשׂ עַל אֲבֹתֶיךָ

When God will again rejoice in His benevolence to you as He rejoiced with your ancestors *(Deuteronomy* 30:9).

One young woman who had recovered from alcoholism wrote to me that after several years of sobriety, she had received a new car as a gift from her father. She added: "I am giving my father a chance to be a father."

During her years of drinking, her father had been forced to stop giving her things, because she used them in a self-destructive manner. It was clear from her letter that although she certainly enjoyed her new car, she had even greater pleasure from allowing her father to give it to her. It is most frustrating when a loving father must suppress his desire to give to his children, because of their improper behavior.

When we receive things from God and express our gratitude to Him, we should be aware how much He enjoys giving to us, and we should rejoice in His happiness even more than in our own gratification. Conversely, we should realize that when we transgress His will, we deprive our loving Father from being kind to us, and that we are causing God much grief when we make Him suppress His infinite kindness.

The Psalmist says, "The righteous rejoice in God" *(Psalms* 97:12), meaning that they rejoice in the Divine gladness, when they give God the opportunity to exercise His kindness.

NOTES

Today I shall ...

... express my thankfulness to God for His kindness to me, and rejoice in the knowledge that God takes pleasure in providing for me.

כָּל מָקוֹם שֶׁנֶּאֱמַר וַיְהִי בִּימֵי אֵינוֹ אֶלָּא צָרָה *From* Every place where it states: "It was in the *the* days of" [the expression] is one of *Sages* anguish (*Vayikra Rabbah* 11:7).

SHEVAT

7

שבט

Jan. 29, 1993
Jan. 19, 1994
Jan. 8, 1995
Jan. 28, 1996
Jan. 15, 1997
Feb. 3, 1998

If someone is preoccupied only with nostalgia, dreaming about how idyllic the past was and seeing nothing good about the present, it is a sign of anguish. If someone looks toward the future, planning for and anticipating what can be, it indicates joy.

All our joyous festivals are tied to the future. Although we commemorate the historic Exodus from Egypt on Passover, the second half of the *Seder* relates to the ultimate Redemption, and we close the *Seder* with the declaration, "Next year in Jerusalem." While Shavuos does commemorate the revelation at Sinai, it is the commitment to observe the Torah given at Sinai in the future that gives the festival its importance. And the festival of Succos, which culminates in the completion of the annual cycle of reading the Torah, is also the beginning of a new cycle. We always rejoice with the future, not the past.

The past is sure, the future is uncertain. Whatever challenges the past had are behind us, while those of the future must yet be confronted. Yet the uncertain and challenging future should generate joy, because it holds the promise and potential of what might be.

If the past has been one of achievement, it is easy to bask in its glory. However, while comfort might feel better than challenge, challenge is constructive, and joy in life should be sought in what *can* be done, rather than in what *has been* done.

NOTES

Today I shall . . .

. . . concentrate on the future, and pray that God give me the wisdom, strength, and courage to confront the challenges the future holds for me.

Jan. 30, 1993
Jan. 20, 1994
Jan. 9, 1995
Jan. 29, 1996
Jan. 16, 1997
Feb. 4, 1998

From the Sages

מְקוֹם שֶׁבַּעֲלֵי תְּשׁוּבָה עוֹמְדִין צַדִּיקִים גְּמוּרִים אֵינָם עוֹמְדִין

The position which baalei teshuvah [penitents] occupy cannot be occupied even by tzaddikim [completely righteous] (*Berachos* 34b).

A surgeon once encountered difficult complications during an operation and asked his assistant to see if there was anyone in the surgical suite who could help. The assistant replied that the only one who was there was the chief of the surgical staff. "There is no point in calling him," the operating surgeon said. "He would not know what to do. He never got himself into a predicament like this."

As far as people's own functioning is concerned, it might be better not to have made mistakes. Still, such perfection makes them relatively useless as sources of help to others who *have* made mistakes, because they have no experience on which to draw to know how to best help them correct their mistakes.

A perfect *tzaddik* may indeed be most virtuous, but may not be able to identify and empathize with average people who need help in correcting their errors. The "position" to which the Talmud is referring may be the position of a *helper*, and in this respect the *baal teshuvah* may indeed be superior to a *tzaddik*.

NOTES

Today I shall . . .

. . . reflect on how I dealt with the mistakes I have made, and share my experience with others who may benefit from them.

וַעֲלִיתֶם אֶת הָהָר וּרְאִיתֶם אֶת הָאָרֶץ מַה *From the*
הִוא *Scriptures*

Climb up the mountain and you will see what the land is like (*Numbers* 13:17-18).

These words are the instructions which Moses gave the spies when he sent them to scout Canaan for the Israelites.

Jan. 31, 1993
Jan. 21, 1994
Jan. 10, 1995
Jan. 30, 1996
Jan. 17, 1997
Feb. 5, 1998

On a visit to a salmon hatchery, I witnessed a wonder of nature. Salmon swim upstream, against the current, to reach the spawning place where they were born. To get there, they must jump against powerful cascades. It is fascinating to observe how they struggle to overcome both the pull of gravity and the force of waterfalls. Nothing stops the salmon from getting to where they "know" they must go.

While humans do not have an instinctual goal, we do have the capacity to discover our goals by the use of our intellect. We must often overcome many hurdles and obstacles to reach our goals, and we must not allow ourselves to be discouraged by the struggles we encounter. Those who do not have the courage to overcome the challenge are likely to rationalize their retreat by saying that the goal is not worth the sacrifice. Instead of admitting their reluctance, they devalue the goal.

Moses knew that the land which was promised by God to Israel was the spiritual goal of the Jewish people, but he knew that when confronted with the difficulties of acquiring the land, some people might retreat and rationalize their reluctance by disparaging the land.

"Only if you are ready to climb mountains," said Moses, "will you be able to truly see what the land is like." The truth can be appreciated only by those who are ready to sacrifice for it.

NOTES

Today I shall . . .

. . . realize that reaching desirable goals may require much courage and effort, and I should not let any challenge divert me from worthwhile goals.

Feb. 1, 1993
Jan. 22, 1994
Jan. 11, 1995
Jan. 31, 1996
Jan. 18, 1997
Feb. 6, 1998

From the Teshuvah [repentance] is so great that it *Sages* can convert sins [of the past] into merits (*Yoma* 86b).

גְּדוֹלָה תְּשׁוּבָה שֶׁזְּדוֹנוֹת נַעֲשׂוֹת לוֹ כִּזְכִיּוֹת

Sins become merits only when the *teshuvah* is done out of an intense love for God.

This type of *teshuvah* is not the average kind of repentance, in which people regret having done wrong and commit themselves to avoid repeating the forbidden act. While that level of *teshuvah* is certainly commendable and indeed may suffice to eradicate a sin, it is not adequate to convert that sin into a merit. We may polish a pewter item to cleanse it of accumulated dirt, and even give it a luster, but it still will remain pewter. If we could find a way to convert pewter into gold, we would be changing its very essence.

In ancient history, some alchemists spent their entire lives trying to discover the magic formula that would enable them to convert base metals into gold. While this task remains impossible for metals, it is not impossible with human behavior. We can turn base acts into virtues. The "magic formula" is to develop so intimate a relationship with God that we not only regret having sinned, but feel the anguish of having displeased someone whom we love intensely.

Rabbi Levi Yitzchok of Berdichev once said to a person who was a known sinner: "How I envy you! When you will do *teshuvah* and convert your sins, you will have many more merits than I do."

Rather than allow the mistakes of the past to depress us, we should try to behave in such a way that we convert them into merits.

NOTES

Today I shall . . .

. . . try to strive for a relationship with God that will be so intense in devotion that my faults will be converted into virtues.

צַדִּיק אֹכֵל לְשֹׂבַע נַפְשׁוֹ *From the*
A righteous person eats to satisfy his *Scriptures*
soul (*Proverbs* 13:25).

Feb. 2, 1993
Jan. 23, 1994
Jan. 12, 1995
Feb. 1, 1996
Jan. 19, 1997
Feb. 7, 1998

When children have poor table manners, their parents will likely reprimand them and say: "You're eating like an animal."

While animals lack the finesse of Emily Post, we can say this much for them: they eat only for their bodily needs. Animals do not overeat, nor do they indulge in the pleasures of eating the way that humans do. Titillating the palate is a uniquely human obsession.

People who sincerely believe they were put on earth solely in order to serve God will eat in order to sustain life and to have the energy to carry out their assignment on earth. While they may enjoy eating, they neither indulge themselves nor constantly seek ways to enhance their food. These people are unlikely to develop obesity, because they would not consume more food than is necessary to maintain optimum bodily function.

In the thirteenth century, Maimonides stated that the majority of human ills come from unhealthy eating practices. Modern medical science substantiates his assertion. However, modern people, instead of developing more body-conscious eating habits, apply their genius to seeking ways to stuff themselves without becoming overweight.

It is a humbling thought that if humans *did* eat like animals, they would live longer and be healthier.

NOTES

Today I shall . . .

. . . try to develop truly healthy eating habits by realizing that the true purpose of eating is to maintain optimum bodily function.

Feb. 3, 1993
Jan. 24, 1994
Jan. 13, 1995
Feb. 2, 1996
Jan. 20, 1997
Feb. 8, 1998

From the Sages

שֶׁהָיָה אַהֲרֹן בּוֹשׁ וְיָרֵא לָגֶשֶׁת אָמַר לוֹ מֹשֶׁה
לָמָּה אַתָּה בּוֹשׁ לְכַךְ נִבְחָרְתָּ

Aaron was ashamed [and was reluctant to assume the position of High Priest] because of his role in the Golden Calf episode, and Moses said, "This is why you were selected" (*Rashi, Leviticus 9:7*).

I was once asked to see a student nurse who was beside herself because she had made an error in medication. While this particular error was harmless, she felt that she lacked the competency to be a nurse, because she saw that she was capable of making even more serious errors.

I told the young woman that I did not know of anyone who can go through life without making any errors. Perfection belongs to God alone. If all nurses who became so upset because of a medication error would leave the field, the only ones who would remain would be those indifferent to making errors, and that would be the worst disservice to mankind.

We must try to do our very best at everything we do, particularly when it concerns others' welfare. We must not be lax, negligent, nor reckless. We should of course be reasonably upset upon making a mistake and learn from such experiences how we might avoid repeating them. However, if in spite of our best efforts we commit errors as a result of our human fallibility, we should not give up. Allowing a mistake to totally shatter us would result in our not doing anything in order to avoid mistakes. This non-action would constitute the greatest mistake of all.

NOTES

Today I shall . . .

. . . try to realize that the distress I feel upon making a mistake is a constructive feeling that can help me improve myself.

בָּז לְרֵעֵהוּ חֲסַר לֵב וְאִישׁ תְּבוּנוֹת יַחֲרִישׁ *From the*

One who degrades another person is *Scriptures*
a fool, and a man of understanding
will make himself deaf to his words
(*Proverbs* 11:12).

When people feel good about themselves, they have no
need to enhance their self-evaluation by berating others.
Those who do so are exposing their own poor self-worth
and to what extremes they will go in order to achieve any
feeling of worth.

Solomon points out that the one who listens to such
prattle is no better than the speaker. Why would anyone
waste time listening to such gossip and slander unless it
served some purpose? A person with good self-esteem
would turn a deaf ear to such talk. Furthermore, one who
listens to gossip provides the talker with an audience,
thereby actually encouraging more gossip.

Solomon calls a wise person "a man of understanding."
The wisdom here consists of understanding the psychology
of gossips. They need to berate others for their own
self-worth, and they are not above lying to disparage
others. You can be certain that the person who speaks
badly about someone else to you will eventually speak
badly about you to someone else. The only approach,
therefore, is to completely shun a gossip.

In his epochal work on *lashon hara* (gossip), the Chofetz
Chaim states that the transgression of listening to *lashon
hara* is every bit as serious as speaking it. If someone tries
to make a listener out of you, leave, or at least politely say
that you are not interested in the subject.

Feb 4, 1993
Jan. 25, 1994
Jan. 14, 1995
Feb. 3, 1996
Jan. 21, 1997
Feb. 9, 1998

NOTES

Today I shall . . .

. . . make a point to avoid listening to gossip and slander as
well as not speaking them.

Feb. 5, 1993
Jan. 26, 1994
Jan. 15, 1995
Feb. 4, 1996
Jan. 22, 1997
Feb. 10, 1998

From the Scriptures

אַל תְּבַהֵל בְּרוּחֲךָ לִכְעוֹס

Do not be hasty in spirit to be angry
(*Ecclesiastes* 7:9).

For what I believe are valid reasons, my home telephone is unlisted. However, this secret has been very poorly kept. While I have made peace with giving free psychiatric advice from my home, I have not been able to make peace with persons whom I do not know who make collect calls in search of free advice. Yet I do not refuse to accept charges. Perhaps the caller is in a desperate crisis and thinks that I can somehow help him.

One evening, a phone call interrupted my already long-delayed dinner. I thought I heard the operator say that it was collect. Although the caller was a stranger, I accepted the call, for the reason given above. The caller asked for some psychiatric advice, but since there was no emergency I expressed outrage for her calling me at home, and particularly for asking me to pay for the call. The woman responded that she had not called me collect, and the operator had perhaps erred, since she had asked that the call be "person to person."

I realized that the mistake was mine; the operator had not asked me to accept the charges, but had asked for me personally. I had therefore reprimanded the caller unjustly, but since I did not know who she was, I had no way to apologize to her.

This incident demonstrates the wisdom of Solomon's words. Had I not hastily jumped to conclusions, but instead had exercised a bit of patience, a gently worded question would have revealed the truth and would have prevented an unjustified reprimand.

NOTES

Today I shall . . .

. . . try to avoid erupting in anger when I feel offended and at least delay an angry response until I have more thoroughly evaluated the situation.

Do not destroy its trees *From the* *Scriptures* לֹא תַשְׁחִית אֶת עֵצָהּ (Deuteronomy 20:19).

Tu B'Shevat
[Rosh Hashanah la'eelanos —
New Year
for the trees]
Feb. 6, 1993
Jan. 27, 1994
Jan. 16, 1995
Feb. 5, 1996
Jan. 23, 1997
Feb. 11, 1998

Although this verse refers specifically to the prohibition of destroying a fruit-bearing tree, the Talmud has extended this principle to prohibit all wanton destruction.

A rabbi and a student were strolling in the street. The student tore a leaf from a tree. "Think about what you have just done," the rabbi said. "There is an ascending scale of matter that parallels each being's function. God wants the inanimate to serve the vegetative, which should in turn serve the animate, which should in turn serve the rational. Our efforts should be directed toward the elevation of matter, and not to its degradation.

"When we cut a tree to fashion from it things that people will use constructively, the tree is elevated by being of service to humanity. But by tearing a living leaf from a tree for no purpose whatsoever, you have degraded the leaf from the vegetative to the inanimate, and you have reversed the ascending order of matter."

If we guided our actions on this scale of elevation to a more sublime state, how different our lives might be! We might also then realize that there is one additional ascent, and that is from the rational to the spiritual. How wonderful our lives would be if everything were directed upward, culminating in the ultimate goal of spirituality!

NOTES

Today I shall . . .

. . . try to think of myself as one who should elevate even the physical items in the world, and certainly be cautious not to cause anything to descend in its status.

Feb. 7, 1993
Jan. 28, 1994
Jan. 17, 1995
Feb. 6, 1996
Jan. 24, 1997
Feb. 12, 1998

From the Sages

מִצְוָה גוֹרֶרֶת מִצְוָה וַעֲבֵרָה גוֹרֶרֶת עֲבֵרָה

A mitzvah draws along another mitzvah, and a sin draws along another sin

(*Ethics of the Fathers* 4:2).

One day I received a panicky call from an alcoholic patient whom I had treated several years earlier. He had been at a gathering at a friend's home, and although he had specified that he wanted a soft drink, his first sip told him that there was alcohol in the drink. He called me for instruction on what he might do, since he knew from past experience that one sip of alcohol sufficed to set in motion a chain reaction that would end in a drunken stupor. He stated that he was prepared to admit himself into a hospital if necessary in order to prevent this brief exposure to alcohol from escalating into a full relapse. Although he had only consumed a small amount and had done so purely accidentally, his fear was legitimate.

Let us suppose that a family which is meticulously observant of kosher laws discovers that a particular product that they ate under the assumption that it was kosher had lost its *hechsher* (rabbinic approval) because a non-kosher ingredient had been added. Although they certainly would regret having ingested something that was not fully kosher, they probably would not call their rabbi for instruction on how to prevent this accidental transgression from dragging them down to other forbidden types of behavior. This mistake may be more serious than their original error.

Doing wrong, even inadvertently, renders us highly vulnerable to further transgressions. Remedial measures, i.e. prompt *teshuvah* and an effort to do better in the future, must be undertaken to avoid deterioration.

NOTES

Today I shall . . .

. . . promptly correct any transgressions and not allow even the slightest improper action to remain uncorrected, lest it lead to my deterioration.

וְלֹא יֵעָנֵשׁ שׁוּם אָדָם בְּסִבָּתִי *From*

M ay no person be made to suffer on my *our*
account (*Siddur, Prayer on Retiring*). *Prayers*

Feb. 8, 1993
Jan. 29, 1994
Jan. 18, 1995
Feb. 7, 1996
Jan. 25, 1997
Feb. 13, 1998

Although the Torah does not require people to *love* their enemies, it does demand *restraint*, in the sense of not seeking revenge (*Leviticus* 19:18). The Talmud extends this concept to forbid not only the act of revenge, but even a prayer that God should punish our enemies. "If someone is punished on account of another person, the latter is not admitted to the Divine Presence, for as Solomon says in *Proverbs* [17:26], 'For the righteous, too, punishment is not good' " (*Shabbos* 149b).

When Rabbi Levi Yitzchok of Berdichev's adversaries expelled his family from town during his absence, his colleagues asked Rabbi Wolf of Zhitomir to invoke the Divine wrath upon them for their heinous deed. "I cannot do anything," Rabbi Wolf said, "because Rabbi Levi Yitzchok has anticipated us and is now standing before the open Ark, praying fervently that no harm come to them."

Actions like this incident may appear to be the ultimate of magnanimity, but it is not necessarily so. To the contrary, they can also be understood as helping one's own interests. If we pray that another person be punished for his or her misdeeds, we become vulnerable ourselves (see 3 Kislev), for the Divine sense of justice may then bring our own actions under greater scrutiny. After all, is it not reasonable to expect a high standard of personal conduct in someone who invokes harsh treatment of his neighbors? Consequently, it is wiser to seek forgiveness for others and thereby merit forgiveness for ourselves than to pray for absolute justice and stern punishment for others' misdeeds and thereby expose ourselves to be similarly judged.

NOTES

Today I shall . . .

. . . try to avoid wishing harm to anyone, even to those who have grievously offended me.

SHEVAT

שבט

Feb. 9, 1993
Jan. 30, 1994
Jan. 19, 1995
Feb. 8, 1996
Jan. 26, 1997
Feb. 14, 1998

From the Sages

כָּל יִשְׂרָאֵל עֲרֵבִים זֶה בְּזֶה

All Jews are responsible for one another (*Shevuos* 39a).

The commentators explain the full extent of our responsibility for one another: If any Jew has been derelict in performance of a given commandment, every other Jew is considered to be derelict in that particular *mitzvah*, even though he or she may have performed it to one's fullest capacity. All Jews are considered to be a single unit. Just as the unit is incomplete if any part of it is missing or broken, so too, no one can consider oneself complete if any other part of the "unit" is incomplete.

A person who sustained an injury causing infection to one arm would not say, "It is only my arm that has been injured; therefore, no other part of my body has been affected." Since the body is a unit, anything that affects the part affects the whole.

People are physically distinct, and their spirituality is an intangible entity; that is why we do not readily perceive the spiritual forces that unite us. Nevertheless they are very real. However, just as it is possible for part of the body to be anesthetized so that it experiences no sensation from what transpires in other parts of the body, so it is possible for there to be a "spiritual anesthesia" which renders us insensitive to the spiritual injury that may occur anywhere within the body of universal Jewry. We must overcome this insensitivity if we are to be a healthy and optimally functioning nation. We must learn the vital lesson that we are enhanced by the spiritual successes of our neighbors, and we are diminished by their failures.

To the question, "Am I my brother's keeper?", the answer is, "Yes!"

NOTES

Today I shall . . .

. . . try to be of assistance in whatever way I can to help other Jews in the fulfillment of their obligations as Jews.

אַל תִּמְנַע טוֹב מִבְּעָלָיו בִּהְיוֹת לְאֵל יָדְךָ *From the*
לַעֲשׂוֹת *Scriptures*

Do not withhold good from one to
whom it is due, when it is in your
power to do it (*Proverbs* 3:27).

Feb. 10, 1993
Jan. 31, 1994
Jan. 20, 1995
Feb. 9, 1996
Jan. 27, 1997
Feb. 15, 1998

Rabbi Samson Raphael Hirsch points out that the word
that is commonly used for charity, *tzedakah*, really does
not mean giving alms. It is derived from the word *tzedek*,
meaning "justice."

When people give *tzedakah*, they may feel that they are
making a sacrifice by giving to another person from their
own money. They may even resent the recipient of
tzedakah for taking away from their assets. The Torah tells
us that this attitude is wrong: "Do not give with a bad
heart" (*Deuteronomy* 15:10), and the reason is in the verse
cited above. What we give the poor is rightfully theirs, and
the person of means is really only the trustee of the poor's
property.

"Do not rob from the poor" (*Proverbs* 22:22). What do
poor people own that we can rob from them? This verse
refers to withholding *tzedakah*, because when people do
so, they keep for themselves what rightfully belongs to the
poor.

People who receive *tzedakah* should not feel humiliated,
and people who give *tzedakah* should not feel magnanimous. It is simply an act of *tzedek*, of justly distributing
what rightfully belongs to each person.

Today I shall . . .

. . . respect someone who needs *tzedakah* and not behave
condescendingly toward that person.

NOTES
_____
_____
_____
_____
_____
_____
_____
_____
_____

Feb. 11, 1993
Feb. 1, 1994
Jan. 21, 1995
Feb. 10, 1996
Jan. 28, 1997
Feb. 16, 1998

From the Sages

יָצְתָה בַת קוֹל וְאָמְרָה יֵשׁ בֵּינֵיכֶם אָדָם אֶחָד שֶׁהוּא רָאוּי לְרוּחַ הַקֹּדֶשׁ אֶלָּא שֶׁאֵין דּוֹרוֹ רָאוּי לְכָךְ

A voice from Heaven proclaimed, "There is one among you who is deserving of the Divine spirit, but his generation is not deserving of it" (*Shir HaShirim Rabbah* 8:11).

We often complain that we lack personalities as great as the leaders of previous generations. We may prefer not to realize that the opposite may also be true: that leaders cannot be totally disproportionate to their generation, and that if we do not have the caliber of leaders of previous generations, the fault may well be our own.

The Talmud tells us that even Moses was demoted when the Israelites sinned, because his greatness was in part for their sake, because they depended on him (*Berachos* 32a). The Baal Shem Tov explained that a leader is like someone who can reach a high place only because he is standing on the shoulders of others. Even the great Moses owed part of his greatness to the people to whom he was devoted.

Sometimes people who could be outstanding leaders never fulfill their potential because no one wishes to receive their message and be guided by them. Just as a nursing mother will soon lose her supply of milk if the infant refuses to nurse, so can the potential of great leaders be stifled if no one will accept their teachings. On the other hand, when people demand that their leaders teach them, the leaders must rise to the occasion, and thereby they gain in stature.

On a very practical level, the rabbi whose congregation demands frequent classes in Torah will learn and grow more, while one whose congregation is more than satisfied with sermons will not be stimulated to further study.

NOTES

Today I shall . . .

. . . examine whether I fully utilize people who could be my mentors, and whether I am willing to accept their counsel.

וּלְאֹם מִלְאֹם יֶאֱמָץ *From the*
One nation shall be mightier than the *Scriptures*
other (*Genesis* 25:23).

Feb. 12, 1993
Feb. 2, 1994
Jan. 22, 1995
Feb. 11, 1996
Jan. 29, 1997
Feb. 17, 1998

These words were part of God's explanation to Rebecca, when she asked why her pregnancy was so difficult. God told her that the two children she carried, Jacob and Esau, were struggling within her, and prophesied that this struggle would be an eternal one. At some points in history, Jacob would triumph; at other times, Esau would triumph.

The *Tanya* (Chapter 9) states that this struggle is not only between the Jewish nation and its adversaries, but that it also exists within each individual. Within each person are a Jacob and an Esau — a Divine soul which strives for sanctity and an animal soul which strives for physical gratifications. Like wrestlers, one may have the superiority at one time, and the other at others.

I strongly disagree with the author of those books which assert that people can attain inner peace and be free of struggle in life. Those who do not attain this desired tranquility therefore feel deprived. They may try many ways — even alcohol or drugs — to attain this assumed freedom from internal strife and tension.

The truth, however, is that inner peace is not even supposed to occur during our earthly existence. Our lives are an eternal struggle between opposing forces. Like opponents in a boxing match, we may get only a brief respite between rounds, only to come out fighting again.

NOTES

Today I shall . . .

. . . try to realize that my mission in life is to make certain that the force of good within me gains mastery over that of evil, and that this struggle will continue throughout my life.

Feb. 13, 1993
Feb. 3, 1994
Jan. 23, 1995
Feb. 12, 1996
Jan. 30, 1997
Feb. 18, 1998

From the Scriptures מַלְתֶּם אֵת עָרְלַת לְבַבְכֶם וְעָרְפְּכֶם לֹא תַקְשׁוּ עוֹד

Y ou shall remove the covering of your hearts and no longer be stiff necked (*Deuteronomy* 10:16).

The Rabbi of Kotzk secluded himself for a long period of time, and none of his many followers could visit him. Several sent in a petition pleading to the rabbi to open his door to them so that they might have an audience with him.

"They want me to open my doors to them?" demanded the rabbi. "Have they opened their hearts so that they will accept what I have to tell them?"

Sometimes we clamor for leadership and insist that if only we had the proper teaching and guidance, we would behave much differently. Let us be honest with ourselves. Are we ready to accept authentic guidance, or are we so set in our own ways that we will only hear that which pleases us?

Spiritual growth does not come easily. In many ways the desires of the body and those of the spirit are mutually antagonistic, and in order to achieve greater spirituality, we may have to divest ourselves of things that offer more immediate gratification. This deprivation may cause considerable resistance; we may even find arguments to refute the authority and teachings of our spiritual leaders. Before finding fault with our leadership, we must do soul-searching to see if we are truly open to change.

NOTES

Today I shall . . .

. . . examine my willingness to deprive myself of some things that have been pleasurable if they stand in the way of spiritual growth.

אֲדוֹן עוֹלָם אֲשֶׁר מָלַךְ בְּטֶרֶם כָּל יְצִיר נִבְרָא *From* **M**aster of the world, Who reigned before *our* **anything was created** (*Siddur*). *Prayers*

Feb. 14, 1993
Feb. 4, 1994
Jan. 24, 1995
Feb. 13, 1996
Jan. 31, 1997
Feb. 19, 1998

The prayer *Adon Olam* is the opening prayer of the morning service; some congregations also recite it at the close of the evening service. It is also included in the extended version of the prayer upon retiring.

Adon Olam's being both the opening and closing prayer is similar to the practice of beginning the reading of *Genesis* on *Simchas Torah* immediately after concluding the last chapter of *Deuteronomy*. There, we indicate that Torah is infinite; like a circle, it has no beginning or end. So it is with prayer, which represents our relationship with God. Since God is infinite, we never reach a finite goal in relating to Him.

Indeed, the cyclical natures of prayer and Torah not only indicate that there is no end, but also that there is no beginning. Secular studies have levels of graduation which indicate that one has completed a certain level. In Torah studies, we do not complete anything. Indeed, each volume of the Talmud begins with page two rather than page one, to teach us that we have not even begun, let alone ever finish.

Growth in spirituality has no limits. The symbolism in the cyclical format of Torah and prayer is that we cannot say that we have even reached the halfway mark in spiritual growth, much less the end. This realization should excite us, not depress us, because our potential is infinite.

NOTES

Today I shall . . .

. . . try to understand that regardless of how much I think I may have advanced in spirituality, I have hardly even made a beginning.

Feb. 15, 1993
Feb. 5, 1994
Jan. 25, 1995
Feb. 14, 1996
Feb. 1, 1997
Feb. 20, 1998

From our Prayers הִתְעוֹרְרִי הִתְעוֹרְרִי כִּי בָא אוֹרֵךְ קוּמִי אוֹרִי עוּרִי עוּרִי שִׁיר דַּבֵּרִי כְּבוֹד ה' עָלַיִךְ נִגְלָה

Arouse yourself, arouse yourself, for your light has come; arise and shine. Awake, awake, utter a song, for the glory of God is revealed upon you (*Siddur*).

An inspiring call to arousal is repeated no less than five times in this liturgical verse. The reason is that merely arousing people to action *once* may not suffice to bring them out of lethargy. A person whose sleep is disturbed by his alarm clock may simply shut off the alarm and return to sleep.

Just as people often resist being awakened from physical sleep, they are much more resistant being awakened from spiritual sleep. Many people have had moments of spiritual awakening, only to ignore them and return to the comfort of their previous routine. Inertia is a powerful force, and repeated urgings are necessary to overcome it.

If we knew that something extremely important or very exciting was awaiting us in the morning, we probably would not silence the alarm clock and return to sleep. Under such circumstances, we usually jump out of bed, anticipating the special event. Children won't get up easily to go to school, but wild horses will not keep them in bed on the morning of a school trip.

If only we knew and understood that spiritual arousal elevates people and makes them worthy of God's Presence upon them, we would welcome the arousal call for spirituality with the anticipation of something great. By failing to appreciate spirituality, we cause ourselves to linger in lethargy.

NOTES

Today I shall . . .

. . . look for experiences that can initiate or enhance my spiritual growth.

שִׂמְחָה לָאִישׁ בְּמַעֲנֵה פִיו וְדָבָר בְּעִתּוֹ מַה *From the*
טּוֹב *Scriptures*

A man has joy in the utterance of his mouth, and a word at the right time, how good it is (*Proverbs* 15:23).

Feb. 16, 1993
Feb. 6, 1994
Jan. 26, 1995
Feb. 15, 1996
Feb. 2, 1997
Feb. 21, 1998

As a rule, silence is golden, and generally we do not regret having held our peace. But exceptions exist to every rule, and sometimes not saying the proper thing is wrong.

We often keep silent because we do not know what to say. Especially in cases where others have suffered great personal losses, what can we say? Every conceivable remark seems so inadequate.

Not only do we tend to remain silent, but the awkwardness of keeping silent may cause us to avoid the discomfort of such a situation. Suppose we hear that an acquaintance lost a child in a traffic accident or to a serious illness. What can we say? It is one thing to pay a condolence call to someone who has lost a parent and say, "Please accept my sympathies." It is the way of the world that parents die before their children. These words are so empty, however, to grieving parents who have lost a child. Since we do not know what to say, we may simply avoid the bereaved family and thereby add loneliness to their suffering.

May God spare us all from such experiences. But if, God forbid, we have heard of a tragedy, we should not stay away or keep silent. If we feel another's pain, we should not hesitate to say so. "I feel along with you" are simple words, and when said in sincerity, can support distressed spirits.

Words cannot restore anyone's loss, but there is truth in the adage that "A sorrow shared is halved."

NOTES

Today I shall . . .

. . . try to be of help to people who are suffering, if only to let them know that I sincerely feel along with them.

Feb. 17, 1993
Feb. 7, 1994
Jan. 27, 1995
Feb. 16, 1996
Feb. 3, 1997
Feb. 22, 1998

From the Scriptures

יִהְיוּ לְרָצוֹן אִמְרֵי פִי וְהֶגְיוֹן לִבִּי לְפָנֶיךָ ה' צוּרִי וְגֹאֲלִי

May the words of my mouth and meditation of my heart find favor before You (*Psalms* 19:15).

Why must we verbalize prayer? Since God knows our innermost thoughts, why don't we just meditate? Furthermore, why should we pray at all? Since God knows what is best for us, we should just trust that He will provide that which we need.

Let us consider the second question first. We do not pray in order to inform God of anything, for indeed He knows our needs better than we do. We pray in order to make ourselves aware of our dependence upon God. We are always at risk of deluding ourselves that we have control of our destinies. We may think that what we do and what transpires are indeed cause and effect. We therefore need to be reminded frequently that except where the principle of moral free choice applies, our destinies are controlled by God.

Why verbalize prayer? Speech alone characterizes us as humans and distinguishes us from lower forms of life. Animals undoubtedly think and feel, but only humans can speak. As we stand before God, we need to remember that we are human, and that as humans our goals and behavior should have the dignity of humanity. If we only pray for our physical needs and welfare, we have not advanced beyond the animal stage, and we are then what science calls *Homo sapiens* — intellectual animals, but animals nevertheless. We need to remember that we are much more than *Homo sapiens,* for we can aspire to spiritual achievements and goals.

NOTES

Today I shall ...

... think about the meaning of prayer and realize that I am a being who is capable of spirituality, and that while my physical life is dependent upon God, I am responsible for my spiritual development.

שֶׁלֹּא תְהֵא צָרָה וְיָגוֹן וַאֲנָחָה בְּיוֹם מְנוּחָתֵנוּ *From*

May there not be anguish nor grief nor *our* sighing on the day of our rest *(Siddur)*. *Prayers*

Feb. 18, 1993
Feb. 8, 1994
Jan. 28, 1995
Feb. 17, 1996
Feb. 4, 1997
Feb. 23, 1998

It is noteworthy that the Hebrew words for these types of distress are all in the singular: *an* anguish, *a* grief, *a* sighing.

Many years ago, when my brother was gravely ill, I visited a rabbi in Israel and asked for a *berachah* (blessing) for his recovery. As I left, the rabbi said to me, "May you have many worries."

Noting my astonishment at this unusual *berachah*, the rabbi said, "When you have many worries, then things are in order. It is when you have only *one* worry that things are bad.

"You see," he explained, "life is never free of worries. Ever since Adam was expelled from *Gan Eden* (paradise), life has never been without problems, but these are the normal stresses of everyday life.

"If something extremely bad occurs, people forget all their usual daily worries and become totally preoccupied with this single, truly serious problem. For example, your worry about your brother's serious illness is pre-eminent and has displaced all other worries, because they all pale in comparison.

"My wish for you is that you have many worries, so that none be of such magnitude as to obscure all others."

NOTES

_____

Today I shall . . .

. . . try to realize that the fact that I can list a number of things that are unpleasant is actually a favorable sign, because none of them is so severe that it obscures all the others.

Feb. 19, 1993
Feb. 9, 1994
Jan. 29, 1995
Feb. 18, 1996
Feb. 5, 1997
Feb. 24, 1998

From our Prayers

עַד הֵנָּה עֲזָרוּנוּ רַחֲמֶיךָ וְלֹא עֲזָבוּנוּ חֲסָדֶיךָ וְאַל תִּטְּשֵׁנוּ ה' אֱלֹקֵינוּ לָנֶצַח

Until now Your compassion has helped us, and Your kindness has not forsaken us, and so, God, never abandon us (*Siddur*).

At a meeting of Alcoholics Anonymous, a man who was sober for several years stated, "I wish that I could tell you that since I have been sober everything has gone my way, but it has not. My wife has recently served me with divorce papers, I have lost my job, my car has been repossessed, and my house is up for sheriff's sale. But I am certain that God did not see me through so many ordeals only to walk out on me now."

I then realized that although I had recited the words of the above prayer many times, I had not grasped their full meaning. At moments of great distress and anguish, we may become bewildered and even lose hope. How foolish for us to think that after all that God has done to sustain us, He would now forsake us!

Perhaps the problem stems from our not realizing that God has sustained us until now. In the *Amidah*, we express our gratitude "for Your miracles that are with us every day." Still, we tend to take many things for granted as though they are natural phenomena rather than Divine miracles, and we fail to see the protective and guiding hand of God, every day of our lives.

A true faith and realization of God's watchfulness over us would reassure us that just as He has not abandoned us in the past, which is attested to by our very existence, He will not abandon us in the future.

NOTES

_____
_____
_____
_____
_____
_____
_____
_____
_____

Today I shall . . .

. . . try to realize that God has looked after me in the past, and when things happen that cause me to have fear, I will find security in the knowledge that God will not forsake me in the future.

מַחֲשָׁבָה טוֹבָה הקב"ה מְצָרְפָהּ לְמַעֲשֶׂה *From* **G**od considers a good intention as *the* though one had performed a good *Sages* deed (*Kiddushin* 40a).

Erev
Rosh Chodesh
[Eve of the
New Month]
Feb. 20, 1993
Feb. 10, 1994
Jan. 30, 1995
Feb. 19, 1996
Feb. 6, 1997
Feb. 25, 1998

Our time is finite, and therefore every moment is precious and irreplaceable. Yet sometimes we waste precious moments because we do not have something constructive to do.

Some people carry a small book with them, so that if they must wait for a bus or sit in a waiting room, they can use the time productively. It may be a book of Psalms or something to study. It may be a notebook to record an idea or jot down plans. While this practice is excellent, what about the times when we are in bed and cannot fall asleep, or are walking down the street and we cannot read?

An excellent idea is to think about how and when to perform a commandment when the opportunity arises. Plan how we can contribute more to charity or other benevolent deeds, or make mental inventory of the sick, lonely, and needy, and think about how we can bring cheer into their lives. One can reflect on the opening phrase of the *Shema*, and reassert one's belief in the unity of God and in His providence. One can dedicate oneself to serve God with all one's heart, soul, and might, as we declare when we recite the *Shema*.

One can also think about self-improvement and how to avoid doing things that one regrets having done. This is part of the commandment to repent, and can be fulfilled at least partially by meditation and concentration.

If one had idle cash and knew that it could be invested for great profit, one would certainly seize the opportunity to do so. We ought to do the same with idle time.

NOTES

Today I shall . . .

. . . try to utilize every moment of the day constructively.

**First Day of
Rosh Chodesh
Adar**

Feb. 21, 1993
Feb. 11, 1994
Jan. 31, 1995
Feb. 20, 1996
Feb. 7, 1997
Feb. 26, 1998

*From
the
Sages*

מִיָּמַי לֹא אָמַרְתִּי דָּבָר וְחָזַרְתִּי לַאֲחוֹרַי

In all my days I have never had to look behind me before saying anything (*Shabbos* 118b).

Lashon hara (gossip or slander) is not necessarily untruthful. The Torah forbids saying something derogatory about a person even if it is completely true.

One of the best guidelines to decide what you should or should not say is to ask: "Does it make a difference who might overhear it?" If it is something that you would rather someone not overhear, it is best left unsaid.

Sometimes the information need not be derogatory. A secret may not be saying anything bad about anyone, but if someone has entrusted you with confidential information, and you have this tremendous urge to share the privileged communication with someone else, you should ask yourself: "Would I reveal this if the person who trusted me with this information were present?"

Sometimes people want to boast. They may even fabricate their story to those who have no way of knowing that it may not be true. Still, they would be ashamed to boast in the presence of someone who knew that their statement was false.

Volumes have been written about what is proper speech and about what constitutes an abuse of this unique capacity to verbalize with which man was endowed. But even if one does not have time to master all of the scholarly works on the subject, a reliable rule of thumb is to ask, "Do I need to look behind me before I say it?" If the answer is yes, do not say it.

NOTES

Today I shall . . .

. . . monitor my speech carefully, and not say anything that I would not wish someone to overhear.

If you eat of the labor of your hands, you will be fortunate, and the good will be yours (*Psalms* 128:2).

יְגִיעַ כַּפֶּיךָ כִּי תֹאכֵל אַשְׁרֶיךָ וְטוֹב לָךְ *From the Scriptures*

The Rabbi of Kotzk had a unique interpretation for this verse. "Yes," he said, "eat of the labor of your hands, but not of your heart and soul. Of course you must work with your hands to earn your bread, but while your hands must work, do not allow your entire being to be absorbed in work. Direct your heart and soul toward goals that are spiritual."

Some Torah commentaries note that when Adam sinned, he was cursed: "By the sweat of your brow shall you eat bread" (*Genesis* 3:19). Since work was established as a punishment, why would anyone want to indulge in punishment? Any thinking person would try to get by with the very minimum penalty.

Today we witness the phenomenon of what happens when people who know nothing but work all their lives reach the age of retirement. Many spend these later years in misery, not having anything else to do; some turn to alcohol in their old age to escape from a burden of an empty life.

If people put their entire being, rather than just their hands, into work, they will not achieve happiness. People who develop spiritual interests have a much happier old age, for as the Psalmist says, "They will bear fruit in their old age, and will remain vigorous and fresh" (*Psalms* 92:15).

Second Day of Rosh Chodesh Adar

[During Hebrew leap years, a thirteenth month called Adar Sheni (the second Adar) is added to the calendar. For those years, two sets of corresponding dates are given below, the first for Adar, and the second for Adar Sheni.]

Feb. 22, 1993
Feb. 12, 1994
Feb. 1, 1995
Feb. 21, 1996
Feb. 8, 1997
Feb. 27, 1998

Adar Sheni

March 3, 1995
March 10, 1997

NOTES

_____
_____
_____
_____
_____
_____
_____
_____
_____
_____

Today I shall . . .

. . . try to realize that although I must work in order to live, I do not live just in order to work, and so I must develop the spiritual aspects of my life.

Feb. 23, 1993
Feb. 13, 1994
Feb. 2, 1995
Feb. 22, 1996
Feb. 9, 1997
Feb. 28, 1998

Adar Sheni

March 4, 1995
March 11, 1997

From the Sages

הַמַּלְבִּין פְּנֵי חֲבֵרוֹ בָּרַבִּים . . . אַף עַל פִּי שֶׁיֵּשׁ בְּיָדוֹ תּוֹרָה וּמַעֲשִׂים טוֹבִים אֵין לוֹ חֵלֶק לָעוֹלָם הַבָּא

One who humiliates another person in public . . . even though he may be a scholar and may have done many good deeds, nevertheless loses his portion in the eternal world (*Ethics of the Fathers* 3:15).

Imagine a situation: you have a fine home, a well-paying job, a comfortable car, and a substantial retirement annuity. If you do a single thoughtless act, you will lose everything you have worked to achieve: home, job, car, and savings. What kind of precautions would you take to avoid even the remotest possibility of incurring such a disaster? Without doubt, you would develop an elaborate system of defenses to assure that this event would never occur.

The Talmud tells us that everything we have worked for during our entire lives can be forfeited in one brief moment of inconsideration: we embarrass another person in public. Perhaps we may say something insulting or make a demeaning gesture. Regardless of how it occurs, the Talmud states that if we cause another person to turn pale because of being humiliated in public, we have committed the equivalent of bloodshed.

Still, we allow our tongues to wag so easily. If we give serious thought to the words of the Talmud, we would exercise the utmost caution in public and be extremely sensitive to other people's feelings, lest an unkind word or degrading gesture deprive us of all our spiritual merits.

NOTES

Today I shall . . .

. . . try to be alert and sensitive to other people's feelings and take utmost caution not to cause anyone to feel humiliated.

From the Scriptures

וְיָדַעְתָּ הַיּוֹם וַהֲשֵׁבֹתָ אֶל לְבָבֶךָ **Y**ou shall know this day and consider it within your heart *(Deuteronomy 4:39).*

Feb. 24, 1993
Feb. 14, 1994
Feb. 3, 1995
Feb. 23, 1996
Feb. 10, 1997
March 1, 1998

Adar Sheni
March 5, 1995
March 12, 1997

Business people who are involved in many transactions employ accountants to analyze their operations and to determine whether or not they are profitable. They may also seek the help of experts to determine which products are making money and which are losing. Such studies allow them to maximize their profits and minimize their losses. Without such data, they might be doing a great deal of business, but discover at the end of the year that their expenditures exceeded their earnings.

Sensible people give at least as much thought to the quality and achievement of their lives as they do to their businesses. Each asks himself, "Where am I going with my life? What am I doing that is of value? In what ways am I gaining and improving? And which practices should I increase, and which should I eliminate?"

Few people make such reckonings. Many of those that do, do so on their own, without consulting an expert's opinion. These same people would not think of being their own business analysts and accountants, and they readily pay large sums of money to engage highly qualified experts in these fields.

Jewish ethical works urge us to regularly undergo *cheshbon hanefesh*, a personal accounting. We would be foolish to approach this accounting of our very lives with any less seriousness than we do our business affairs. We should seek out the "spiritual C.P.A.s," those who have expertise in spiritual guidance, to help us in our analyses.

NOTES

Today I shall . . .

. . . look for competent guidance in doing a personal moral inventory and in planning my future.

Feb. 25, 1993
Feb. 15, 1994
Feb. 4, 1995
Feb. 24, 1996
Feb. 11, 1997
March 2, 1998

Adar Sheni

March 6, 1995
March 13, 1997

From the Sages

שֶׁיִּהְיוּ עֲלֵיכֶם חֲדָשִׁים כְּאִלּוּ שְׁמַעְתֶּם בּוֹ בַּיּוֹם

The words of Torah should be as fresh to you as if you first heard them today *(Rashi, Deuteronomy 11:13)*.

Excitement often comes from novelty, but novelty is exciting only as long as it is new. Someone who buys a car fully loaded with options may feel an emotional high, but after several weeks, the novelty wears off and it is just another vehicle.

Spirituality, too, suffers from routine. Human beings may do all that is required of them as moral people and observe all the Torah's demands in terms of the performance of commandments, yet their lives may be insipid and unexciting because their actions have become rote, simply a matter of habit. The prophet Isaiah criticizes this when he says, "Their reverence of Me has become a matter of routine" *(Isaiah* 29:13). Reverence must be an emotional experience. A reverence that is routine and devoid of emotion is really no reverence at all.

Thus, the excitement that is essential for true observance of Torah depends upon novelty, upon having both an understanding of Torah today that we did not have yesterday and a perception of our relationship to God that is deeper than the one we had yesterday. Only through constantly learning and increasing our knowledge and awareness of Torah and Godliness can we achieve this excitement.

Life is growth. Since stagnation is the antithesis of growth, it is also the antithesis of life. We can *exist* without growth, but such an existence lacks true life.

NOTES

Today I shall . . .

. . . try to discover new things in the Torah and in my relationship to God.

From the Scriptures

לֵךְ אֶל נְמָלָה עָצֵל רְאֵה דְרָכֶיהָ וַחֲכָם

Go to the ant, you sluggard, consider her ways and become wise (*Proverbs* 6:6).

Feb. 26, 1993
Feb. 16, 1994
Feb. 5, 1995
Feb. 25, 1996
Feb. 12, 1997
March 3, 1998

Adar Sheni
March 7, 1995
March 14, 1997

The Talmud states that had the Torah not been given, we would have been held accountable to learn proper behavior from observance of lower forms of life. As Solomon says, we could have learned diligence from the ant. The Talmud adds that we could have learned modesty, fidelity, and respect of others' possessions by observing certain animals' behaviors.

We might ask: "Without Torah to teach us, how would we have known which animal traits to emulate? Perhaps we would have learned indolence from the alligator, which basks in the sun all day, and ruthlessness from predatory animals!"

People are endowed with an inherent sense of decency and morality. We are expected to use this innate power to judge right and wrong. The Torah only clarifies and emphasizes for us what we could have achieved on our own.

The Talmud thus teaches us that corruption is not only wrong and sinful, but actually unnatural. People do not sin because they have unnatural desires, but because they fail to exercise their innate intellect. If we think before we act, weighing the pros and cons of what we do, we are less likely to go astray.

NOTES

Today I shall . . .

. . . be aware that the dignity of a human being lies in the capacity to think before acting. I will not allow myself to be less than a dignified human being.

ADAR

6

אדר

Feb. 27, 1993
Feb. 17, 1994
Feb. 6, 1995
Feb. 26, 1996
Feb. 13, 1997
March 4, 1998

Adar Sheni

March 8, 1995
March 15, 1997

From the Sages

וַיֶּחְכַּם מִכָּל הָאָדָם (מלכים א ה:יא) אֲפִילוּ מִן הַשׁוֹטִים

[S]olomon] was wiser than all men (*I Kings* 5:11), **even wiser than fools** (*Midrash*).

What does the Midrash mean by "wiser than fools"?

A man of means was once a Sabbath guest at the home of the Chofetz Chaim. He insisted upon paying the sage in advance for the Sabbath meals — an insulting demand. To everyone's surprise, the Chofetz Chaim accepted the money.

After the Sabbath the Chofetz Chaim forced the guest to take the money back. He explained, "Had I refused to accept the money before the Sabbath, the thought that he was imposing upon me might have distracted from the man's enjoying the spirit of the Sabbath. Although it was foolish of him to feel this way, I wished to put his mind at rest."

Not everyone thinks wisely all the time. Some people have foolish ideas. Yet if we oppose them, they may feel they have been wronged. Insisting on the logic of our own thinking may not convince them in the least. In such instances, it may require great wisdom to avoid offending someone, yet not submitting to his folly.

By accepting his guest's money, knowing that he would return it to him after the Sabbath, the Chofetz Chaim wisely accommodated this man's whim without compromising on his own principles.

A wise person may be convinced by a logical argument, but outsmarting a fool truly requires genius.

NOTES

_____
_____
_____
_____
_____
_____
_____
_____
_____

Today I shall . . .

. . . try to avoid offending people whom I feel to be in the wrong, without in any way compromising myself.

וַיֹּאמֶר ה' אֵלָיו זֹאת הָאָרֶץ אֲשֶׁר נִשְׁבַּעְתִּי *From the*
לְאַבְרָהָם לְיִצְחָק וּלְיַעֲקֹב *Scriptures*

[Just before Moses' death] God said
to him, "This is the Land that I
promised to Abraham, to Isaac, and to
Jacob" (*Deuteronomy* 34:4).

Feb. 28, 1993
Feb. 18, 1994
Feb. 7, 1995
Feb. 27, 1996
Feb. 14, 1997
March 5, 1998

Adar Sheni
March 9, 1995
March 16, 1997

The Midrash says that Moses pleaded to live long enough
to be able to enter the Promised Land. He surrendered his
soul only after God instructed him to enter Heaven and
inform the Patriarchs that the Israelites had come to their
Land and that God had indeed fulfilled His promise to give
the Land of Israel to their descendants. To fulfill God's will
was dearer to Moses than his craving to enter the Land.

It is only natural to cling to life, and the thought of leaving
this world is depressing. However, if a person develops the
attitude that he lives only in order to fulfill God's will, then
life and death are no longer polar opposites, because he
lives to do the will of God, and when that will requires that
he leave this world, he will be equally obedient.

The seventh day of Adar is the anniversary of Moses'
death. He wanted to enter the Promised Land so that he
could fulfill the commandments and thereby have a new
opportunity to fulfill the Divine wish. He surrendered his
soul willingly when he was told that there was a special
commandment for him to perform, one that could only be
achieved after leaving this earth.

We refer to Moses as *Rabbeinu*, our teacher. He not only
taught us didactically, but by means of everything he did in
his life — and by his death, as well.

NOTES

Today I shall . . .

. . . try to dedicate my life to fulfilling the will of God, so
that even when that will contradicts my personal desires, I
can accept it with serenity.

March 1, 1993
Feb. 19, 1994
Feb. 8, 1995
Feb. 28, 1996
Feb. 15, 1997
March 6, 1998

Adar Sheni
March 10, 1995
March 17, 1997

From the Scriptures

לְמַעַן תִּזְכְּרוּ וַעֲשִׂיתֶם אֶת כָּל מִצְוֹתָי

In order that you remember and perform all My commandments (*Numbers* 15:40).

Memory is a unique Divine gift. Indeed, to this very day, neuropsychologists have not discovered the secret of exactly how memory operates. The turnover of the chemicals in our bodies is such that after a period of time not a single atom remains in the brain that was there several months earlier, yet a person's brain retains memories for years, decades, a lifetime.

This unique gift should not be abused. Many times the Torah tells us what we should remember and cautions us against forgetting. The concepts and events that we must retain are goals that are vital to our spiritual well-being. Most *siddurim* list six verses of the Torah that we should recite each day to remind us of who we are and to caution us against idolatry and *lashon hara* (harmful talk).

However, if we use this wonderful gift to remember those who have offended us and to harbor grudges against them, or if we remember the favors we have done for others and expect them to be beholden to us, we are abusing this Divine gift.

The key to discerning what we should remember and what we should forget is contained in the above verse: "In order that you remember and perform all My commandments." Any memory that does not assist us in working toward the ultimate goal of serving God does not deserve being retained.

NOTES

Today I shall . . .

. . . try to retain in my mind only those things that contribute to my devotion to God, and dismiss those things that may deter me therefrom.

הָאָסְפוּ וְאַגִּידָה לָכֶם אֵת אֲשֶׁר יִקְרָא אֶתְכֶם *From the* בְּאַחֲרִית הַיָּמִים *Scriptures*

Gather together and I will tell you what will befall you at the end of days (*Genesis* 49:1).

Prior to his death, the Patriarch Jacob wished to disclose to his children the future of the Jewish nation. We know only too well what those prophecies were, and Jacob knew that revealing the enormous suffering that the Jews were destined to experience would be devastating to his children. The only way they could hear these things was if they "gathered together" and, by virtue of their unity, could share their strengths.

March 2, 1993
Feb. 20, 1994
Feb. 9, 1995
Feb. 29, 1996
Feb. 16, 1997
March 7, 1998

Adar Sheni
March 11, 1995
March 18, 1997

What was true for our ancestors holds true for us. Our strength and our ability to withstand the repeated on-slaughts that mark our history lie in our joining together.

Jacob knew this lesson well. The Torah tells us that "Jacob remained alone, and a man wrestled with him" (*Genesis* 32:25). Jacob discovered that he was vulnerable only when he remained alone.

Some people feel that they must be completely independent. They see reliance on someone else, be it others or God, as an indication of weakness. This destructive pride emanates from an unhealthy ego. In my book *Let Us Make Man* (CIS 1987), I address the apparent paradox that a humble person is one who is actually aware of his strengths, and that feelings of inadequacy give rise to egocentricity and false pride.

Not only are we all mutually interdependent, the Torah further states that when we join together, our strengths are not only additive, but increase exponentially (*Rashi*, *Leviticus* 26:8). Together, we can overcome formidable challenges.

NOTES

Today I shall . . .

. . . try to join with others in strengthening Judaism and in resisting those forces that threaten spirituality.

March 3, 1993
Feb. 21, 1994
Feb. 10, 1995
March 1, 1996
Feb. 17, 1997
March 8, 1998

Adar Sheni

March 12, 1995
March 19, 1997

From the **D**o not throw a stone into the well from *Sages* which you drank (*Bava Kama* 92b).

בֵּירָא דְּשָׁתִית מִינֵיהּ לָא תִשְׁדֵּי בֵּיהּ קָלָא

The Talmud states that this folk saying is related to the Torah commandment, "Do not reject an Egyptian, because you were a dweller in his land" (*Deuteronomy* 23:8). Since Egypt hosted the Israelites, we, their descendants, must acknowledge our gratitude.

The brief period of tranquility that our ancestors enjoyed in Egypt was followed by decades of ruthless enslavement and brutal oppression. Thousands of newborn Israelite children were murdered. This unspeakable horror more than obscured any favorable treatment they had received earlier, and our natural inclination is to despise the Egyptians with a passion.

The Torah tells us to take a different path. Although we celebrate, every Passover, our liberation from this tyrannical enslavement and commemorate the triumph over our oppressors, we have no right to deny that we did receive some benefit from them. Even though a denial of gratitude might appear well justified in this particular case, it might impact upon us in such a manner that we might also deny gratitude when it is fully deserved.

If people cast stones into the well from which they drank, the well will not be hurt in the least, because it is an inanimate and insensitive object. The act, however, might impact negatively upon those who do it: they might subsequently behave with a lack of gratitude to people as well.

NOTES

Today I shall . . .

. . . try to remember to be considerate of anyone who has any time been of help to me, even though his later actions might have been hostile.

נְשָׁמָה יְתֵירָה נוֹתֵן הַקָּב"ה בְּאָדָם עֶרֶב שַׁבָּת *From the Sages*

Cod instills an additional neshamah (soul) in a person on the eve of the Sabbath (*Beitzah* 16a).

ADAR

אדר

March 4, 1993
Feb. 22, 1994
Feb, 11. 1995
March 2, 1996
Feb. 18, 1997
March 9, 1998

Adar Sheni
March 13, 1995
March 20, 1997

We know that two things cannot occupy the same space at the same time. Although spiritual substance need not be subject to the law of physics, we might still ask, "Where does this additional *neshamah* fit? Was there previously a vacuum in the space it now occupies?"

As the Sabbath approaches, we create a place for the additional *neshamah* by discarding much of the weekday matter we have accumulated. To the extent that we rid ourselves of the weekday problems, to that extent we can receive the additional *neshamah* of the Sabbath.

We are instructed to approach the Sabbath with an attitude that all our weekday work has been totally completed, and so nothing has been left undone that could cause us to think about it on the Sabbath. Weekday activities relate to the means of living, while the Sabbath represents the goal of life. It is the time when, freed from all other activities, we can direct attention to the study of Torah, to prayer, and to contemplating on what God wants of us. Vacating the thoughts, stresses, and worries of weekday life leaves "space" for that extra *neshamah*.

We can begin preparing to receive the additional *neshamah* during the week: we can consider our weekday activities as merely the means to earn a livelihood, and then look forward to the Sabbath, on which we will be able to focus on the purpose of life.

Today I shall . . .

. . . try to realize that work is a means rather than a goal, and to look forward to the Sabbath, when I will be able to more fully concentrate on the goals of life.

NOTES

GROWING EACH DAY / 161

March 5, 1993
Feb. 23, 1994
Feb. 12, 1995
March 3, 1996
Feb. 19, 1997
March 10, 1998

Adar Sheni

March 14, 1995
March 21, 1997

From the **W**ith exercising patience you could have
Sages saved yourself **400 zuzim** (*Berachos* 20a).

מָתוּן מָתוּן אַרְבַּע מֵאוֹת זוּזָא שָׁוְיָא

This Talmudic proverb arose from a case where someone was fined 400 *zuzim* because he acted in undue haste and insulted someone.

I was once pulling into a parking lot. Since I was a bit late for an important appointment, I was terribly annoyed that the lead car in the procession was creeping at a snail's pace. The driver immediately in front of me was showing his impatience by sounding his horn. In my aggravation, I wanted to join him, but I saw no real purpose in adding to the cacophony.

When the lead driver finally pulled into a parking space, I saw a wheelchair symbol on his rear license plate. He was handicapped and was obviously in need of the nearest parking space. I felt badly that I had harbored such hostile feelings about him, but was gratified that I had not sounded my horn, because then I would really have felt guilty for my lack of consideration.

This incident has helped me to delay my reactions to other frustrating situations until I have more time to evaluate all the circumstances. My motives do not stem from lofty principles, but from my desire to avoid having to feel guilt and remorse for having been foolish or inconsiderate.

NOTES

Today I shall . . .

. . . try to withhold impulsive reaction, bearing in mind that a hasty act performed without full knowledge of all the circumstances may cause me much distress.

מִפִּי עוֹלְלִים וְיֹנְקִים יִסַּדְתָּ עֹז *From the*

From the mouths of babes and suck- *Scriptures*
lings You established strength
(*Psalms* 8:3).

The Talmud tells us that when Haman threatened to annihilate the Jews, Mordechai gathered the children and led them in prayer to God. Why children? Because they are likely to be more sincere, and their prayers more genuine.

A Chassidic master said that one of the things we should learn from an infant is that it cries for whatever it wants. When an infant wants something, it wants it with all its being, and nothing else either interests it or distracts it from the object of its desire. The baby will cry relentlessly until it gets what it wants.

We pray for the redemption of Israel. We tell ourselves that we really want the Exile to end. We ask for redemption no less than three times a day in our prayers. But just one question: If we really wanted it as much as we say we do, why do we not cry for it?

An infant does not play intellectual games. It does not rationalize. It does not debate why it is preferable to get its way or not get it. The item of its desire may be only a brightly colored ball or a wooden block, but at that moment, it is as important to the infant as life itself, and it makes its desire well known to all with ears to hear.

Parents respond to the infant's cry because, in their intense love for the child, they do not wish to deprive it of something it wants so desperately.

God loves us more than a parent loves a child. If we would cry for our redemption, we would certainly get it.

Fast of Esther
[During Hebrew
leap years, the fast
is observed in
Adar Sheni. When
13 Adar falls on
the Sabbath, the
fast is observed on
the preceding
Thursday.]
March 6, 1993
Feb. 24, 1994
Feb. 13, 1995
March 4, 1996
Feb. 20, 1997
March 11, 1998

Adar Sheni
March 15, 1995
March 22, 1997

NOTES

_____
_____
_____
_____
_____
_____

Today I shall . . .

. . . try to understand how being in Exile prevents me from attaining maximum intimacy with God, to the point where I will cry to Him for redemption.

_____
_____

Purim

*[During
Hebrew leap
years, Purim is
celebrated in
Adar Sheni.]*

March 7, 1993
Feb. 25, 1994
Feb. 14, 1995
March 5, 1996
Feb. 21, 1997
March 12, 1998

Adar Sheni

March 16, 1995
March 23, 1997

*From the
Scriptures*

וַיֹּאמֶר מָרְדֳּכַי לְהָשִׁיב אֶל אֶסְתֵּר אַל תְּדַמִּי
בְנַפְשֵׁךְ לְהִמָּלֵט בֵּית הַמֶּלֶךְ מִכָּל הַיְּהוּדִים

Mordechai said to respond to Esther, "Do not think that you can save yourself [from Haman's decree of annihilation] because you are in the royal palace" (*Esther* 4:13).

Esther, the heroine of the Purim episode, received this sharp rebuke from Mordechai. No Jew should ever assume that anti-Semitism will affect only others but not oneself. No one has immunity. Every Jew must know that he or she is part of a unit, and a threat against any Jew anywhere in the world is a threat to all Jews.

History has unfortunately repeated itself many times. Spanish Jews who held powerful governmental positions were sent into exile along with their brethren. Jewish millionaires and members of European parliaments were cremated in Auschwitz ovens. Throughout the ages, those who had thought to escape anti-Semitic persecution by concealing their Jewish identities sadly learned that this effort was futile.

Esther accepted Mordechai's reprimand and risked her life to save her people. In fact, the *Megillah* (*Book of Esther*) tells us that Esther had not revealed her Jewish identity because Mordechai had instructed her to keep it a secret. She never would have stayed hidden in the palace and watched her people perish. Mordechai spoke his sharp words not to her, but to posterity.

Some people simply refuse to accept history's painful lessons. In defiance, they continue to say that *they* will be different. Neither any individual who feels secure for any reason nor any community that lives in what it considers to be a safe environment should have this delusion of immunity.

Mordechai's message reverberates throughout the centuries: "Do not think that you can save yourself by hiding when other Jews are being persecuted."

NOTES

_____
_____
_____
_____
_____
_____
_____
_____
_____

Today I shall . . .

. . . be forthcoming and proud of my Jewish identity and at all times retain a firm solidarity with my people.

כִּי מָרְדֳּכַי הַיְּהוּדִי . . . וְרָצוּי לְרֹב אֶחָיו *From the*
דֹּרֵשׁ טוֹב לְעַמּוֹ וְדֹבֵר שָׁלוֹם לְכָל זַרְעוֹ *Scriptures*

For Mordechai . . . was approved by
most of his brethren. He sought the
good of his people and spoke in peace
to all their descendants (*Esther* 10:3).

The great Mordechai, who saved the Jewish people from total annihilation, won the approval of only *most* of his brethren. Most, but not all.

Some people need to be liked by everyone. If one person out of several hundred does not approve of them, they are devastated. They are likely to become "people pleasers," going out of their way to obtain universal approval.

This attitude comes from low self-esteem. People who feel secure about themselves believe that they are generally likable and do not feel threatened if one or more people does not like them. They realize that some personalities are simply incompatible with certain other personalities. The "chemistry" between two people may be of such a nature that one person simply does not like the other, but that need not be a reflection on the latter's worth.

People who are insecure and feel unlikable expect to be rejected. They therefore interpret innocent comments or gestures as confirmations of their unlikability. Since they fear such "rejections," they do things in order to be liked, in other words, they try to "buy" affection.

Mordechai sought everyone's welfare and spoke peacefully to all, but he was not perturbed that he did not achieve universal approval. If some did not approve of him, that was *their* problem, not his.

Shushan Purim
[During Hebrew
leap years,
Shushan Purim
is celebrated
in Adar Sheni.]
March 8, 1993
Feb. 26, 1994
Feb. 15, 1995
March 6, 1996
Feb. 22, 1997
March 13, 1998

Adar Sheni
March 17, 1995
March 24, 1997

NOTES

_____
_____
_____
_____
_____
_____
_____

Today I shall . . .

. . . try to avoid using universal approval as the measure of my self-worth and avoid buying friendship and affection.

March 9, 1993
Feb. 27, 1994
Feb. 16, 1995
March 7, 1996
Feb. 23, 1997
March 14, 1998

Adar Sheni
March 18, 1995
March 25, 1997

From the Sages

לֹא עָלֶיךָ הַמְּלָאכָה לִגְמוֹר

It is not incumbent upon you to complete the work (*Ethics of the Fathers* 2:21).

In economics, the bottom line measures success and failure. Someone who goes into a business venture with complete recklessness, yet makes a great deal of money, is considered a successful entrepreneur. Another person who was extremely cautious and applied sound business principles, yet went bankrupt, is considered a failure.

Unfortunately, we tend to apply these values to our personal, non-business lives. If things do not turn out the way we wish, we may think that we have performed badly. This is not true. If parents abuse and neglect their children, yet one child wins the Nobel Prize, or discovers the cure for cancer, they do not suddenly become good parents. On the other hand, if they did their utmost to raise their children well, yet one becomes a criminal, they are not necessarily bad parents.

We must understand that we have no control over outcome. All we can control is process, i.e. what we do. If we act with sincerity and with the best guidance available, then what we are doing is right.

Parents whose children turn out to be anti-social invariably fault themselves and may be consumed by guilt. Their pain is unavoidable, but their guilt is unjustified.

Humans do not have the gift of prophecy, nor do we always have the most accurate knowledge. We should hold ourselves responsible for that which we can control, but we should not hold ourselves responsible for that which is beyond our control.

NOTES

_____
_____
_____
_____
_____
_____
_____
_____

Today I shall . . .

. . . try to realize that I must judge the correctness of my actions by how I arrive at them, and not by what results from them.

אָנֹכִי עֹמֵד בֵּין ה' וּבֵינֵיכֶם *From the*

I stand between God and you (Deu- *Scriptures*
teronomy 5:5).

We can also read the verse to mean that it is the "I" that
stands between God and you. Indeed, many commentaries
make the illuminating interpretation that the ego not only
forms the barrier between God and people, but it also
separates us from our fellow men and women.

Self-centeredness renders us unable to empathize with
others — to share in their distress or participate in their
success. When we are completely preoccupied with
ourselves, we lack the time and capacity to be attentive to
others, and barriers to communication inevitably develop.

The great works of *mussar* and *chassidus* stress that
people must efface themselves before God, because to the
degree that they are occupied with their own importance,
to that degree they separate themselves from God. Even sin
cannot separate a person from God the way vanity does. It
is of the vain person that God says, "I cannot coexist in his
presence" (*Sotah* 5a).

Self-effacement does not mean low self-esteem. How? If
people realize that their abilities are gifts from God, they
can then be both humble and aware of their skills and
talents.

If we allow awareness of our potential to go to our heads,
however, we begin to consider others inferior to ourselves.
Our hollow feelings of superiority not only disrupt our
sense of belonging with others, but also cause the vanity
and arrogance which repel the Divine Presence.

March 10, 1993
Feb. 28, 1994
Feb. 17, 1995
March 8, 1996
Feb. 24, 1997
March 15, 1998

Adar Sheni
March 19, 1995
March 26, 1997

NOTES

Today I shall . . .

. . . try to recognize my self-worth, while being aware that
my strengths are a Divine gift. I am no better than any of
God's creatures, and I should not allow barriers to develop
between myself and them.

ADAR

אדר

March 11, 1993
March 1, 1994
Feb. 18, 1995
March 9, 1996
Feb. 25, 1997
March 16, 1998

Adar Sheni

March 20, 1995
March 27, 1997

From the Scriptures אֱלֹקַי בֹּשְׁתִּי וְנִכְלַמְתִּי לְהָרִים אֱלֹקַי פָּנַי אֵלֶיךָ

My God, I am ashamed and embarrassed to lift, my God, my face unto **You** (*Ezra* 9:6).

People may be tempted to do many things, but refrain from doing them for fear of the consequences. For example, they may have the opportunity to enrich themselves dishonestly, but they refrain because they fear that the possible exposure of the crime may lead to heavy fines and/or imprisonment. The deterrent to this improper behavior is thus the fear of the punishment that may follow.

This deterrent effect is not unique to humans. A hungry jackal will not try to take a carcass from the possession of a tiger or lion, because it fears that it will be beaten or killed. Even animals will forego satisfying a bodily drive rather than risk punishment.

Human beings can go a step further. We can deny a bodily drive even without the threat of punishment. If we know that indulging a particular urge is not proper, we can refrain from doing so. Making moral free choices is thus distinctly and uniquely human, and this kind of behavior should give us the pride of being human.

Animals are slaves to their drives. Human beings are capable of making free choices and thus being masters over themselves.

Only when we are embarrassed to show our face before God for having done wrong and when we are ashamed of behaving immorally, without feeling any punishment, are we truly dignified human beings.

NOTES

_____
_____
_____
_____
_____
_____
_____
_____
_____

Today I shall . . .

. . . try to realize that the essence of my humanity involves correct moral free choices, to behave properly because it is right, and to avoid improper behavior simply because it is wrong.

יַעֲלוּ שָׁמַיִם יֵרְדוּ תְהוֹמוֹת נַפְשָׁם בְּרָעָה From the
תִּתְמוֹגָג Scriptures

They rise to the Heavens and descend to the depths; their souls melt
for fear of harm (*Psalm* 107:26).

March 12, 1993
March 2, 1994
Feb. 19, 1995
March 10, 1996
Feb. 26, 1997
March 17, 1998

Adar Sheni
March 21, 1995
March 28, 1997

If we were permitted to design the course of our lives, we would undoubtedly eliminate all crises. Indeed, if we were given the authority to design the course of the world, we would eliminate many types of unpleasantness, both physical and emotional.

However, we did not design the world, and so we must adapt to its laws. Everyone has crises; some are major, some are minor. If we triumph over a certain crisis, we ascend to a new strength of character. If we succumb to the crisis, we lose character strength.

Very often, triumph consists of making a change, and failure consists of being adamant and continuing to do things as before. That resistance to change often comes from fear. We feel more secure with what is familiar, and so we plod along the familiar path even though it may be ruinous.

"I will fear no evil, for You are with me" (*Psalms* 23:4). Faith and trust in God will give us a sense of security and the courage to take advantage of the opportunities for growth that are contained in a crisis, and instead of descending into the depths, we can rise to new heights.

NOTES

_____
_____
_____
_____
_____
_____
_____
_____
_____

Today I shall . . .

. . . consider a crisis an opportunity for growth, and with trust in God have the courage to make constructive changes in my life.

March 13, 1993
March 3, 1994
Feb. 20, 1995
March 11, 1996
Feb. 27, 1997
March 18, 1998

Adar Sheni

March 22, 1995
March 29, 1997

From the Scriptures

תְּמוֹתֵת רָשָׁע רָעָה

It is the evil that kills the wicked (*Psalms* 34:22).

Chassidic philosophy teaches that God gives vitality, a life-sustaining force, only to the good and positive in the world. Evil can exist only because it derives its "nutrition" from that which is good and positive, just as a parasite derives its nutrition from the host. Evil could not continue to exist unless it somehow attached itself to the good, but while it is the nature of good to give of itself, the parasitic evil only takes and thus drains the good of its strength.

Parasites ultimately destroy themselves. Because a parasite can only exist by feeding on its host, and since it thereby weakens the host, it is essentially working toward its own destruction. If it never lets go, it will kill the host, its source of sustenance, and it too will die.

Fear of punishment need not be our only deterrent from doing wrong. Just as the parasite that sucks the lifeblood from its host can temporarily thrive, so may wrongdoing appear to be profitable for a short term. Ultimately, however, evil destroys itself.

Looking only at the short-term consequences and ignoring the inevitable is a common mistake. The Talmud states that truly wise people look to the future and give serious thought to the ultimate consequences of their behavior, rather than focusing upon the momentary gratification.

NOTES

_____
_____
_____
_____
_____
_____
_____
_____
_____

Today I shall . . .

. . . think responsibly about what I do. I shall not let the enticement of immediate gratification blind me to the long-term consequences of my behavior.

Blessed are You, HASHEM, our God, King **our** of the Universe . . . (*Siddur*)   *Prayers*

... בָּרוּךְ אַתָּה ה' אֱלֹקֵינוּ מֶלֶךְ הָעוֹלָם   *From*

March 14, 1993
March 4, 1994
Feb. 21, 1995
March 12, 1996
Feb. 28, 1997
March 19, 1998

Adar Sheni
March 23, 1995
March 30, 1997

Many times each day, we recite various blessings to remind ourselves that God is King of the Universe.

While a person may be tempted to do things that defy the Divine will, the Baal Shem Tov suggests a simple technique that can help withstand temptation.

He gave the parable of a king who wished to test the loyalty of his subjects. He summoned one of his officers and instructed him to go among the masses and attempt to incite a rebellion. By observing who acceded to this agitator, the king could gauge the loyalty or disloyalty of his subjects. One wise man approached by the instigator reasoned that it was unthinkable that so powerful a monarch would allow such a traitor to move about so freely. Hence, he concluded, the rebel must be acting with the king's consent, and his ultimate purpose was to test the loyalty of the populace. So the wise man immediately rejected the instigator.

Our recognition of God as a monarch, as the Absolute Ruler of the Universe, should make it apparent that any instigation to defy the Divine will is a test of our loyalty. Indeed, the evil inclination [*yetzer hara*] is merely carrying out its mission to seduce us to sin, but since the *yetzer hara* too is in the Divine service, it really does not wish us to submit to its seduction. Ironically, one who submits to the seduction of the *yetzer hara* is not only transgressing the Divine will but even disappointing the *yetzer hara*. It is like the diabetic who submits to his desire for sweets. Far from indulging himself, he is harming himself.

NOTES

_____
_____
_____
_____
_____
_____
_____
_____
_____
_____

Today I shall . . .

. . . try to realize that nothing in the world can exist other than by the Divine will, and that anything that appears to be in defiance of the Divine will can only be a test.

ADAR

22

אדר

March 15, 1993
March 5, 1994
Feb. 22, 1995
March 13, 1996
March 1, 1997
March 20, 1998

Adar Sheni

March 24, 1995
March 31, 1997

From the Do *Sages*

אַל תָּדִין אֶת חֲבֵרְךָ עַד שֶׁתַּגִּיעַ לִמְקוֹמוֹ

Do not judge your neighbor until you are in his place (*Ethics of the Fathers* 2:5).

While this Talmudic dictum is generally understood to mean that we should not be critical of another's action because we may not be aware what circumstances led to the behavior, there is also another possible interpretation.

I once heard a recovering alcoholic say, "I used to judge my *insides* by everyone else's *outsides*. I felt deprived because I saw other people smiling, but I did not feel like smiling. I saw other couples communicating, while my wife and I did not. Only later did I realize that when other people smiled, I didn't known whether they *felt* like smiling, and that when I observed other couples communicating, they were in company, but it was certainly possible that when they were alone they did not communicate at all."

Externals are all we can observe. How often do we smile or otherwise act as though we were pleased, while internally we are a cauldron of dissatisfaction? Just as others may mistakenly think that we are happy, so may we mistakenly think that they are happy and that we are missing out. In all likelihood, we are no more and no less satisfied or dissatisfied than anyone else. We should not gauge our *insides* by others' *outsides,* but should set our individual goals and do our utmost to achieve them.

NOTES

_____
_____
_____
_____
_____
_____
_____
_____
_____
_____

Today I shall . . .

. . . try to avoid comparing myself to others and avoid feelings of discontent on the basis that others must be happier than I am.

וְדִבַּרְתָּ בָּם וְלֹא בִּדְבָרִים אֲחֵרִים *From*

You shall converse in the words of *the* Torah and not in other things (*Yoma* 19b). *Sages*

The Talmud explains "other things" as referring to idle, meaningless things.

The Hebrew language has words that mean rest, play, relaxation, and pleasant activities, while it has no word for "fun." A "fun" activity has no goal, as is implied in the colloquial expression, "just for the fun of it." In other words, the goal of the activity is within itself, and fun does not lead to or result in anything else.

March 16, 1993
March 6, 1994
Feb. 23, 1995
March 14, 1996
March 2, 1997
March 21, 1998

Adar Sheni
March 25, 1995
April 1, 1997

This concept is alien to Judaism. Every human being is created with a mission in life. This mission is the ultimate goal toward which everything must in one way or another be directed. Seemingly mundane activities can become goal directed; we eat and sleep so that we can function, and we function in order to achieve our ultimate goal. Even relaxation and judicious enjoyable activities, if they contribute to sound health, can be considered goal directed if they enhance our functioning. However, fun as an activity in which people indulge just to "kill time" is proscribed. Time is precious, and we must constructively utilize every moment of life.

Furthermore, since people conceptualize their self-worth in terms of their activities, doing things "just for the fun of it" may in fact harm their self-esteem.

NOTES

Today I shall . . .

. . . try to direct all my activities, even rest and relaxation, to the ultimate purpose of my life.

March 17, 1993
March 7, 1994
Feb. 24, 1995
March 15, 1996
March 3, 1997
March 22, 1998

Adar Sheni

March 26, 1995
April 2, 1997

From the אָנֹכִי ה' אֱלֹקֶיךָ אֲשֶׁר הוֹצֵאתִיךָ מֵאֶרֶץ
Scriptures מִצְרָיִם

I am your God Who has delivered you from the land of Egypt (*Exodus* 20:2).

This verse states the *mitzvah* of *emunah*, or faith in God. However, since all *mitzvos* take the form of commandments, they take as a given that Someone exists Who commanded them. Therefore, belief in God must come before accepting any *mitzvah*. How, then, can there be a *mitzvah* to believe in God? The reasoning comes out circular. Because we believe in God, we believe that He commanded us to believe in Him.

This *mitzvah* does not only involve believing that God exists, but believing that God rules the universe and is in charge of its functioning. Thus, the first of the Ten Commandments tells us to believe in Divine Providence, that God attends to the operation of the universe and that things do not occur accidentally or spontaneously. Therefore, the first commandment does not state, "I am your God Who created the universe," because creation of the universe does not assume an ongoing participation in its function.

Some believe that God, after creating the universe, abandoned it to the physical laws of nature. Judaism teaches that God continues His interest in everything that happens in the universe. With the exception of free moral choice, which God has delegated to us, everything that occurs in the universe is of Divine origin, although He may operate through the vehicle of the physical laws of nature.

We maintain our relationship to God, to a Father Who not only begot us, but remains involved in our lives.

NOTES

Today I shall . . .

. . . try to remember that God is not only present everywhere, but that He maintains a constant participation in everything that transpires in the universe.

M y sin is forever before me (*Psalms* 51:5).

The human soul may be compared to gold. The more we polish an object made of gold, the brighter it gets. While a certain degree of shine may indeed be beautiful, it may be less than the maximum possible, and hence, relatively defective.

The word חֵטְא, which we generally translate as "sin" or "mistake," can also mean "a defect." The above verse can thus read, "My *defect* is forever before me." Since growth is an endless path, we can always strive to reach a higher level than where we are now. Therefore, we can always consider ourselves relatively "defective" in the sense that we can always find room to improve.

However, the result of such consideration should not be dejection. To the contrary, just as graduation from one level of education prepares and enables us to move to a higher level, and we are certainly not saddened by moving up, so should our awareness of our own "defectiveness," i.e. that we can reach ever-greater heights, never be a cause for sadness. Progress should bring us joy.

March 18, 1993
March 8, 1994
Feb. 25, 1995
March 16, 1996
March 4, 1997
March 23, 1998

Adar Sheni
March 27, 1995
April 3, 1997

NOTES

Today I shall . . .

. . . try to realize that what I have achieved so far allows me to proceed even further.

March 19, 1993
March 9, 1994
Feb. 26, 1995
March 17, 1996
March 5, 1997
March 24, 1998

Adar Sheni
March 28, 1995
April 4, 1997

From the Sages אַל תֹּאמַר לִכְשֶׁאֶפָּנֶה אֶשְׁנֶה שֶׁמָּא לֹא תִפָּנֶה

Do not say, "I will study Torah when I will have free time," because you may never have free time (*Ethics of the Fathers* 2:5).

When we have a certain task before us, the lazy bone in ourselves (and we all know it well) has two ways of thwarting our good intentions — outright refusal and delay. Since outright refusal will likely arouse the resistance of our conscience, we sometimes do an "end run" and achieve the same goal with procrastination. People who have destructive addictions — whether alcohol, drugs, or food — are notorious for saying that they will quit "tomorrow." They may say so with utmost sincerity, but laziness does not affect good intentions, only constructive action.

Furthermore, procrastination feeds upon itself, for it not only delays constructive action, it actually makes that action more difficult. As the deadline approaches, we have less time to do it right.

That which should be done, should be done *now*. Myriad reasons will invariably come to mind. "I cannot learn now. My mind is tired from an exhausting day. I will be able to understand and retain what I learn better when I arise early in the morning." These "reasons" are generally nothing but excuses for laziness.

NOTES

_____
_____
_____
_____
_____
_____
_____
_____
_____

Today I shall . . .

. . . try to do that which I know to be my duty, and avoid the pitfalls of procrastination.

הַשְׁמֵן לֵב הָעָם הַזֶּה וְאָזְנָיו הַכְבֵּד וְעֵינָיו *From the*
הָשַׁע *Scriptures*

The hearts of this nation are fattened, and their ears are heavy, and their eyes are sealed (*Isaiah* 6:10).

Some people's conduct may be exemplary in every way, yet they lack a deep emotional relationship with God. They may even have an intellectual awareness of the infinite greatness of God, yet they may fail to experience the sense of reverence that such an awareness should evoke. They may firmly believe that God is their Provider and Protector, yet fail to love Him and be devoted to Him. This insensitivity of the heart and dullness of the senses, states Rabbi Schneur Zalman in *Tanya*, is due to an insulating barrier with which the *yetzer hara* has enveloped the thought processes of an individual. Finding itself unable to seduce a person into frank transgressions of the Divine will, the *yetzer hara* does the next best thing for its purpose. It renders him insensitive in his relationship to God, even when he goes through the motions of performing the commandments. Since the person is technically complying with the Divine will, he may not recognize that his insensitivity is keeping him distant from God.

Drastic measures may be required to overcome this insensitivity and penetrate its shell of insulation. An individual may need a crisis to shatter his ego and thereby overwhelm the *yetzer hara*. But such a course carries with it the danger of falling into a mood of dejection, which would drain the person's energy and paralyze his functioning. That would hand the *yetzer hara* a triumph. Conversely, a carefully controlled dismantling of the ego, with proper and competent guidance, can free the individual from the constrictive shell, allow him to feel a closeness to God, and rebuild his healthy ego.

March 20, 1993
March 10, 1994
Feb. 27, 1995
March 18, 1996
March 6, 1997
March 25, 1998

Adar Sheni
March 29, 1995
April 5, 1997

NOTES

Today I shall . . .

. . . try to discover whether I feel love and reverence for God, and if not, seek spiritual guidance how to achieve these.

March 21, 1993
March 11, 1994
Feb. 28, 1995
March 19, 1996
March 7, 1997
March 26, 1998

Adar Sheni
March 30, 1995
April 6, 1997

From the Scriptures שֶׁבַע יִפּוֹל צַדִּיק וָקָם

A just person may fall seven times and rise (*Proverbs* 24:16).

Although we may have realized that we learn our most valuable lessons the hard way, and that therefore we may tolerate our mistakes because of their educational value, we are apt to be intolerant of a mistake that we repeat. "I should have known better from last time," one says.

We should stop berating ourselves. Some lessons are not learned so easily, even from experience. The reason? We may understand something with our intellect, yet it may not have filtered down into our hearts and bones and muscles. In other words, if we lack an emotional grasp of a concept, the intellectual awareness alone may not suffice to deter us from repeating a mistake.

We are human. Rather than blame ourselves for a repetitive mistake, we should realize that the anguish we feel when we have failed to learn from a previous experience might just give us the emotional insight that can prevent that same mistake in the future.

In fact, new mistakes can shed light on old mistakes. When we do something wrong once, we may make only a superficial repair. Soon afterwards, in a different situation, we again fall flat. We may continue to fall until we realize that all our failures point to a flaw in ourselves that we had never noticed. Once we have uncovered the real reason for our mistakes, we can correct it and greatly, genuinely improve ourselves.

NOTES

Today I shall . . .

. . . try to maintain faith in myself even when I make the same mistake over and over again.

יֵשׁ קוֹנֶה עוֹלָמוֹ בְּשָׁעָה אַחַת *From*

A person may acquire an entire world of *the* reward in just a brief period of time *Sages* (*Avodah Zarah* 10b).

Someone once challenged the Rabbi of Gur: "We read in the *Shema* that if we observe the *mitzvos*, we will be rewarded, and if we transgress, we will be punished. I am not observant and in fact have many, many transgressions to my credit, yet I am wealthy and content with my life. Therefore, the *Shema* is incorrect."

The Rabbi of Gur responded: "My child, you would not have been familiar with the *Shema* unless you had at some time recited it. When you did so, you performed a *mitzvah*, and to put it mildly, you have been rewarded."

Negative behavior tends to perpetuate itself. If we berate ourselves, we may discourage ourselves from behaving properly, for one may think: "What's the use? I am beyond help anyway."

We can all find some positive deeds in our life. They can serve as nuclei for feelings of self-worth that stimulate us to do more positive things, rather than despair of ourselves and resign ourselves to lower standards of behavior.

Erev **Rosh Chodesh** *[Eve of the New Month]*

March 22, 1993
March 12, 1994
March 1, 1995
March 20, 1996
March 8, 1997
March 27, 1998

Adar Sheni

March 31, 1995
April 7, 1997

NOTES

Today I shall . . .

. . . find something for which I can give myself approval, and use that positive act as a springboard for more positive acts.

**First Day of
Rosh Chodesh
Adar Sheni**

*[During most
years, Adar has
29 days. During
Hebrew leap
years, Adar has 30
days, while Adar
Sheni has 29.]*

March 2, 1995
March 9, 1997

*From the
Scriptures*

מַחְשְׁבוֹת חָרוּץ אַךְ לְמוֹתָר

The deliberations of the industrious always lead to an advantage *(Proverbs 21:5)*.

What are a person's moral obligations? How much is a person required to do, and when may one say, "I have done enough?"

Inertia is a powerful force, which operates to maintain things at rest until overcome by a greater force. For many people, the driving force that gets them up in the morning is the need to provide for themselves and/or the family. Once financial and social obligations have been met, many people retire to the easy chair or to any of many pastimes.

The Torah perspective is that a person is responsible to do whatever one *can* do rather than what one *must* do. While a person must certainly have the rest, relaxation, and entertainment that is conducive to optimum physical and emotional health, one is not free to become inactive just because one's immediate personal obligations have been satisfied. There are always people in need of help, and deserving causes that should be supported. There is an infinite store of Torah wisdom, and a *mitzvah* to learn more about how one can enhance one's relationship to God.

There are some *mitzvos* that can be fulfilled by meeting minimum standards, such as eating a small portion of matzah at the Seder. Other *mitzvos*, especially those involving extending a helping hand to people in need, have no upper limits. Whatever one can do is what one should do.

NOTES

Today I shall . . .

. . . carefully examine whether I am doing all that is within my means to do.

הַחֹדֶשׁ הַזֶּה לָכֶם רֹאשׁ חֳדָשִׁים *From the*

This month shall be unto you the first *Scriptures*
of the months (*Exodus* 12:2).

NISSAN

ניסן

Rosh Chodesh
March 23, 1993
March 13, 1994
April 1, 1995
March 21, 1996
April 8, 1997
March 28, 1998

The Jewish calendar has two New Years. Rosh Hashanah, the first day of Tishrei, which marks the beginning of the calendar year, is a day of judgment, signifying that we are held accountable for our behavior. The first day of Nissan marks the beginning of the month of our liberation from Egypt, an event which teaches us that God watches us, that He cares about us, and that even distressful experiences, such as the bitter enslavement in Egypt, are part of a Divine master plan.

Six months separate the two New Years. The personal inventory and the analysis of our mistakes and character defects which we do during the solemn days of Tishrei are very sobering tasks. On the other hand, realizing that we hold a lofty status as children of God and that we are constantly under His vigilance, which is emphasized in Nissan, is exhilarating and elating. Both attitudes are indeed essential, but if one tries to achieve them simultaneously, one may end up in a state of confusion.

In the third chapter of *Ecclesiastes*, Solomon points out that we should dedicate appropriate times in life for conflicting acts and attitudes. He says, "There's a time to plant and a time to uproot" (3:2), and "There is a time to cry and a time to laugh" (3:4), etc. A healthy adjustment to life is a delicate balancing act. With proper learning and guidance, we can learn to determine appropriate times for what we are supposed to do.

NOTES

Today I shall . . .

. . . give thought to scheduling my hours and days, so that I can achieve a healthy balance of diverse attitudes.

March 24, 1993
March 14, 1994
April 2, 1995
March 22, 1996
April 9, 1997
March 29, 1998

From the Sages כָּךְ הִיא דַרְכָּהּ שֶׁל תּוֹרָה פַּת בַּמֶּלַח תֹּאכֵל וּמַיִם בִּמְשׂוּרָה תִּשְׁתֶּה וְעַל הָאָרֶץ תִּישָׁן

This is the way of Torah: eat bread with salt, drink water by measure, and sleep on the earth (*Ethics of the Fathers* 6:4).

Does observance of Torah require living a life of poverty and depriving ourselves of all the niceties of the world?

Certainly not. The Talmud is elaborating upon another Talmudic statement: "Who is wealthy? One who is content with his portion" (*Ethics of the Fathers* 4:1).

People who can be happy with the basics of life — food, clothing, and shelter — can truly enjoy the luxuries of life, because they can be happy even without them. Those whose happiness depends upon having luxuries are likely to be perennially dissatisfied, in constant need of more, and consequently unhappy, even if they have everything they desire.

A wise man once observed a display of various items in a store window. "I never knew there were so many things I can get along without," he said.

If bread and water can satisfy us, then we can enjoy a steak. If we are not satisfied unless we have caviar, we will discover that even caviar is not enough.

NOTES

_____
_____
_____
_____
_____
_____
_____
_____
_____
_____

Today I shall . . .

. . . try to be content with the essentials of life and consider everything else as optional.

הַהִרְהוּרֵי עֲבֵירָה קָשׁוּ מֵעֲבֵירָה *From*
Contemplating sin is more serious than *the*
the sin itself (*Yoma* 29a). *Sages*

March 25, 1993
March 15, 1994
April 3, 1995
March 23, 1996
April 10, 1997
March 30, 1998

Although actions generally have much greater impact than thoughts, thoughts may have a more serious effect in several areas.

The distance that our hands can reach is quite limited. The ears can hear from a much greater distance, and the reach of the eye is much farther yet. Thought, however, is virtually limitless in its reach. We can think of objects millions of light years away, and so we have a much greater selection of improper thoughts than of improper actions.

Thought also lacks the restraints that can deter actions. One may refrain from an improper act for fear of punishment or because of social disapproval, but the privacy of thought places it beyond these restraints.

Furthermore, thoughts create attitudes and mindsets. An improper action creates a certain amount of damage, but an improper mindset can create a multitude of improper actions. Finally, an improper mindset can numb our conscience and render us less sensitive to the effects of our actions. We therefore do not feel the guilt that would otherwise come from doing an improper act.

We may not be able to avoid the occurrence of improper impulses, but we should promptly reject them and not permit them to dwell in our mind.

NOTES

Today I shall . . .

. . . make special effort to avoid harboring improper thoughts.

March 26, 1993
March 16, 1994
April 4, 1995
March 24, 1996
April 11, 1997
March 31, 1998

From the **M**ay goodness and kindness pursue *Scriptures* me all the days of my life (*Psalms* 23:1).

אַךְ טוֹב וָחֶסֶד יִרְדְּפוּנִי כָּל יְמֵי חַיָּי

What a strange expression! Goodness and kindness should *pursue* me, as though I was fleeing from them?!

Perhaps the Psalmist had in mind the verse: "You shall pursue righteousness, only righteousness" (*Deuteronomy* 16:20). Many people have things reversed. They pursue goodness and kindness for themselves, but leave righteousness to somehow catch up with them. The Torah dictates a different order. A person should pursue righteousness and allow goodness and kindness to catch up.

If we asked people for their goal for life, many would say, "to achieve happiness." While this answer is certainly understandable, happiness is not the primary goal of creation of man. Indeed, the Scripture states very clearly: "Man was created in order to toil" (*Job* 5:7). And the Talmud explains that this means to work on the Divine mission, to fulfill the Divine will. If our primary goal is happiness, we are certain to be frustrated. The average person's life is abundant in distressful happenings. If the primary goal is to do the Divine will, then those times of happiness that do occur can be enjoyed, and the times of distress are borne without bitterness.

NOTES

_____
_____
_____
_____
_____
_____
_____
_____
_____

Today I shall . . .

. . . try to remember that I was created to do the will of God rather than to lead a blissful life.

בֶּן שְׁלֹשׁ עֶשְׂרֵה לַמִּצְוֹת *From the Sages*

At the age of thirteen, one becomes obligated to perform the mitzvos (*Ethics of the Fathers* 5:25).

March 27, 1993
March 17, 1994
April 5, 1995
March 25, 1996
April 12, 1997
April 1, 1998

Jewish law does not recognize any such entity as adolescence. A child is a minor until the age of legal majority, which is the twelfth birthday for a girl and the thirteenth for a boy. One moment prior to the sunset of the eleventh or twelfth year, the person is a minor; the next moment, she or he is an adult. Parents and teachers still must provide guidance of course, but the "child" is no longer a child, and must assume responsibility for him or herself.

Parents take responsibility for their *children's* behavior, but once those children reach the age of majority, they are accountable for their actions. A Jew never has a single moment of diminished responsibility; he or she always advances.

In the general culture, however, adolescence constitutes a "no man's land," a period of diminished responsibility. Adolescents are too old for their behavior to be dismissed as childish, yet too young to be held accountable for their actions.

The problem is that once youths experience a period of diminished responsibility, they may never advance to a sense of full responsibility. Similarly, Western legal systems abound with legal factors that diminish individuals' culpability for misbehavior. It stands to reason, therefore, that once people have a window of lessened responsibility, they have even less reason to take full responsibility for themselves. This may be one factor in Western civilization's worsening problem of individuals and groups blaming others for their problems and shortcomings.

NOTES

_____

Today I shall . . .

. . . hold myself accountable and responsible for everything I do or have done.

March 28, 1993
March 18, 1994
April 6, 1995
March 26, 1996
April 13, 1997
April 2, 1998

From the **M**an is judged each day (*Rosh Hashanah* *the* 16a).
Sages

אָדָם נִידוֹן בְּכָל יוֹם

A disciple of the Baal Shem Tov remarked to him that the above statement appears to contradict another Talmudic statement, which states that a person is judged on Rosh Hashanah for the entire year.

The Baal Shem Tov noticed a water carrier passing by. "How are things with you, Chaikel?" he asked. "What can I tell you?" Chaikel answered. "In my old age, I still have to earn my meager bread with backbreaking work." The Baal Shem Tov told his disciple to remember Chaikel's words.

Several days later, the water carrier again passed by. Again, the Baal Shem Tov inquired as to how things were with him. "Thank God," Chaikel said, "if at my age I can still provide for myself by *shlepping* water up the hill, I have no cause to complain."

The Baal Shem Tov then told his disciple: "Both Talmudic statements are true. On Rosh Hashanah, it was decreed that Chaikel will be a water carrier this year, but how Chaikel reacts to this decree can vary from day to day."

While our particular station in life may be the same, we react to it differently from day to day. We thus have the option to react more favorably and less favorably to the very same conditions.

NOTES

Today I shall . . .

. . . try to realize that some things that irritate me today did not bother me at other times, and I have the option not to be irritated today.

I lift my eyes to the mountains (*Psalms* 121:1). אֶשָּׂא עֵינַי אֶל הֶהָרִים: אֶל הַהוֹרִים *From the Scriptures*

The Hebrew word for mountains can also be read phonetically to mean "ancestors" (*Bereishis Rabbah* 68:2). *From the Sages*

March 29, 1993
March 19, 1994
April 7, 1995
March 27, 1996
April 14, 1997
April 3, 1998

Every culture has its heroes. In Western civilization, the heroes for youth are apt to be sports figures or popular entertainers who make a great deal of money. More mature people are likely to admire financiers and industrialists who have achieved great success. In either case, the role models are not people of great spiritual achievement.

Judaism has as its role models the Patriarchs and Matriarchs — Abraham, Isaac, Jacob, and Sarah, Rivkah, Rochel, Leah — who are known not for their worldly success, but for their total devotion to God.

Parents tremendously influence their children. If the parents choose heroes of great spirituality, so will the children.

Acknowledging the Patriarchs by referring to them in prayers (e.g. "the God of Abraham, Isaac, and Jacob") is not enough. If children are given tangible evidence that their parents value and wish to emulate the virtues of the Patriarchs, they will follow their elders and seek the spiritual, rather than the material alone, in their lives.

Today I shall . . .

. . . try to demonstrate to my children that I truly value people of great spiritual achievement, rather than those who have been materially successful.

NOTES

NISSAN

8

נִיסָן

March 30, 1993
March 20, 1994
April 8, 1995
March 28, 1996
April 15, 1997
April 4, 1998

From the Sages

כֵּיוָן שֶׁבָּא לִכְלַל כַּעַס בָּא לִכְלַל טָעוּת

Once he entered the category of rage, he entered the category of error (*Sifri, Matos* 48).

The Talmud says that this passage refers to Moses, and that if it holds true of Moses, how much more so for people of lesser spirituality.

The difference between rage and anger is profound. While anger comes from an external stimulus (and therefore our feeling that it is beyond our control), rage comes from people permitting their anger to feed upon itself and intensify into fury.

Note that the above quote states that those who enter the "category" of rage have entered the "category" of error. In other words, even if they have not actually been violent in word or deed, but have lost their composure to the degree that they *could* lose control, they have thereby already entered the realm of error. Anything they say or do in such a state is likely to be wrong.

If we feel our anger is intensifying within ourselves, we should stop whatever we are doing. We will regret the harsh words and acts that we are likely to do. We should instead allow time to pass and then confide our feelings to a trusted friend, thus defusing the rage and allowing it to dissipate.

NOTES

Today I shall . . .

. . . avoid responding in word or deed when I feel intensely angry.

נֶקֶב קָטָן בַּגּוּף גּוֹרֵם לְנֶקֶב גָּדוֹל בַּנְּשָׁמָה *From the Sages*

O ne who creates a small defect in the body creates a great defect in the soul (*Maggid of Mezritch*).

March 31, 1993
March 21, 1994
April 9, 1995
March 29, 1996
April 16, 1997
April 5, 1998

A student spied the great Hillel leaving his academy. He approached the Sage and asked him where he was going. "I am going to do a *mitzvah* for someone poor and forsaken," Hillel answered. Noting his student's bewilderment, he then explained: "I am going to feed my body. It is totally dependent upon me to look after it."

If someone gives us an object for safekeeping, we have a responsibility to look after it and cannot be derelict in its care. Likewise, our bodies have been entrusted to us, and we have a full obligation to care properly for them.

Too many of us violate our trust by taking unnecessary risks or doing things which are detrimental to our bodies, such as smoking, overeating, or abusing alcohol and drugs. Is it not strange that one who would never think of drinking a non-diet soft drink might not have the least hesitance in smoking a cigarette, even though the harmful effects of smoking are now established beyond a shadow of a doubt?

A Chassidic master observed one of his followers who looked lean and weak. On inquiring, he learned that this man was fasting frequently to atone for his sins. He then told him: "First you set out to ruin your soul, and having achieved this, you are now out to ruin your body as well."

NOTES

Today I shall . . .

. . . remember that I am fully responsible for the well-being of my body, and I shall take every means to protect it from harm.

April 1, 1993
March 22, 1994
April 10, 1995
March 30, 1996
April 17, 1997
April 6, 1998

From our Prayers

הִנְנִי מוּכָן וּמְזֻמָּן לְקַיֵּם מִצְוַת עֲשֵׂה

I am prepared and ready to fulfill the positive commandment (*Siddur*).

The above phrase should be said before the performance of every commandment.

Soldiers must undergo extensive training and frequent drilling. They are put through exercises in various simulations of actual battle, so that they will be ready when the enemy attacks. Obviously, to wait until the attack and then prepare oneself would be suicidal. The preparation must come long before the attack.

People should view the evil inclination as an enemy that is seeking to destroy them. It is a most cunning enemy, with a huge array of tactics and a singlemindedness of purpose. It never tires and has infinite patience, lurking in stealth and waiting for an opportunity to attack. Confronted with such a persistent and formidable foe, a person must be prepared at all times.

We begin this preparation as soon as we awaken, by expressing our gratitude towards God for another day of life. This acknowledgment that God is the source of life leads one to dedicate himself to His service, and this is reinforced many times a day, as one accepts His sovereignty in prayers and blessings. Study of the Torah and performance of the commandments further increase one's capacity to resist the destructive maneuvers of the *yetzer hara*, for they train the mind and accustom the body in how to think and act.

NOTES

Today I shall . . .

. . . try to maintain a state of alertness and preparedness against the attempts of the *yetzer hara* to mislead me.

דֶּרֶךְ בְּרִיָּתוֹ שֶׁל אָדָם לִהְיוֹת נִמְשָׁךְ בְּדֵעוֹתָיו אַחַר רֵעָיו וַחֲבֵרָיו *From the Sages*

It is the nature of a person to be influenced by his fellows and comrades (*Rambam, Hil. De'os* 6:1).

April 2, 1993
March 23, 1994
April 11, 1995
March 31, 1996
April 18, 1997
April 7, 1998

We can never escape the influence of our environment. Our life-style impacts upon us and, as if by osmosis, penetrates our skin and becomes part of us.

Our environment today is thoroughly computerized. Computer intelligence is no longer a science-fiction fantasy, but an everyday occurrence. Some computers can even carry out complete interviews. The computer asks questions, receives answers, interprets these answers, and uses its newly acquired information to ask new questions.

Still, while computers may be able to think, they cannot feel. The uniqueness of human beings is therefore no longer in their intellect, but in their emotions.

We must be extremely careful not to allow ourselves to become human computers that are devoid of feelings. Our culture is in danger of losing this essential aspect of humanity, remaining only with intellect. Because we communicate so much with unfeeling computers, we are in danger of becoming disconnected from our own feelings and oblivious to the feelings of others.

As we check in at our jobs, and the computer on our desk greets us with, "Good morning, Mr. Smith. Today is Wednesday, and here is the agenda for today," let us remember that this machine may indeed be brilliant, but it cannot laugh or cry. It cannot be happy if we succeed, or sad if we fail.

NOTES

Today I shall ...

... try to remain a human being in every way — by keeping in touch with my own feelings and being sensitive to the feelings of others.

April 3, 1993
March 24, 1994
April 12, 1995
April 1, 1996
April 19, 1997
April 8, 1998

From the
Scriptures

כִּי נַעַר יִשְׂרָאֵל וָאֹהֲבֵהוּ

For Israel is a young lad, therefore I love him (*Hosea* 11:1).

Historically, the Jewish nation is one of the oldest in existence. In terms of behavior and reactions, it is the youngest.

One prominent difference between children and the elderly is that children heal much more rapidly. Children are resilient. When they fall, their bones do not break as easily, and therefore they are quickly back in action. An elderly person who falls is likely to sustain a severe fracture and may remain disabled for a long period of time.

No nation has experienced the traumas that have repeatedly befallen the Jewish nation. Expelled from its homeland and subjected to inquisitions, pogroms, holocausts, and hostility everywhere, the Jewish nation reacts with the resilience of a child. Its bones bend rather than break. Injuries heal quickly, and while still smarting from its wounds, it rises and is back into action.

We individuals should learn from the nation to never grow old in this sense. No one's life is free of distressful experiences and trauma. At any age, we can retain the vigor and resilience of youth and go on with the business of creativity and constructive living.

NOTES

Today I shall . . .

. . . try to retain a youthful spirit and learn to rebound quickly from any adverse circumstance.

כִּי תִפְגַּע שׁוֹר אֹיִבְךָ אוֹ חֲמֹרוֹ תֹּעֶה הָשֵׁב *From the*
תְּשִׁיבֶנּוּ לוֹ *Scriptures*

If you encounter your enemy's ox or
donkey wandering astray, you must
return it to him (*Exodus* 23:4).

April 4, 1993
March 25, 1994
April 13, 1995
April 2, 1996
April 20, 1997
April 9, 1998
[The search for
chametz takes
place tonight.]

In this *mitzvah*, the Torah makes two demands: (1) to go
out of our way to return a lost animal to its rightful owner,
and (2) to overcome our hostile feelings towards our
enemy if the lost animal is his.

If this is what is demanded toward a mere *belonging* of
an *enemy*, how much more are we responsible when we
see *friends* going astray and acting improperly? Yet, how
often do we avoid telling them that we feel what they are
doing is wrong? We rationalize by saying: "We do not wish
to interfere in their private affairs. How they run their life is
their own business," or "We don't want to offend them."

A popular billboard declares: "A true friend does not
allow a friend to drive drunk." If you truly care for others,
you will take the necessary steps to protect them from
themselves, even if they may be angry at you for doing so.

Honesty is more potent than sympathy. A person who
has suffered from grievous mistakes often says: "If only
someone had stopped me!"

Drunk driving is not the only destructive behavior which
a true friend would try to stop. Whenever we see that a
friend is doing something which we sincerely believe to be
wrong, we have a responsibility to convey our opinion to
him or her. Failure to do so comes from either of two
rationalizations: (1) I am not really his or her friend, or (2) I
really do not believe the behavior is wrong. In either case,
we are guilty of insincerity.

NOTES

Today I shall . . .

. . . examine my own convictions and the sincerity of my
friendship and let this determine whether I will share my
opinions with my friends.

Erev Pesach
[Eve of Passover]
April 5, 1993
March 26, 1994
April 14, 1995
April 3, 1996
April 21, 1997
April 10, 1998

From the Scriptures

לֹא תִזְבַּח עַל חָמֵץ

Do not sacrifice [the Passover offering] while you are in possession of chametz (leaven) (*Exodus* 23:18).

Chametz and *matzah* have many symbolic explanations. Whatever the symbolic meaning may be, one fact cannot be denied. For the few days of Passover, *chametz* and *matzah* are antithetical. The Passover *seder* cannot coexist with *chametz*. This point is clearly stated in the first of the traditional four questions near the beginning of the *Haggadah*: "All other nights we eat both *chametz* and *matzah*; but this night, only *matzah*."

Passover tells us that we cannot maintain two opposites, but must make a commitment one way or the other. As Elijah said to the Jews who worshiped idols: "How long will you vacillate between two contradictory ideologies? If Hashem is God, then follow Him. If Baal is god, then follow him" (*I Kings* 18:21).

People who can take a definite stand can also open themselves to any needed change when they are shown that they are wrong. However, people who constantly vacillate can always find excuses to slither out of improving themselves.

The above verse taught the about-to-be-liberated Israelites and their descendants a vital principle: Do not try to maintain mutually contradictory ideologies.

NOTES

_____
_____
_____
_____
_____
_____
_____
_____
_____

Today I shall . . .

. . . try to rid myself of mutually contradictory concepts, and instead make a commitment to a way of life that I can fully accept.

אֲנִי הִכְבַּדְתִּי אֶת לִבּוֹ . . . לְמַעַן שְׁתִי *From the*
אֹתֹתַי אֵלֶּה בְּקִרְבּוֹ *Scriptures*

I have hardened his [Pharaoh's] heart
. . . in order to execute My miracles
within him (*Exodus* 10:1).

Many commentaries raise the question: If God rendered
Pharaoh unable to learn from experience, why did He then
punish him for refusing to release the Israelites?

The answer lies in an understanding of free will. Many
psychologists believe in "psychic determinism," that various circumstances can so affect people that they have no
freedom of choice. People therefore act in certain ways
because they must do so. Such concepts have been
introduced in trials of those who have committed heinous
crimes. So many lawyers have pleaded to the jury: "He was
raised in such a terrible environment that he did not know
better."

Torah rejects this idea. While many circumstances may
impact upon a person, no human being with an intact brain
is ever deprived of freedom of choice. We are always
responsible for our actions. This concept is a pillar of the
Torah's concept of human freedom.

The about-to-be-liberated Israelites were thus told: "I
will indeed harden Pharaoh's heart and put great pressure
upon him, but that will not deprive him of freedom of
choice. Pharaoh will remain free and therefore will be held
responsible for his behavior. In preparation for your
liberation and ultimate acceptance of the Torah, you must
retain this principle: people are *always* responsible for their
actions."

*First Day of
Pesach*
April 6, 1993
March 27, 1994
April 15, 1995
April 4, 1996
April 22, 1997
April 11, 1998

NOTES

_____
_____
_____
_____
_____
_____

Today I shall . . .

. . . try to realize that I have free will, and that whatever my
circumstances may be, I will always retain freedom of
choice to do good or evil.

**Second Day
of Pesach**

*[In the Land of
Israel, this is the
first day of Chol
Hamoed, the In-
termediate Days.]*

April 7, 1993
March 28, 1994
April 16, 1995
April 5, 1996
April 23, 1997
April 12, 1998

*From the
Scriptures* **Y**ou shall love your God (*Deuteronomy* 6:5).

וְאָהַבְתָּ אֵת ה' אֱלֹקֶיךָ

You shall fear your God (*Leviticus* 19:14).

וְיָרֵאתָ מֵאֱלֹקֶיךָ

Love and fear of the same subject are obviously incompatible emotions. Love implies a desire to be close to the loved one, while fear is associated with the desire to be more remote from the object of one's fear. How does the Torah expect a person to relate to God in both ways simultaneously?

Rabbi Schneur Zalman explains in *Tanya* that when one fulfills the Divine will, one is drawn closer to God, and that when one transgresses the Divine will, one detaches oneself from God. Inasmuch as a person is constantly tempted by the *yetzer hara* to flout the Divine will, one should fear succumbing to the *yetzer hara* because one would thereby lose the closeness to God. Thus, fear of God is not a fear of being punished, but a fear of losing one's relationship with the object of one's love, and this fear is perfectly compatible with love of God.

In a love relationship between two people, it is easily understood that one would not wish to offend the beloved person in any way, even though there is no fear of punishment. We can develop a loving relationship with God that will result in a similar type of fear, the fear of offending Him. The Talmud tells us that one can never be certain that one will never sin, and, given the human frailty to temptation and the constant incitement by the *yetzer hara*, we can understand why one should always have this type of fear of God, for it is a fear that is perfectly compatible with love.

NOTES

Today I shall . . .

. . . cherish my relationship with God so that the thought of losing my closeness with Him becomes frightening to me.

לֹא תַחְמֹד בֵּית רֵעֶךָ . . . אֵשֶׁת רֵעֶךָ . . . *From the*
וְכֹל אֲשֶׁר לְרֵעֶךָ *Scriptures*

Do not covet your neighbor's house
. . . your neighbor's wife . . . and
anything that belongs to your neighbor
(*Exodus* 20:14).

Chol Hamoed
Pesach
April 8, 1993
March 29, 1994
April 17, 1995
April 6, 1996
April 24, 1997
April 13, 1998

Some ask: How can a person be commanded to not
desire something? Is not wanting something a spontaneous
feeling and therefore not subject to rational control?

A noted psychologist says: "In order to feel love for some
object, be it a human being, pet, or a new home, a man
must see some possibility of an action he can take in regard
to it, otherwise his appraisal of 'good' is merely an abstract
judgment without personal significance" (Branden, N., *The
Psychology of Self Esteem*, Bantam Books [New York, 1973]
p. 77).

This important psychological insight tells us that something which is completely beyond attainability cannot
become an object of desire. Hence, if we desire something
belonging to our neighbor, it is because somehow,
however remote, we think we might get it.

When we become aware of a desire for something
belonging to someone else, it is time to take steps to avoid
any improper behavior. Sincere commitment to avoid
improper behavior can help eliminate improper desires.

NOTES

_____
_____
_____
_____
_____
_____
_____

Today I shall . . .

_____

. . . make my commitments to respect another person's
possessions so absolute that a desire for them should never
occur.

_____

_____

Chol Hamoed
Pesach

April 9, 1993
March 30, 1994
April 18, 1995
April 7, 1996
April 25, 1997
April 14, 1998

From the Sages

הָעוֹלָם הַזֶּה נִקְרָא עוֹלָם הַתִּיקוּן

This world is known as the "World of Rectification" (*The Works of Kabbalah*).

I wonder what the ancient Kabbalists would say about the modern world. Our everyday life certainly does not appear to be a "world of rectification."

To rectify means to repair or correct an existing defect. This practice has become almost extinct. Years ago, things that went wrong were repaired; today, they are simply replaced. Replacing an item is cheaper than going to the trouble of having it repaired. When we add the vast numbers of disposable items that have become commonplace, we have a life-style where "rectifying," at least of objects that we use are concerned, is a rather infrequent phenomenon.

Unfortunately, this attitude of replacing items rather than trying to repair them has extended itself from object relationships to people relationships. The most dramatic evidence is the unprecedented number of divorces. In the past, a couple that developed problems would try to repair the relationship. Most often, the attempt succeeded. Today, people do not want to waste time and effort; rather, they simply terminate the relationship and replace it with a new one. Human beings, much like styrofoam cups and contact lenses, have become "disposable."

We would do well to make at least our interpersonal relationships comply with the Kabbalistic concept of "World of Rectification."

NOTES

_____
_____
_____
_____
_____
_____
_____
_____
_____

Today I shall . . .

. . . try to appreciate the unique character of an interpersonal relationship and make every effort to preserve it.

יוֹדוּ לַה' חַסְדּוֹ וְנִפְלְאוֹתָיו לִבְנֵי אָדָם *From the*
They praise God for His kindness and *Scriptures*
relate His wonders to other people
(*Psalms* 107:8).

**Chol Hamoed
Pesach**

April 10, 1993
March 31, 1994
April 19, 1995
April 8, 1996
April 26, 1997
April 15, 1998

This verse is repeated four times in this chapter, emphasizing the obligation people have to express their gratitude to God for His kindnesses.

Human beings have the capacity for complaining about their distress as well as being thankful for benevolence. Unfortunately, in many people these traits are not balanced, and the capacity to complain may outweigh that of being grateful.

There is a story about a mother who was walking along the seashore with her son. Unexpectedly, a huge wave descended upon them and carried the child out to sea. The distraught mother began begging to God: "Please, God, save my child! Give me back my little son!" Shortly afterwards, another huge wave deposited the child, unharmed, right at her feet.

The mother embraced the child, and turning her eyes toward heaven, exclaimed, "Thank You, God. Thank You, thank You forever." A moment later, she looked at her child, then turned her eyes to heaven once again and asked: "Where is the hat he was wearing?"

Many humorous stories have a kernel of truth. How often do we forget kindnesses and focus instead on annoyances, even when the disparity between them is in the magnitude of the saving of a child versus the loss of a hat.

NOTES

_____

Today I shall . . .

. . . try to bear in mind the many great kindnesses that God has done for me, and ignore the relatively insignificant displeasures in my life.

**Chol Hamoed
Pesach**
*April 11, 1993
April 1, 1994
April 20, 1995
April 9, 1996
April 27, 1997
April 16, 1998*

*From the
Scriptures*

וְאִם לֹא קָרוֹב אָחִיךָ אֵלֶיךָ וְלֹא יְדַעְתּוֹ

And if your brother is not close to you
and you do not know him (*Deuteronomy* 22:2).

Perhaps the reason that other people are not close to you
is because you do not know them.

The Chassidic master of Apt said: "As a young man, I was
determined to change the world. As I matured, I narrowed
my goals to changing my community. Still later, I decided
to change only my family. Now I realize that it is all I can do
to change myself."

Some things in the world are givens, and others are
modifiable. The only thing we can really modify is
ourselves. All other people are givens. Unfortunately, many
people assume the reverse to be true. They accept
themselves as givens and expect everyone else to change to
accommodate them.

(There is one limited exception. When our children are
small, we can teach and guide them. When they mature,
however, we can no longer mold them.)

Trying to change others is both futile and frustrating.
Furthermore, we cannot see other people the way they
truly are, as long as we are preoccupied with trying to
change them to the way we would like them to be.

The people we should know the most intimately are
those who are closest to us. Yet it is precisely these people
whom we wish to mold into the image we have developed
for them. As long as this attitude prevails, we cannot see
them for what they are. How ironic and tragic that those we
care for the most may be those we know the least!

NOTES

Today I shall . . .

. . . try to focus any desires to change on myself and let
other people determine for themselves who and what they
wish to be.

נַעֲנָה ר' עֲקִיבָא חֲבִיבִין יִסּוּרִין *From*

Rabbi Akiva spoke up: "Suffering can be *the* precious" (*Sanhedrin* 101a). *Sages*

Rabbi Akiva made this point when he and a group of colleagues visited their revered teacher, Rabbi Eliezer, who was gravely ill. When all the other students heaped abundant praise on Rabbi Eliezer, he turned a deaf ear to them. Only Rabbi Akiva's remark elicited a response. "Let me hear what my son Akiva has to say," he said.

When we have our health and full capacities, we can do countless things and make all kinds of choices. This personal freedom gives life so much of its meaning. But if we are gravely ill and bedridden, and disease has drained all of our energies, we can do virtually nothing and are no longer free to make any choices. This loss of personal freedom can be felt as a loss of our very humanity.

Rabbi Eliezer, in his state of severe illness, felt that his loss of freedom had cost him his human identity. His students' praises were empty to him, for even a glorious past could not give him the freedom of choice so vital to his being.

Rabbi Akiva pointed out that he still had one choice: a choice of attitude. Although all other choices had been taken from him, Rabbi Eliezer could still choose to either accept his suffering with serenity, or swallow it with bitterness. Rabbi Akiva had restored his freedom to him.

Seventh Day of Pesach

[In the Land of Israel, this is the last day of Pesach.]

April 12, 1993
April 2, 1994
Apri 21, 1995
April 10, 1996
April 28, 1997
April 17, 1998

NOTES

_____
_____
_____
_____
_____
_____
_____
_____
_____
_____

Today I shall . . .

. . . realize that even when many things in my life are not subject to change, how I accept them is a freedom that no one can take from me.

**Eighth Day
of Pesach**

[Yizkor]

April 13, 1993
April 3, 1994
April 22, 1995
April 11, 1996
April 29, 1997
April 18, 1998

*From
our* **T**his day of the festival of matzos (*Siddur*).
Prayers

אֶת יוֹם חַג הַמַּצּוֹת הַזֶּה

Outside the Land of Israel, today is observed as the last day of Passover. In Israel, Passover lasts seven days, so it ended yesterday.

This discrepancy has its origin in the beginning of the dispersion of the Jewish people, before a set calendar had been established. In those days the High Court in Jerusalem declared the first day of a new month, based on sighting the new moon. Jewish communities outside of Israel could not know whether the High Court of Jerusalem had determined the previous month of Adar to be one of twenty-nine or of thirty days, so that they did not know which day was the first of Nissan. Not knowing when Passover began, communities in the diaspora observed an additional day.

Since we now have an established calendar, why do we continue this practice? The months are set; we have no doubt when Passover begins.

The Talmud states that because our condition in the diaspora is always one of uncertainty, the possibility exists that Jewish communities may lose contact with the established calendar. Hence, Jews have preserved the tradition of keeping an additional day. This idea is not farfetched; ninety percent of Jews today live in a different country than did their ancestors a century ago.

Why, then, is Israel different? Has history not taught us so painfully that we have no certainty of permanence, even in our own homeland? Do Jews in Israel have some guarantee?

The answer is that living with uncertainty in the Land of our roots is still far superior to the security of being firmly established in the diaspora. The observance of the additional day of the festival is a reminder that our roots and our future, as well as our past, are in the Land of Israel.

NOTES

_____
_____
_____
_____
_____
_____
_____
_____
_____
_____

Today I shall . . .

. . . remember that only *Eretz Yisrael*, the Land promised us by God, is the eternal homeland of every Jew.

בַּטֵּל רְצוֹנְךָ מִפְּנֵי רְצוֹנוֹ *From*
N egate your own will in favor of God's *the*
will (*Ethics of the Fathers* 2:4). *Sages*

April 14, 1993
April 4, 1994
April 23, 1995
April 12, 1996
April 30, 1997
April 19, 1998

If I surrender my will and turn my life over completely to the will of God, do I not thereby abrogate my power of free choice?

Certainly not. Take the example of a child who receives money for his birthday. An immature child may run off to the toy store or candy store and spend the money on everything his heart desires. He may indeed have several moments of merriment (although a stomach ache from indulging too heavily in confections is a possibility). Without doubt, however, after a short period of time those moments of enjoyment will be nothing but a memory, with the candy long since consumed and the broken toys lying on the junk heap.

A wiser child would give the money to a parent and ask that it be put into some type of savings account where it can increase in value and be available in the future for things of real importance.

Did the second child abrogate his prerogative of free choice by allowing the parent to decide how to invest the money? Of course not. In fact, this was a choice, and a wise choice as well as a free choice.

We can choose to follow our own whims or we can choose to adopt the will of an omniscient Father. We are wise when we make the second choice.

Today I shall . . .

. . . turn my will over to God, and seek to do only that which is His will for me.

NOTES

April 15, 1993
April 5, 1994
April 24, 1995
April 13, 1996
May 1, 1997
April 20, 1998

From the מַה טֹּבוּ אֹהָלֶיךָ יַעֲקֹב מִשְׁכְּנֹתֶיךָ יִשְׂרָאֵל
Scriptures How good are your tents, O Jacob,
your dwelling places, O Israel
(*Numbers* 24:5).

While visiting a community for a lecture, I awoke to a cold, drizzly, dreary day, which only added to my rather depressed spirits at that particular time.

As I entered the *shul* for the morning service, I realized that in this community, where I did not know a single soul, I was not alone. Several people greeted me with *Shalom Aleichem*. One person asked me if there was anything he could do for me and then invited me to his kosher home for breakfast. As we left the *shul,* even the cold dampness could not subdue the warmth I felt.

I now have another reason to pray with a *minyan* each day. Strangers may be traveling through town, and the *shul* is the place where they should feel their loneliness lifted and be welcomed among their people.

In our prayer, we ask God to attend to and provide for our needs. The Talmud states that God relates to people according to how they relate to others. When they are concerned with providing for others' needs, they thereby merit Divine concern for their own needs.

No wonder the Talmud stresses the greater efficacy of communal prayer. Attending *shul* enables one to be of service to others, a *mitzvah* which is rewarded with Divine response to one's prayers.

NOTES

_____
_____
_____
_____
_____
_____
_____
_____
_____

Today I shall . . .

. . . put myself in a position to be of service to people who may be in need.

וַיִּקְרָא אֶת שְׁמָם אָדָם בְּיוֹם הִבָּרְאָם *From the* *Scriptures*

He called their names Adam on the day they were created (*Genesis* 5:2).

April 16, 1993
April 6, 1994
April 25, 1995
April 14, 1996
May 2, 1997
April 21, 1998

The Biblical term for a human being, *adam*, has a dual origin. It derives from the word *adamah* (earth), indicating that man was fashioned out of dust, and also from the word *adameh* (to emulate), indicating that people are capable of emulating God.

This dual nature is not contradictory, any more than is the raw material, the clay from which sculptors form a work of art, a contradiction to the completed work. The artist's idea of her work is an abstraction, something which exists only in her imagination. The pure idea cannot be enjoyed or appreciated, and only when the artist forms the clay into the finished work can others share in the beauty of her idea.

When we observe *tzaddikim* in their daily lives, how they champion truth, have love for others, easily forgive when they are offended, and see only the good in everything, then we can begin to have a concept of God. The *tzaddik* is the being that was created in the Divine image. Although God is completely beyond comprehension, His attributes are known to us, and when we emulate the Divine attributes, such as kindness and compassion, we achieve our mission of making other people aware of Godliness. We thereby achieve the *adameh*, being like unto God. If we fail to do so, we remain nothing but the *adam*, the lifeless dust from which we originated.

People are capable of achieving the highest heights, but they can also descend to the nethermost depths of being.

NOTES

_____
_____
_____
_____
_____
_____
_____
_____
_____

Today I shall . . .

. . . try to exercise my potential for spirituality, and emulate God by behaving according to the Divine attributes.

NISSAN

ניסן

April 17, 1993
April 7, 1994
April 26, 1995
April 15, 1996
May 3, 1997
April 22, 1998

From our **M**y God, the soul You have placed within *Prayers* me is pure (*Siddur*).

אֱלֹקַי נְשָׁמָה שֶׁנָּתַתָּ בִּי טְהוֹרָה הִיא

As we all know, self-esteem is essential for optimum mental health, and a lack of self-esteem can result in any of many emotional problems. Many of us don't know, however, that self-esteem is not at all antithetical to humility.

Self-esteem comes from a sense that one is competent and worthy of the respect of others. Often a person who lacks this sense of personal worth may try to compensate for it by achieving greater competence in one or more skills, but this attempt will not work, because it does not remedy the underlying source of the problem.

The excess of competence cannot compensate for a lack of self-esteem any more than large doses of vitamin B can compensate for a lack of vitamin C. The only cure is for one to respect and value oneself.

A person should have this basic sense of worthiness by virtue of the awareness that he possesses a Divine *neshamah*, or soul, and the daily prayer, "My God, the *neshamah* You have placed within me is pure," should affirm this sense of self-worth. If one has behaved in a manner that has soiled his pure *neshamah*, one can restore its purity through repentance. A sense of self-worth is therefore always attainable through proper behavior and by correcting any improper behavior via *teshuvah* or repentance. Of course, every person should work to achieve his personal maximum — but he should do so for its own sake, and not in order to compensate for a lack of self-worth.

NOTES

Today I shall . . .

. . . try to understand that I am worthy by virtue of my *neshamah,* and though I will try to develop my skills, it will not be to compensate for a lack of self-worth.

וְיָדַעְתָּ הַיּוֹם . . . כִּי ה׳ הוּא הָאֱלֹקִים *From the*
בַּשָׁמַיִם מִמַּעַל וְעַל הָאָרֶץ מִתָּחַת אֵין עוֹד *Scriptures*

And you should know this day. . . that Hashem is God, in the heavens above and on the earth below, there is none other (*Deuteronomy* 4:39).

One Torah commentary explains this passage to mean that if one has an awareness of God, there is nothing more to know. This idea requires clarification.

April 18, 1993
April 8, 1994
April 27, 1995
April 16, 1996
May 4, 1997
April 23, 1998

The principles of faith of Judaism that were revealed at Sinai and through the prophets are absolutes, and, as axioms, are not subject to argument. In this sense, it is proper to state that "about God," there is nothing more to know.

Judaism does not require stagnation of the mind, however. Within the framework of the basic principles, Judaism has always encouraged the persistent search for truth. Throughout Jewish history, great scholars — the Ari in Kabbalah, the Baal Shem Tov in Chassidus, Rabbi Yisroel of Salant in *Mussar*, and Rabbi Chaim Soloveitchik in Talmudic analysis, to name several more-recent leaders — have electrified their contemporaries and future generations with their original insights.

Judaism is vibrant, and the Jewish mind must be productive. Just as we cannot have a valid geometry if we postulate that two parallel lines intersect, so we cannot develop valid ideas of Judaism by abrogating any of the basic principles of the faith. The search for an ever-deeper understanding of Torah, however, should never end.

NOTES

Today I shall . . .

. . . keep my mind fresh and vibrant by continuing to search for an ever-deeper understanding of Torah.

April 19, 1993
April 9, 1994
April 28, 1995
April 17, 1996
May 5, 1997
April 24, 1998

From the Scriptures

מֶלֶךְ זָקֵן וּכְסִיל

[The yetzer hara] is an old, foolish king (cf. Ecclesiastes 4:13).

The Rabbi of Rhizin was imprisoned by the Czarist government. He said that until his imprisonment he never fully understood the above description of the *yetzer hara,* the evil inclination within people. "A king, yes," he observed, "because he rules over so many people. Old, yes, because he is as old as creation. But why 'foolish'? He seems to be very sly and cunning.

"When I was in prison, however, I found that the *yetzer hara* was there with me too. Now, I had no choice about being in prison, because gendarmes took me there at gunpoint. But no one forced the *yetzer hara*, and if he came there of his own free will, he is indeed a fool."

We must be aware that the *yetzer hara* never leaves people but will follow them into the most undesirable circumstances. People may be gravely ill and in pain, hardly a desirable condition, but the *yetzer hara* will stay with them. Soldiers may be at the battlefront under mortal fire, yet there too, the *yetzer hara* will accompany them.

The *yetzer hara* has his assignment and does not take "no" for an answer. He never leaves his post, even under the most dire circumstances. In this respect, he should serve as a model for us, that we too should never defect from an assignment, regardless of adverse conditions.

NOTES

_____
_____
_____
_____
_____
_____
_____
_____

Today I shall . . .

. . . dedicate myself to doing my assignment irrespective of what circumstances may be.

הַמּוֹחַ שָׁלִיט עַל הַלֵּב *From*
The rational mind can rule over the heart *the*
(*Tanya* ch. 12). *Sages*

Erev
Rosh Chodesh
[Eve of the
New Month]
April 20, 1993
April 10, 1994
April 29, 1995
April 18, 1996
May 6, 1997
April 25, 1998

Two hundred years ago, Rabbi Schneur Zalman stated this fundamental principle: our minds can control our emotions. When people do not use their minds to their full capacity, their emotions take charge.

Anxiety is one of the most frequent symptoms that bring people to the psychotherapist's office. It is defined as a feeling of intense fear that occurs in complete absence of any actual threat. Anxious people readily admit that the fear is groundless, yet emotionally they cannot subdue it.

A method of treatment of anxiety, known as "Mental Health Through Will Training," was developed by Dr. William Low. His system strengthens people's rational capacity in order to master their runaway emotions. While some types of anxiety come from biochemical causes, and therefore require medical treatment, his method has proven itself to be an effective approach to conquering anxiety.

Too often, people resign themselves to a state of helplessness and allow themselves to be overwhelmed by stressful emotions. We ought to have greater respect for and confidence in our rational power.

NOTES

Today I shall . . .

. . . realize that my rational mind is far more powerful than I had assumed, and I will seek ways to develop it to its full capacity.

**First Day of
Rosh Chodesh
Iyar**

April 21, 1993
April 11, 1994
April 30, 1995
April 19, 1996
May 7, 1997
April 26, 1998

*From
the
Sages*

אֵין לְךָ שִׂמְחָה גְּדוֹלָה מֵהַתָּרַת סְפֵיקוֹת

There is no joy like the resolution of
doubts (*Tzel HaMaalos,* 38).

Many people's insecurity leads them to suffer from
self-doubt. They are never certain about what they should
do or whether what they have done is right. While this
degree of doubt may not be so intense that it renders them
incapable of making decisions (and therefore requiring
psychiatric care), it can cause them enough distress to
prevent them from enjoying life.

Self-doubt is one aspect of low self-esteem. Somewhere
in these people's past, they failed to develop trust in their
capacity to make good judgments.

All of us must make many decisions every day. Since we
lack prophetic foresight, we cannot predict the outcomes of
our decisions. Our control of events is limited. We should
realize that all we can do is to take the best information
available and be sincere in trying to do what we believe is
right.

NOTES

_____
_____
_____
_____
_____
_____
_____
_____

Today I shall . . .

. . . try to gain joy in life by overcoming self-doubt through
trying my very best.

בִּזְכוּת סְפִירַת הָעוֹמֶר שֶׁסָּפַרְתִּי הַיּוֹם יְתֻקַּן מַה *From*
שֶׁפָּגַמְתִּי *our*

By virtue of the mitzvah of counting the *Prayers*
omer of today, may my defects be
rectified (*Siddur*).

The theme of correcting a defect each day is specially
employed in the *mitzvah* of counting the *omer*, during the
forty-nine days that begin with the celebration of the
Exodus on Passover and end with the commemoration of
the receiving of the Torah at Sinai on Shavuos. On each of
these days, we pray that we become better, more refined
people.

Rosh Chodesh
April 22, 1993
April 12, 1994
May 1, 1995
April 20, 1996
May 8, 1997
April 27, 1998

While the emphasis of this book has been on character
development and spiritual growth via daily improvement of
personality traits, the *mitzvah* of counting the *omer* goes
one step further. The above-cited prayer continues: "May I
be purified and sanctified from Above; and through this,
may there be an abundant outpouring of Divine bounty in
all the universe."

The concept here tells us that the impact of a personal
defect is not limited to oneself or even to one's immediate
environment, but it impacts the entire universe. Just as a
watch works only when all its parts are in good shape, the
world functions optimally only according to the Divine law,
part of which is people's developing good character traits.
Any transgression can have a much greater impact than we
think.

We therefore share a sense of responsibility. People
cannot claim that their lives are their own private business,
any more than a passenger in a boat can drill a hole under
his or her own seat and tell others to mind their own
business.

A vivid proof of this concept comes from today's
exploitation of world resources and pollution of the
environment. No one can say that an oil spill is a private
matter.

NOTES

Today I shall . . .

. . . try to remember that my actions and behavior, even
when they may seem to me to be a private affair, do affect
others, and that I have an obligation to refrain from
affecting others negatively.

April 23, 1993
April 13, 1994
May 2, 1995
April 21, 1996
May 9, 1997
April 28, 1998

From the
Scriptures

טוֹב לָלֶכֶת אֶל בֵּית אֵבֶל מִלֶּכֶת אֶל בֵּית
מִשְׁתֶּה

It is better to go to the house of a mourner than to the house of feasting (*Ecclesiastes* 7:2).

Progress and achievement in life come from identifying the challenges of reality and dealing with them effectively. Anything that constitutes an escape from reality is destructive, because an escape from reality is actually an escape from life itself.

The house of feasting which Solomon criticizes is literally "a house of drinking." In his era, like modern times, the participants at some social gatherings put themselves into an alcoholic stupor, talked senselessly, and made believe that the world was free of stresses and problems. Such "feasting" constituted an escape from reality and contributed nothing to the betterment of the participants.

The house of the mourner is a solemn place, which confronts people with the reality of their own mortality. There we recognize, at least momentarily, that our stay on earth has a limit, and that so many of the things that we spend our lives to attain are left behind when we die. Our only permanent acquisitions are our spiritual achievements, such as our good deeds and our positive effects on others. The house of the mourner actually brings us to an enhanced appreciation of reality.

Is it more pleasant to go to the house of the mourner? Of course not. It is "better," however, because it can contribute to our betterment.

NOTES

Today I shall . . .

. . . try to avoid activities that provide an escape from reality and realize that growth consists only of dealing with reality.

אָנָה אֵלֵךְ מֵרוּחֶךָ וְאָנָה מִפָּנֶיךָ אֶבְרָח *From the* W**here can I go that I will be away** *Scriptures* **from Your spirit, and where can I flee from You?** (*Psalms* 139:7).

April 24, 1993
April 14, 1994
May 3, 1995
April 22, 1996
May 10, 1997
April 29, 1998

The Psalmist goes on to say that there is no escaping from God because He is present everywhere and knows everything. The Psalmist then concludes: "Search me, O God, and know that which is in my heart" (ibid. 23). Once we realize that God is omniscient, we must abandon all efforts to escape or to hide from Him, since they are futile, and instead open ourselves up to Him.

Just as this concept applies to people's relationship to God, it is equally true of people's relationship to themselves. We cannot escape from ourselves, regardless of what techniques we may employ. We cannot run away to the next neighborhood, nor the next country, nor throw ourselves into our work. We cannot use alcohol or drugs to escape. We cannot even conceal ourselves with denial, repression, and other means of psychological self-deception. Ultimately, we must confront ourselves. It is therefore only logical to cease and desist from these futile efforts and submit ourselves to a thorough journey to self-awareness. Let us say to ourselves: "Search me and know my heart."

Facing ourselves may not be easy. Doing a thorough moral inventory may force us to look at parts of ourselves that we might prefer to disown. However, adjusting to reality requires a thorough self-knowledge. We can only adjust effectively to reality if we have not distorted it.

NOTES

_____

_____

_____

_____

_____

_____

Today I shall . . .

_____

. . . try to realize that optimum living can only be with a valid self-awareness.

April 25, 1993
April 15, 1994
May 4, 1995
April 23, 1996
May 11, 1997
April 30, 1998

From the Sages

אַף צְבָת בִּצְבַת עֲשׂוּיָה

ongs could only be made by tongs (*Ethics of the Fathers* 5:8).

The Talmud states that God gave man the first pair of tongs, because it is impossible to forge a pair of tongs without already having another pair to hold the metal in the fire.

A wise man said that the way to really make an apple pie from scratch is to first invent the universe.

These ideas should be sobering thoughts for people who consider themselves self-sufficient. Self-sufficiency is obviously a myth; we all must rely on others, in varying degrees.

Many people find it hard to accept their dependency. They see it as demeaning and a sign of weakness. They may take radical measures to prove to themselves and to others that they can stand on their own two feet. This rejection of healthy dependency can give rise to many problems.

Certainly, being lazy and expecting others to do everything for us is wrong, but going to the opposite extreme and denying our need of both emotional and physical support is equally wrong. We should be able to accept our dependence upon others, and their dependence upon us, as a part of life.

NOTES

Today I shall . . .

. . . try to realize that absolute self-sufficiency is an impossibility. Rather, I will be able to accept appropriate help without considering it demeaning.

From the Scriptures

הַחַיִּים וְהַמָּוֶת נָתַתִּי לְפָנֶיךָ הַבְּרָכָה וְהַקְּלָלָה וּבָחַרְתָּ בַּחַיִּים

I have placed before you life and death, blessing and curse, and you should choose life (*Deuteronomy* 30:19).

April 26, 1993
April 16, 1994
May 5, 1995
April 24, 1996
May 12, 1997
May 1, 1998

Some people who commit improper acts defend themselves by insisting that the temptation was too intense to resist. They are wrong.

A law of human behavior states that when given two options, people can choose only that which they perceive as being the lesser distress. However, individual choice decides which distress is greater and which is lesser. For example, when a hungry baby cries in the middle of the night, the parents will get up. They naturally choose to forego the greater distress — staying in bed and listening to their baby — for the lesser — getting up and feeding the baby. Extreme cases come from martyrs who choose death rather than violate principles which are sacred to them. Here, death hurts less than compromised life.

People can evaluate for themselves what is good and what is evil. Everyone is responsible for his or her own evaluations, and so submitting to the temptation to do a forbidden or improper act indicates failure to evaluate properly.

NOTES

_____
_____
_____
_____
_____
_____
_____
_____

Today I shall . . .

. . . program myself with correct evaluations of what is right and wrong so that I may make the correct choices.

April 27, 1993
April 17, 1994
May 6, 1995
April 25, 1996
May 13, 1997
May 2, 1998

From the Sages

לַמֵּד לְשׁוֹנְךָ לוֹמַר אֵינִי יוֹדֵעַ

Accustom your tongue to say "I do not know" (*Berachos* 4a).

While no human being can know everything, some people cannot admit any ignorance about anything. For them, any admission of lack of knowledge threatens their fragile egos. Although they try to impress others with their omniscience, they accomplish the reverse, because the more they try to conceal their ignorance, the more prominent it becomes.

Furthermore, the only way we can acquire knowledge is by accepting that we do not have it. People who claim to know everything cannot learn. Therefore, many opportunities to learn pass them by, and their denying their ignorance actually increases their ignorance.

We do not have to know everything, and no one expects us to. Today, more than ever, with the unprecedented amount of information available, no one can be a universal genius. The simple statement, "I don't know," is actually highly respected.

We should also open ourselves to acquiring knowledge from every source. Learning from someone whom we consider to be inferior to ourselves should not be demeaning. As the Psalmist says, "I became wise by learning from all my teachers" (*Psalms* 119:99). A willingness to learn from everyone is a sign of greatness, while affecting omniscience actually betrays ignorance.

NOTES

Today I shall . . .

. . . admit that there are many things that I do not know. Instead, I will become willing to learn from anyone and everyone.

וְלֹא יֵרַע לְבָבְךָ בְּתִתְּךָ לוֹ *From the*

Do not feel badly in your heart when *Scriptures* you give to him [the poor] (*Deuteronomy* 15:10).

April 28, 1993
April 18, 1994
May 7, 1995
April 26, 1996
May 14, 1997
May 3, 1998

When people come to collect charity, we may sometimes feel annoyed with them, especially if they come frequently. The Torah here is cautioning us not to bear any resentment when we give to them.

A recovered alcoholic, sober for many years, gave much of his time to help newcomers to sobriety. He therefore made himself available to them twenty-four hours a day, so that whenever they called, he could help them resist the urge to drink. Someone once asked him, "Doesn't it irritate you to be repeatedly awakened during the night?" "Of course not!" he answered. "I just have to remember that *I'm* not the one who is doing the calling."

This man knew that many years earlier, he himself had needed to call for help. Now that he was in a position to *give* help instead of receiving it, his deep gratitude precluded any irritation at being bothered at strange hours.

If we ever feel put upon by people who ask for charity, one need only realize that since we are in a position to give instead of needing to receive, we should be so overwhelmed with gratitude that there should be no room for annoyance. As we give charity, we might also give our blessings and good wishes to the recipients, that God should help them soon be in a position to give to others.

NOTES

Today I shall . . .

. . . give *tzedakah* with an open hand and willing heart, and be grateful that I am in a position to give instead of needing to receive.

IYAR

8

אייר

Apri 29, 1993
April 19, 1994
May 8, 1995
April 27, 1996
May 15, 1997
May 4, 1998

From the Scriptures

הַצּוּר תָּמִים פָּעֳלוֹ כִּי כָל דְּרָכָיו מִשְׁפָּט קֵל אֱמוּנָה וְאֵין עָוֶל

The Mighty Rock, Whose deeds are perfect, because all His ways are good. He is a faithful God in Whom there is no iniquity (*Deuteronomy* 32:4-5).

These very sobering words are often invoked at moments of great personal distress to express our faith and trust in the Divine wisdom and justice.

People who have suffered deep personal losses, such as destruction of their home by fire or the premature death of a loved one, or who have observed the widespread suffering caused by a typhoon or an earthquake, may be shaken in their relationship with God. How could a loving, caring God mete out such enormous suffering?

It is futile to search for logical explanations, and even if there were any, they would accomplish little in relieving the suffering of the victims. This is the time when the true nature of faith emerges, a faith that is beyond logic, that is not subject to understanding.

The *kaddish* recited by mourners makes no reference to any memorial concept or prayer for the departed. The words of *kaddish*, "May the name of the Almighty be exalted and sanctified," are simply a statement of reaffirmation, that in spite of the severe distress one has experienced, one does not deny the sovereignty and absolute justice of God.

Our language may be too poor in words and our thoughts lacking in concepts that can provide comfort when severe distress occurs, but the Jew accepts Divine justice even in the face of enormous pain.

NOTES

Today I shall . . .

. . . reaffirm my trust and faith in the sovereignty and justice of God, even when I see inexplicable suffering.

218 / GROWING EACH DAY

וַיַּחֲלֹם עוֹד חֲלוֹם אַחֵר . . . וְהִנֵּה הַשֶּׁמֶשׁ *From the*
וְהַיָּרֵחַ וְאַחַד עָשָׂר כּוֹכָבִים מִשְׁתַּחֲוִים לִי *Scriptures*
[Joseph] dreamt another dream . . .
the sun, moon, and the eleven stars
were bowing before me (*Genesis* 37:9).

IYAR

9

אייר

April 30, 1993
April 20, 1994
May 9, 1995
April 28, 1996
May 16, 1997
May 5, 1998

Joseph dreamt of greatness, and he achieved it. Still, he paid a steep price for that greatness, suffering years of enslavement and imprisonment.

Some people are satisfied with their status quo and choose not to rock the boat. Others are dreamers, people of great ambition.

Dreams and fantasy are very different. Fantasy is mere wishful thinking, something we know is beyond reach, but a dream is something that may be in the remote future, yet is conceivably achievable.

Suppose Joseph had known that, in order to obtain the promise of the dream, he would have to endure years of suffering. Would he have foregone the greatness, or would he have accepted the pain? Since Joseph understood the dream to be a revelation of the Divine plan for him, he undoubtedly would have chosen to accept the suffering it entailed.

We may be frequently confronted with a decision whether to resign ourselves to the status quo or to try to advance ourselves at considerable cost. We should avail ourselves of expert counseling and pray for Divine guidance to know what the Divine plan for us is. If we feel secure in the knowledge that God wants us to advance to our optimum potential, we should not retreat because of the personal cost entailed.

Infants are fortunate; they do not have to choose whether to remain toothless or to accept the distress of teething. While we do have such choices, we also have the wisdom to make the right choice.

NOTES

Today I shall . . .

. . . pray for enlightenment as to what is God's will for me and for the fortitude and courage to achieve it.

May 1, 1993
April 21, 1994
May 10, 1995
April 29, 1996
May 17, 1997
May 6, 1998

From the **W**rongdoers are referred to as having died even while they live (*Berachos* 18b).

רְשָׁעִים שֶׁבְּחַיֵּיהֶן קְרוּיִין מֵתִים

From the Sages

Animals grow and develop until they reach physical maturity. Thereafter, animals do only those actions necessary to survive, but they do not grow significantly in any way.

Human beings are distinctly different. While they do stop growing at physical maturity, their minds have a limitless capacity to grow intellectually and spiritually. This difference leads to another. Animals survive by adapting themselves to the world, but human beings can change the world according to their desires.

We can thus subdivide human life into an animal-physical phase, where growth ends with physical maturity, and a human-intellectual/spiritual phase, which should continue as long as we live. If people neglect intellectual-spiritual growth and indulge only in physical needs and desires, their human phase of life has stopped growing and therefore has essentially died, and only the animal phase continues to live.

The Talmud's reference to wrongdoers is to those people who neglect their intellectual-spiritual growth and seek only to maintain their physical lives. They have therefore allowed their unique human aspect to die.

No self-respecting, rational people would ever degrade themselves to a subhuman existence. While we pray to God to grant us life, it is our task to make that life truly human.

NOTES

Today I shall . . .

. . . try to realize that abandoning myself completely to actions that merely maintain my physical self is degrading, and I therefore shall take pride in being fully human.

אִם לֹא תַאֲמִינוּ כִּי לֹא תֵאָמֵנוּ *From the*
If you do not believe, it is because you *Scriptures*
are not trustworthy (Isaiah 7:9).

May 2, 1993
April 22, 1994
May 11, 1995
April 30, 1996
May 18, 1997
May 7, 1998

In these few pungent words, the Prophet explains why people may have difficulty in believing in God: they are not themselves trustworthy. In other words, if I am reliable, and I know that people can trust that I will keep my word as best I can to perform and deliver, then I will have little difficulty in having trust in God and in His ability to perform and deliver. Lack of trust in God is thus a reflection of one's own lack of trustworthiness.

Projection, a psychological defense mechanism, consists of attributing to others those attitudes and motives that we ourselves harbor. The Talmud summarizes this concept in the dictum that those who find defects in others must themselves be defective in the same way. Isaiah is simply applying this principle to trust and faith.

Some people struggle with faith and therefore consult various philosophic works on the subject. The authoritative works — such as *Duties of the Heart* by Rabbeinu Bachaye, the *Kuzari*, and others — certainly deserve study, but while they define very well various aspects of faith, they cannot be expected to have much impact on someone who lacks the basic capacity to trust, because of his or her own lack of trustworthiness. One can fine-tune a radio, but the dial will not do much without an electric current.

NOTES

Today I shall . . .

. . . try to develop my integrity so that I should be fully trustworthy.

May 3, 1993
April 23, 1994
May 12, 1995
May 1, 1996
May 19, 1997
May 8, 1998

From the
Scriptures

פּוֹתֵחַ אֶת יָדֶיךָ וּמַשְׂבִּיעַ לְכָל חַי רָצוֹן

You open Your hand and satisfy all living things with will *(Psalms* 145:16).

This verse is usually understood to mean that God provides for all living things, satisfying their wills and desires. Another interpretation is that God provides all living things *with will;* i.e. with desire, so that all living things should have desire.

When we say the Grace After Meals, we thank God for the food He provides for us; we do not give thanks for being hungry. However, if we talk with people who suffer with any of the diseases which cause loss of appetite, we will discover that we must be grateful for the sensation of hunger as well as for the means provided for us to satisfy that hunger.

This concept applies to wants of all sorts. An ancient Chinese curse goes, "May all of your wishes come true." Why is this a curse? Pause a moment and reflect. What would we do if *all* of our desires were fulfilled? Since sensation of needs cause actions, without any sensation we would have no motivation to act. Satisfaction of all our needs would essentially mean an end to life itself.

As a physician, I frequently encounter people who are very depressed and who have no appetite at all. Other patients have diseases that affect their digestive systems, so that they cannot even tolerate the sight of food (let alone crave it). We must remember, then, that when we feel the pangs of hunger and thirst, we should appreciate them.

NOTES

Today I shall . . .

. . . try to be aware that feeling hunger or having other needs is a Divine blessing for which I should be grateful.

אִם בְּחֻקֹּתַי תֵּלְכוּ . . . וְנָתַתִּי גִשְׁמֵיכֶם בְּעִתָּם *From the Scriptures*

If you will go in the way of My ordinances . . . I will give your rain in the proper time (*Leviticus* 26:3-4).

May 4, 1993
April 24, 1994
May 13, 1995
May 2, 1996
May 20, 1997
May 9, 1998

Rashi explains that "going in the way of My ordinances" means that one will "toil in the Torah." This toil and labor itself causes the abundant blessings that follow.

Our culture highly values achievement, and it confers various kinds of reward for academic and scientific excellence. But the world is interested in results, not in the effort expended. If one person of limited capacity were to labor continuously at a given project without achieving success, while another person who is extremely gifted achieves success in the project with a minimum expenditure of effort, the latter will reap the reward. This is not the Jewish attitude. The Talmud states, "Reward is commensurate with effort." In the study of Torah, in the performance of *mitzvos*, and in the development of character, God measures virtue not by how much we accomplish, but by how hard we try.

The Talmud further states that not only are people rewarded for extreme effort; they are also blessed with those very goals for which they have worked. They receive not only the many material blessings listed in the chapter cited above, but also the spiritual goals for which they strove, and which might not have been attainable through human effort alone.

NOTES

_____
_____
_____
_____
_____
_____
_____

Today I shall . . .

. . . try to advance myself spiritually, and realize that God wants me to try — the reward will come from God.

May 5, 1993
April 25, 1994
May 14, 1995
May 3, 1996
May 21, 1997
May 10, 1998

From the Sages

כָּל הַתְחָלוֹת קָשׁוֹת

All beginnings are difficult (*Rashi, Exodus* 19:5).

We are creatures of habit. Learning something new may take effort, but once we make something a part of our routine, it becomes not only effortless, but automatic. For example, when we learned to walk, it required conscious effort, as we can see when we observe children taking their first steps. Later on in life, walking takes no thought at all. The same holds true for many other behaviors. Whenever we begin something new, we are, by definition, initiating some new type of behavior. The body naturally tends to return to the old, effortless pattern. If the new behavior holds promises of significant gain (such as a new job, new business, or new learning), which we anticipate will be profitable, this anticipation of reward overcomes the resistance to change, and we make the adjustment to the new. When we see no tangible gain, such as in spiritual advancement, the ease of routine is likely to draw us back to well-established habits.

Let's face it. If we were offered a significant promotion at work which would necessitate arising half an hour earlier than usual, we would certainly set the alarm clock and get up promptly. If, however, we resolve to devote that half-hour to bettering ourselves, we would have trouble getting up.

We must value our spiritual goals so much that we will be willing to make the changes in our routine that are necessary to achieve them.

NOTES

_____
_____
_____
_____
_____
_____
_____
_____
_____

Today I shall . . .

. . . try to overcome any resistance to spiritual growth that requires changing well-established routines.

כָּל הַמֵּשִׂים שָׁלוֹם בְּתוֹךְ בֵּיתוֹ כְּאִילוּ מֵשִׂים *From*
שָׁלוֹם בְּיִשְׂרָאֵל *the*

If one brings peace to one's own - *Sages*
household, it is as though one brought
peace to all of Israel (*Avos De R' Nosson*
28:3).

IYAR

אייר

May 6, 1993
April 26, 1994
May 15, 1995
May 4, 1996
May 22, 1997
May 11, 1998

A scourge has plagued our people throughout its entire history — internal strife. A unified Jewish people has such strength that the Talmud states that when there is brotherhood among all Jews, God overlooks even their worst transgressions.

How can such peace be achieved? The Talmud suggests a simple approach: start with the family.

Domestic peace is achieved only when husbands, wives, parents, and children learn to respect each other's wishes, to yield personal preferences, to listen to others' points of view, and to resolve differences amicably. Children who grow up in a family where there is no strife or envy and where everyone makes an effort to accommodate and maintain peace will incorporate these attitudes as part of their character. They will then practice them when relating to people outside the family.

Expecting people to behave in ways to which they have not been accustomed previously is unrealistic. Children who were raised in homes where there was frequent bickering, with no yielding and no compromise among the parents, and where sibling rivalry was not appropriately resolved are unlikely to build a harmonious and peaceful society.

NOTES

_____
_____
_____
_____

Today I shall . . .

_____
_____

. . . beginning with myself, try to establish peace within my home by avoiding harsh speech and actions, being tolerant of others' opinions, and being willing to compromise.

_____

GROWING EACH DAY / **225**

May 7, 1993
April 27, 1994
May 16, 1995
May 5, 1996
May 23, 1997
May 12, 1998

From the Scriptures

חֵץ שָׁחוּט לְשׁוֹנָם

Their tongue is like a sharp arrow (*Jeremiah* 9:7).

Some people would never physically injure another person. The sight or even the thought of violence makes them cringe. They may not realize that their words can cause more damage than their fists ever could. A physical injury eventually heals and may even be forgotten, but an insulting word can penetrate to the depths of someone's being and continue to reverberate, long after a mere physical wound would have healed.

I have seen this phenomenon in my own practice. Many children are spanked by their parents. Still, with the exception of cases of severe abuse, my patients rarely, if ever, mention the spanking as a trauma. Not so with degrading words. After thirty or more years, patients will remember having been called "stupid," "rotten," or "a no-good bum." A child who was not spanked, but was instead disciplined with shame and made to feel that he or she was a disgrace, is likely to retain that feeling for decades and may harbor an attitude of shame that affects everything that he or she does.

While we are taught to refrain from striking out in anger, we are far less restrained when it comes to verbal lashings. Whether we direct them towards spouses, children, or peers, we should be aware of the impact that words can have. The verse cited above correctly describes the tongue as a sharp, penetrating arrow, which can be every bit as lethal as any physical weapon.

Some people have a wise custom. When they become angry, they clamp their lips tightly. The anger will safely dissipate and the words which could have stung for years never come out.

NOTES

Today I shall . . .

. . . try to avoid words that may be injurious to another person.

אֵין אָדָם חוֹטֵא אֶלָּא אִם כֵּן נִכְנַס בּוֹ רוּחַ שְׁטוּת *From* A person does not sin unless he is seized *the* by a spirit of folly (*Sotah* 3a). *Sages*

IYAR

17

אייר

May 8, 1993
April 28, 1994
May 17, 1995
May 6, 1996
May 24, 1997
May 13, 1998

Some people try to defend a misdeed by claiming "temporary insanity." The Talmud is telling us that while all wrongdoing does result from temporary insanity, people are still held accountable for their behavior.

No sane person would do things that are self-destructive. Small children who do not know any better may eat things that are harmful, but when adults submit to temptation and eat things that are harmful, they have essentially taken leave of their adult senses. This form of temporary insanity accompanies every wrong act.

Civil law does not accept ignorance as a defense, and although Jewish law does consider ignorance a mitigating factor, it holds a person responsible for being derelict in not having obtained the requisite knowledge and information necessary to act properly.

Jewish law holds that while true psychosis may be an exonerating factor, a non-psychotic person is capable of overcoming the "temporary insanity" that leads to wrong-doing. The Talmud states that in evaluating any act, we should calculate the gain from the act versus the loss it entails. A reasonable person will conclude that a brief pleasure of indulgence is certainly not worth the price, whether it is in terms of negative physical effects or of spiritual deterioration. People are certainly accountable for failure to exercise their reason and come to correct conclusions.

NOTES

Today I shall . . .

. . . exercise my rational powers to avoid making foolish decisions, especially when subjected to temptation.

May 9, 1993
April 29, 1994
May 18, 1995
May 7, 1996
May 25, 1997
May 14, 1998

*From the
Scriptures*

אֱלֹהֵי כֶסֶף וֵאלֹהֵי זָהָב לֹא תַעֲשׂוּ לָכֶם

Do not make for yourselves gods of gold and silver (*Exodus* 20:20).

While the plain meaning of this verse is an injunction against making idols, it has also been interpreted to mean, "Do not worship gold and silver."

Rabbi Schneur Zalman once approached a wealthy man, a known miser, for a donation to redeem someone from captivity. He was given one penny. Instead of throwing the penny in the miser's face, as others had done, Rabbi Schneur Zalman thanked the man politely and turned to leave. The man called him back, apologized, and gave him a slightly larger sum. Again, the rabbi blessed him, thanked him, and turned to leave, only to be called back. This scene repeated itself numerous times with progressively intense apologies and larger donations, until the man donated the entire sum needed.

Rabbi Schneur Zalman explained that when people had previously refused the one-cent donation, the miser, who had come to worship money as his god, took it as a personal insult and reacted as though his god had been disgraced. By thanking him for the penny, the rabbi set in motion an approach which allowed the miser to shed his defenses and respond with compassion.

This concept is important both in our relating to others as well as in developing attitudes of our own. Because money is so vital in our lives, we must remember that we, as well as other people, are at risk of deifying it. We must be both cautious to prevent ourselves from falling into this trap and also understand that others may have fallen into it.

NOTES

Today I shall . . .

. . . be on the alert to avoid money from becoming unduly important in my life and think about how to relate to others who may have developed this mistaken attitude.

אֵין שָׁלִיחַ לִדְבַר עֲבֵירָה . . . דִּבְרֵי הָרַב וְדִבְרֵי *From*
תַּלְמִיד דִּבְרֵי מִי שׁוֹמְעִים *the*

Sages

There is no such thing as an agent for committing a wrong act . . . if a master's instructions conflict with the student's, whom would you obey? (*Kiddushin* 42b).

With this principle, the Talmud places responsibility for any wrongdoing squarely on the person who carries out the action. "I was told to do it" is not a defense.

The same principle applies to projecting blame on anyone else in any way. Alcoholics frequently employ this device. "We drink because we've been harassed by our wives / jobs / employers / the police," they often say. We understand their motive; placing the blame on others not only exonerates them, it also gives them a way out of facing reality and changing themselves. Instead, they blame others. "If those responsible for our distress will change, the problems will be solved, and we will have no need to drink" is a frequently used line.

This phenomenon is not limited to alcoholics. People in general prefer to continue their accustomed behavior. If they hurt anyone, including themselves, they often try to both justify their behavior and avoid the need to make any changes which seem inconvenient by blaming others.

Regardless of what circumstances may be, we are fully accountable for our own behavior.

May 10, 1993
April 30, 1994
May 19, 1995
May 8, 1996
May 26, 1997
May 15, 1998

NOTES

Today I shall . . .

. . . avoid finding scapegoats and placing blame on others. Instead, I will do my utmost to make the necessary changes in myself.

May 11, 1993
May 1, 1994
May 20, 1995
May 9, 1996
May 27, 1997
May 16, 1998

From the Scriptures

וְאָהַבְתָּ לְרֵעֲךָ כָּמוֹךָ

You shall love your neighbor as you do yourself (*Leviticus* 19:18).

The usual translation is printed above and indeed is the way the verse is generally interpreted. As a result, the question is often raised, "How can people have the same love for others as they have for themselves? Isn't this demand unrealistic?"

If, however, we look more carefully at the original Hebrew, the question disappears. The Torah is stating here a definition of "love": *ve'ahavta*, the sensation or the experience of love, is *lerei'acha kamocha*, when you wish for another that which you wish for yourself.

What some people consider love may be nothing more than a self-serving relationship. They may "love" something because it satisfies their needs, but when the object cannot satisfy the need, or the need itself disappears, the love evaporates.

True love is not self-serving, but self-giving. We love only when we have as intense a desire to please the other person as to be pleased ourselves. Such an attitude calls for sacrifice, because it may be that we will have to deprive ourselves in order to provide what will please the other person.

As children, we are selfish. As we mature, we should develop a spiritual love, which is quite different from our childish physical love. This spiritual, other-directed love can withstand all challenges. As the *Song of Songs* says, *Even abundant waters cannot extinguish love* (8:7).

NOTES

Today I shall . . .

. . . try to avoid the self-centered love of my childhood and replace it with a true love for the person I claim to love, even when it demands great personal sacrifice.

יְהִי רָצוֹן מִלְּפָנֶיךָ . . . שֶׁתּוֹלִיכֵנוּ לְשָׁלוֹם . . . *From*
וְתַגִּיעֵנוּ לִמְחוֹז חֶפְצֵנוּ לְחַיִּים וּלְשִׂמְחָה וּלְשָׁלוֹם *our*

May it be Your will . . . that You lead us *Prayers*
toward peace . . . and enable us to
reach our desired destination for life,
gladness, and peace (*Prayer of the Traveler*).

May 12, 1993
May 2, 1994
May 21, 1995
May 10, 1996
May 28, 1997
May 17, 1998

Before we take a long trip in a car, we first consult a map to determine the best route. If we know people who have already made that particular trip, we ask them whether there are certain spots to avoid, where the best stopovers are, etc. Only a fool would start out without any plan, and stop at each hamlet to figure out the best way to get to the next hamlet.

It is strange that we do not apply this same logic in our journey through life. Once we reach the age of reason, we should think of a goal in life, and then plan how to get there. Since many people have already made the trip, they can tell us in advance which path is the smoothest, what the obstacles are, and where we can find help if we get into trouble.

Few things are as distressful as finding oneself lost on the road with no signposts and no one to ask directions. Still, many people live their lives as though they are lost in the thicket. Yet, they are not even aware that they are lost. They travel from hamlet to hamlet and often find that after seventy years of travel, they have essentially reached nowhere.

The Prayer of the Traveler applies to our daily lives as well as to a trip.

NOTES

Today I shall . . .

. . . see what kind of goals I have set for myself and how I plan to reach these goals.

May 13, 1993
May 3, 1994
May 22, 1995
May 11, 1996
May 29, 1997
May 18, 1998

From our Prayers

בָּרוּךְ אַתָּה ה' אֱלֹקֵינוּ מֶלֶךְ הָעוֹלָם אֲשֶׁר קִדְּשָׁנוּ בְּמִצְוֹתָיו וְצִוָּנוּ . . .

Blessed are You, our God, King of the Universe, Who has sanctified us with His commandments and has commanded us . . . (*Siddur*).

The above *berachah* (blessing) was intentionally left unfinished because it represents a blessing that does not exist: the *berachah* for the *mitzvah* of *tzedakah* (charity). Why does this *mitzvah*, which ranks so high among the *mitzvos*, not merit a *berachah*?

One reason is that a *berachah* is supposed to be said with meditation and concentration on its words, reflecting on the infinity of God and His sovereignty, and the significance of our having been chosen to observe the *mitzvos*. Unfortunately, it is easy to mumble a *berachah* without giving it the thought that it deserves.

Tzedakah must be performed promptly, without any delay whatsoever. If someone needy requests help from us, we have no time for meditation. The needy person needs help without delay and should not be made to wait while we prepare ourselves to perform the *mitzvah*, and certainly should not be sent away to return at a later time.

But why did the Sages not formulate a *berachah* for this wonderful *mitzvah* and simply specify that it should be said quickly and without meditation? That kind of a *berachah* is hardly worth saying.

The absence of a *berachah* for *tzedakah* thus teaches us two things: (1) *tzedakah* should be given promptly, and (2) *berachos* require adequate time for meditation and concentration.

NOTES

Today I shall . . .

. . . react promptly when asked for *tzedakah*, and give much thought when reciting a *berachah*.

כָּל מִי שֶׁנַּעֲשָׂה רַחֲמָן בִּמְקוֹם אַכְזָרִי סוֹף *From*
שֶׁנַּעֲשָׂה אַכְזָרִי בִּמְקוֹם רַחֲמָן *the*

O ne who acts with compassion when *Sages*
firmness is called for will eventually act
with cruelty when compassion is needed
(*Koheles Rabbah* 7:33).

May 14, 1993
May 4, 1994
May 23, 1995
May 12, 1996
May 30, 1997
May 19, 1998

While mercy and compassion are highly valued character traits, sometimes they are inappropriate; instead, harsh discipline must be applied.

A young alcoholic woman who had been in several automobile wrecks related that one winter night, she totally ruined her father's new car because she was driving under the influence. She pleaded with the police officer to report this episode as a skidding accident, because she feared her father's wrath. The officer complied with her request.

This young woman subsequently was in another accident due to drunk driving. This time she sustained facial injuries; in spite of excellent cosmetic surgery, her former features were never fully restored. "That police officer thought he was being kind to me," she later said. "Had I been arrested for drunk driving, I might have been forced into treatment for my alcoholism, and maybe I never would have sustained the facial injuries."

True kindness which comes from our minds guiding our emotions will bring more kindness in its wake. Misguided kindness, brought on by our uncontrolled emotions, generally causes pain.

How can we avoid misguided kindness? One way is to ask others who are not influenced by our emotions for their opinion.

NOTES

Today I shall . . .

. . . try to be aware that even my highly commendable character traits, such as kindness, may be misapplied. I should look for guidance to avoid such mistakes.

May 15, 1993
May 5, 1994
May 24, 1995
May 13, 1996
May 31, 1997
May 20, 1998

From the Sages

כָּל הַמַּחֲנִיף לַחֲבֵרוֹ לְשֵׁם כָּבוֹד לְסוֹפוֹ נִפְטַר בְּקָלוֹן

One who flatters another person in order to win favor will ultimately suffer disgrace (*Avos De R' Nosson* 29:4).

The insatiable need to receive praise from others can be one of the most powerful, albeit destructive, motivating forces in human behavior. People who have the need for praise generally suffer from such low self-esteem that they need constant assurance that they are really worthy. Since this low self-esteem has no place in reality, measures such as praise or other affirmation can never counteract it. The pit of low self-esteem is bottomless; nothing ever fills it.

Desperately trying to receive external affirmation, people flatter and fawn to please others, so that they may react positively toward them. While giving false compliments may appear innocent, the attempts to win favor may snare this flatterer in relationships and obligations that are likely to backfire, so that they suffer embarrassment, not the expected admiration.

A healthy self-awareness would obviate the need for such tactics, and a devotion to honesty would prevent indulging in the falsehoods that initially bring about the desired response, but eventually result in further loss of both one's self-respect and the respect of others.

NOTES

Today I shall . . .

. . . avoid fawning and flattering. Instead, I will try to achieve a self-esteem which will render these unnecessary.

וְאַבְרָהָם וְשָׂרָה זְקֵנִים בָּאִים בַּיָּמִים *From the*
braham and Sarah were old, they *Scriptures*
came into days (*Genesis* 18:11).

IYAR
25
אייר

May 16, 1993
May 6, 1994
May 25, 1995
May 14, 1996
June 1, 1997
May 21, 1998

"Coming into days" means making each day count.

Sometimes we feel "down" at the end of a day without really knowing why. Some people try to obliterate that feeling by drinking; others glue themselves to the television screen so that the inane dialogues can drown out their thoughts; and yet others find different escape routes. A few make a simple reckoning that could be constructive.

Was the day spent doing something important? If so, there is no reason to be dejected. If the day was utilized in a positive way, we should feel good about it. On the other hand, if the day was spent doing unimportant things, and we are annoyed with ourselves for exchanging a day of life for nothing of value, then we should think about what we must do to keep tomorrow from being a repetition of today. What changes must we make so that tomorrow should be a day of substance?

The latter question should lead to specific answers that themselves lead to planning a more meaningful tomorrow. Having planned a constructive day, we can feel a measure of accomplishment. Even if anything should happen tomorrow to thwart our well-laid plans, we can then plan again how to avoid such pitfalls on the following day. Each day can thus turn out to be a profitable day either in its own right, or a lesson in which changes we must make to make the next day better.

Coping leads to progress. Escaping not only leaves problems unresolved, but it also adds to the previous problems by bringing about a negative attitude.

NOTES

_____
_____
_____
_____
_____
_____
_____
_____
_____

Today I shall . . .

. . . try to make each day positively productive and analyze each unproductive day to enable me to make the next day better.

May 17, 1993
May 7, 1994
May 26, 1995
May 15, 1996
June 2, 1997
May 22, 1998

לְעוֹלָם יְהֵא אָדָם רַדְ כְּקָנֶה וְאַל יְהֵא קָשֶׁה כְּאֶרֶז

A person should always be flexible like a reed, and not rigid like a cedar (*Taanis* 20a).

Some people forget that they have the right to be wrong. They may see being wrong as showing weakness. They grossly misunderstand the true concept of strength.

In the physical world, many substances that are very rigid are also fragile. Glass, for instance, is hard but shatters into many splinters, and metals which lack resilience are apt to break under pressure.

Rigidity in people frequently shows ignorance. If people do something without understanding why they are doing it, they are likely to become very defensive when challenged. The reason is obvious: if they do not understand the reason for their actions, they of course do not know if they have any room for compromise. Since they can respond only in an all-or-nothing manner, they perceive any questioning of their principles or practices as a threat or even as a hostile attack. They therefore react defensively.

Willingness to listen to advice, to consider it, and to alter our opinion when the advice appears to be the correct thing to do are signs of strength, not of weakness. Honor means being honest, not being right all the time. As the Talmud says, "You should not say, 'You must accept my opinion,' because the others may be right and not you" (*Ethics of the Fathers* 4:10).

NOTES

Today I shall . . .

. . . try to be flexible, to listen to other opinions, and not be obstinate in insisting that I am always right.

עֲקַבְיָא בֶּן מַהֲלַלְאֵל הֵעִיד אַרְבָּעָה דְבָרִים. *From*
אָמְרוּ לוֹ: עֲקַבְיָא, חֲזֹר בָּךְ ... וְנַעַשְׂךָ אַב *the*
בֵּית דִּין לְיִשְׂרָאֵל. אָמַר לָהֶן מוּטָב לִי לְהִקָּרֵא *Sages*
שׁוֹטֶה כָּל יָמַי וְלֹא לֵיעָשׂוֹת שָׁעָה אַחַת רָשָׁע
לִפְנֵי הַמָּקוֹם

May 18, 1993
May 8, 1994
May 27, 1995
May 16, 1996
June 3, 1997
May 23, 1998

Akavia testified on four laws [that he heard from his teachers]. [The Rabbis] said to him, "Akavia, change your rulings, and we will appoint you Chief Judge of the highest court in Israel." He responded, "It is better that I be considered a fool all my life rather than an unjust person for even one moment before God" (*Eidiyos* 5:6).

Yesterday, we discussed the virtue of flexibility and the fault of obstinacy. In the above quote from the Talmud, Akavia is praised for his refusal to yield. Can these two attributes be reconciled?

The distinction should be obvious. If Akavia had been championing his own opinion, he would gladly have considered cogent arguments by his colleagues and even deferred to them. However, the Talmud states that Akavia *testified*; i.e. he conveyed the rulings that he had heard from his teachers and that therefore carried their authority. However convincing the arguments of his colleagues may have been, he held that he could not override the rulings of his teachers.

Public opinion was obviously in favor of Akavia conceding to his colleagues and thereby being elevated to the highest court in the land, which was certainly an attractive position. Certainly, no one would have criticized Akavia had he changed his position. Still, Akavia stood firm and was willing to forego the coveted position of honor rather than compromise on his principles.

While flexibility in one's own opinion is commendable, firmness in adhering to principles is essential.

NOTES

Today I shall . . .

. . . be unyielding when my basic principles are put to the test.

May 19, 1993
May 9, 1994
May 28, 1995
May 17, 1996
June 4, 1997
May 24, 1998

From the Scriptures

אֲשֶׁר יַרְשִׁיעֻן אֱלֹהִים יְשַׁלֵּם שְׁנַיִם לְרֵעֵהוּ

If the court finds [the thief] guilty, he shall pay twofold (*Exodus* 22:8).

The Talmud explains that an armed robber can make restitution simply by returning the stolen item. A thief, who steals in stealth, must return the object and pay a heavy fine.

Why is the thief punished more severely? By operating in stealth, he indicated that he feared being observed by humans, but was not concerned that God saw his deeds. In other words, he essentially denied the providence of God. While the robber's act was just as dishonest, he at least equated people with God, in that he operated in full view of both. Hence, although his attitude was one of defiance of God, it was not necessarily one of denial.

Sometimes we do things that are not ethically sound, and in order to avoid social sanction and to maintain a reputation of decency, we may act in such a manner that it appears to be ethically proper. While we may indeed succeed in this deception, we must remember that there is One Who cannot be deceived, and Who knows the truth of our behavior. We should realize that acting in such a manner is essentially a denial as well as a defiance of God.

It is evident now why the thief pays double. The robber pays only for defiance of God, whereas the thief must pay for defiance *and* denial.

People who think they are willing to sacrifice their very lives rather than deny God should reflect on whether they might not actually deny God for the sake of mere monetary gain. The acid test of loyalty to God is not just in martyrdom, but in living honestly.

NOTES

Today I shall . . .

. . . rededicate myself to honesty in all my affairs and realize that dishonest behavior constitutes a denial of God.

לְמַעַן יְבָרֶכְךָ ה' אֱלֹהֶיךָ בְּכֹל מַעֲשֵׂה יָדֶיךָ *From the*
In order that God will bless you in all *Scriptures*
the work of your hands (*Deuteronomy*
24:19).

May 20, 1993
May 10, 1994
May 29, 1995
May 18, 1996
June 5, 1997
May 25, 1998

Sometimes we dream up a worthwhile project, but we hesitate to undertake it because it seems beyond our capacities. Obviously, people must be realistic and should not embark on something which is totally outlandish because it would require means or knowledge which they lack. However, we still shy away from many things that are achievable.

There is a folk saying: "The appetite comes with the eating." A person may not be hungry, yet when he or she sits at the table, and the food is served, the initial course actually stimulates the appetite.

When we make a beginning and exert some effort, a Divine blessing may come. A composer may have but one melody in mind, but as he or she begins to write, one idea seems to inspire another, and an entire symphony comes to life.

I once heard a recovered alcoholic with many years of sobriety give instructions to a newcomer who was unable to comprehend how anyone could abstain from drinking for so many years when it was so difficult for him to abstain even for one day. "You just begin," he said. "It's like standing on the shore and wanting to get across when there is no boat. Someone says to you, 'Start rowing,' and you say, 'How can I start rowing when there is no boat?' 'Never mind,' the man responds, 'Just start rowing, and the boat will appear.' "

We must make the effort, and God will help us bring it to fruition.

NOTES

Today I shall . . .

. . . not hesitate in making a beginning of things that I know that I should do, even if they may seem formidable.

Rosh Chodesh
May 21, 1993
May 11, 1994
May 30, 1995
May 19, 1996
June 6, 1997
May 26, 1998

From the Scriptures

מַה גָּדְלוּ מַעֲשֶׂיךָ ה'

How great are Your ways, O God *(Psalms 92:6).*

The *Midrash* states that when King David completed his *Psalms*, he was elated that he had been able to compose such wonderful praises to God. A frog then appeared and said, "Do not let your compositions go to your head. Every day I sing more beautiful hymns to God than you do."

While we may be proud of our achievements, we should realize how they pale before the majestic natural phenomena that are the immediate handiwork of God.

We can marvel at a highly sophisticated computer that can process complicated calculations in a fraction of a second. However, the most efficient computer is nothing more than a simple juvenile tinker toy in comparison with the central nervous system of any living thing, let alone the human brain. The brain is comprised of more than fourteen *billion* units, all intrinsically interconnected, to convey multiple messages simultaneously to one another at unimaginable rates of speed. The brain also stores far more information than a warehouse full of computers; furthermore, it can be creative and generate new ideas, while a computer can only do what it has been programmed to do.

We may be proud of the radar that allows airplanes to take off, fly, and land in darkness and fog, but the radar of the lowly bat is by far superior to that of the most advanced aircraft. Similarly, the sonar of many aquatic animals is superior to our most highly developed soundwave technology.

While we may be justly proud of our achievements as humans, they should not go to our head. We can remain humble if we compare our works with those devised by God.

NOTES

Today I shall . . .

. . . try to be aware that while my accomplishments may be significant, there is no reason for me to become vain because of them.

הַיּוֹם יִפְנֶה הַשֶּׁמֶשׁ יָבֹא וְיִפְנֶה נָבוֹאָה שְׁעָרֶיךָ *From*

our

Prayers

The day is coming to a close. The sun is about to set. Let us enter into Your gates

(*Concluding service of Yom Kippur*).

May 22, 1993
May 12, 1994
May 31, 1995
May 20, 1996
June 7, 1997
May 27, 1998

Sometimes the first part of a typical day may be disappointing to us. A transaction that we had hoped for may have fallen through, a job that we had applied for was denied, or we turned in a poor performance on a test for which we had studied. Such negative experiences may depress us so much that the rest of the day is a waste; we simply do not have the energy or initiative to do anything.

While adverse occurrences certainly may be depressing, we should not allow them to affect us so profoundly.

The Chofetz Chaim encountered a person who had suffered a reversal and was complaining that the loss had so severely affected him that he was unable to get on with his life.

The Chofetz Chaim told him a parable of a young boy who was selling apples from a cart. Some hoodlums fell upon him and began running off with his apples. The boy stood there helplessly and cried. An observer said to him, "Don't just stand there crying! You will lose everything. Go ahead and grab as many apples as you can and run off with them, too. At least that way, you will salvage something."

The Chofetz Chaim said, "If you allow this adverse incident to disable you, you will be adding to your losses. Go ahead and grab what you still can, and you will at least salvage something."

If the first part of our day does not go as we wished, we should try to salvage the rest of the day. By allowing ourselves to be paralyzed by whatever adversity occurred, we only add to our losses.

NOTES

Today I shall . . .

. . . try to avoid any emotional paralysis from unpleasant incidents and instead salvage whatever I can.

May 23, 1993
May 13, 1994
June 1, 1995
May 21, 1996
June 8, 1997
May 28, 1998

From the Sages

קָרָא וְשָׁנָה וְלֹא שִׁמֵּשׁ תַּלְמִידֵי חֲכָמִים הֲרֵי זֶה עַם הָאָרֶץ

If one read and reviewed his studies but did not serve an apprenticeship to scholars, he remains unlearned (*Berachos* 47b).

We can learn more about tennis by seeing a pro in action than by reading a book about how to play good tennis. Book learning certainly has value, but observing a professional performance is much more impressive.

One of the *mitzvos* the Torah lists is to say *Shema Yisrael* twice daily. I had learned about the proper *kavanah* (concentration) needed when saying the *Shema*, and I had heard lectures on the subject regarding the intensity of meditation required. One day, I attended the *vasikin minyan* (sunrise communal service) at the *Kotel* (the Western Wall), and I heard the *Shema* being recited the way it should be said. All that I had read and heard beforehand now became galvanized and took on new meaning.

If you have the opportunity to watch any expert performing in his or her field, do so. Watch a *tzaddik* pray, a matriarch light the Shabbos candles, and a scholar learning Torah. These indelible experiences can give life and spirit to your own actions and convert the knowledge you have accumulated through book learning into more meaningful experiences.

The Torah states that at Sinai, the entire nation *saw the sounds* (*Exodus* 20:15). Many commentaries ask how sounds can be seen. Perhaps the Torah is saying that the Israelites observed how their leader Moses acted, and so were able to *see* that which they had previously heard.

NOTES

Today I shall . . .

. . . try to reinforce those character traits that I know are correct by observing how good people implement them.

מָשָׁל לְמַרְגָּלִית שֶׁנָּפְלָה בֵּין הַחוֹל *From*

It may be compared to a pearl which fell *the*
into the sand. [One sifts great amounts of *Sages*
sand, casting them aside until one finds
the gem] (*Rashi, Genesis* 37:1).

SIVAN
4
סיון

May 24, 1993
May 14, 1994
June 2, 1995
May 22, 1996
June 9, 1997
May 29, 1998

During the Gold Rush, prospectors patiently panned water all day long just to wash out a few grains of gold. The great value of those particles motivated them so much that they were able to be patient with this otherwise endless, monotonous panning of water.

Sometimes we find ourselves impatient. We may be waiting a long time for something or enduring monotonous work. Our patience may be exhausted, and we may abandon the project.

We should ask ourselves what we are waiting for. If it has real value to us, then, like the gold prospector, we should not even feel the monotony.

Of course, if we are working to earn a living, the importance of our economic survival may overcome our impatience. If we are working towards spiritual goals, whose attainment is not as palpably vital to our survival, we may become bored more easily.

We must assign proper values to spiritual achievement. Like those grains of gold, it may appear only after we have worked long hours, gleaning it from the sand and water of everyday life. Solomon correctly stated that spiritual treasures will come only to those who seek them with the same diligence and perseverance as one who seeks material treasures (*Proverbs* 2:4).

NOTES

Today I shall . . .

. . . try to realize that the real values in life are spiritual treasures, and that I should persevere in attaining them.

Erev Shavuos

[Eve of Shavuos]

May 25, 1993
May 15, 1994
June 3, 1995
May 23, 1996
June 10, 1997
May 30, 1998

From the Scriptures

וַיּוֹצֵא מֹשֶׁה אֶת הָעָם לִקְרַאת הָאֱלֹקִים מִן הַמַּחֲנֶה

Moses brought the people forth out of the camp to meet God (*Exodus* 19:17)

It is traditional to spend the entire night of Shavuos reciting or studying Torah until daybreak. This has its origin in the *Midrash* that relates that some of the Israelites overslept on the morning of the revelation at Sinai, and that Moses had to arouse them for the momentous event. It is generally assumed that denying ourselves sleep on this night is a kind of rectification for our ancestors' lethargy.

Far more important than being an atonement for our ancestors is the message this custom has for us. It is not unusual for us to fail to take advantage of opportunities. We too may "oversleep" for momentous occasions.

Whether opportunity knocks only the proverbial once or several times, each missed opportunity is a loss we can ill afford. Some people regret having overlooked opportunities to buy properties that subsequently escalated greatly in value. Since we lack prophetic foresight, we can hardly fault ourselves for this. But there are opportunities which do not require prophecy, such as when Moses tells the Israelites that tomorrow morning there will be an unprecedented Divine revelation, and that they will be hearing the words of God directly from the Almighty Himself. Our Sages related this *Midrash* so that we should be aware of our vulnerability, that our inertia may result in our failure to take advantage even of a once-in-the-history-of-the-world event.

To avoid overlooking opportunities, we must forever be on the alert. Habit and routine are our greatest impediments. We may have opportunities for spiritual growth today that were not there yesterday, and if we become complacent, we may not notice them.

NOTES

Today I shall. . .

. . .maintain a state of alertness for opportunities that will allow me to grow in character and spirituality.

וַיְדַבֵּר אֱלֹקִים אֵת כָּל הַדְּבָרִים הָאֵלֶּה *From the* לֵאמֹר אָנֹכִי ה' אֱלֹקֶיךָ *Scriptures*

God spoke all these words saying, "I am the Lord, your God" (*Exodus* 20:1-2).

SIVAN

6

סיון

First Day of Shavuos

[In the Land of Israel, Shavuos is only celebrated one day.]

May 26, 1993
May 16, 1994
June 4, 1995
May 24, 1996
June 11, 1997
May 31, 1998

The word *leimor*, usually translated as quoted above, *saying*, can also mean, "to say." The phrase *all these words* may refer to the entire text of the Torah that precedes the Ten Commandments, from the moment of Creation in *Genesis*, through the accounts of the lives of the Patriarchs and the bondage in Egypt. Everything that the Torah relates prior to the Ten Commandments may thus be understood as preparatory to them.

The lives of the Patriarchs; the absolute devotion of Abraham, Isaac and Jacob; the episode of Joseph and his brothers; the enslavement in Egypt; and the miracles of the Exodus — all are a necessary prelude to the acceptance of trust and faith in God, which constitutes the foundation and the first of the Ten Commandments.

The Talmud and *Midrash* provide many additional details about the history of our people prior to Sinai, and the wealth of writings in the commentaries and in homiletics by Torah scholars through the ages clarify and elaborate on the Talmud and Midrashic statements, thereby enabling us to draw from them the principles that are to guide us in living ethical and moral lives.

The Torah is not a history text. Nothing appears in the Torah that does not provide a teaching that we can apply to our lives. It is our responsibility to study and utilize these valuable teachings.

Every word in the Torah was Divinely dictated, and it was all *leimor*, to make possible the statement, "I am the Lord, your God."

NOTES

Today I shall . . .

. . . dedicate myself to the comprehensive study of Torah in order to gain the knowledge necessary for living Jewishly.

**Second Day of
Shavuos**

[Yizkor]

May 27, 1993
May 17, 1994
June 5, 1995
May 25, 1996
June 12, 1997
June 1, 1998

From the Sages

אִם אֵין אֲנִי לִי מִי לִי

If I am not for myself, who is for me (*Ethics of the Fathers* 1:14).

Every human being appreciates approval. We naturally desire to hear good things about ourselves and to have our feelings of worth confirmed.

Those totally dependent on the approval of others for a sense of self-worth, however, have a different story. An analogy will explain the difference. We all need oxygen in order to survive. A healthy person derives sufficient oxygen from breathing air. Someone with an impairment of the heart or lungs may require constant inhalation of pure oxygen, and any interruption may cause serious damage and even death.

In usual daily activities, we generally obtain affirmation of ourselves via two routes: our own accomplishments and the love, recognition, and appreciation that we receive from family and friends. Together, they provide us with an adequate feeling of self-worth. For a person whose ego is seriously impaired and who feels inwardly impoverished, they do not suffice, and the constant need for outside approval places the fragile ego in jeopardy. Even momentary lapses may not be tolerable.

Hillel said it well: "If I do not have a good feeling about myself, there is no one who can give it to me," which means that total dependency on external sources for affirming self-worth is unrealistic. The supply can never meet the demand.

NOTES

_____
_____
_____
_____
_____
_____
_____
_____
_____

Today I shall . . .

. . . check whether I am in constant need of affirmation of my self-worth, and if so, seek to improve my own sense of self-esteem by remembering the many good aspects of myself.

רְאֵה אָנֹכִי . . . שֶׁהֱעִירָם כִּי אֵלָיו יִרְאוּ *From*
לְהִדַּמּוֹת אֵלָיו *the*

See, I . . . [in see me] Moses alerted them *Sages*
to see him and emulate him (*Or
HaChayim, Deuteronomy* 11:26).

May 28, 1993
May 18, 1994
June 6, 1995
May 26, 1996
June 13, 1997
June 2, 1998

In yesterday's message, we distinguished between a healthy and a pathological drive for approval, in that the latter is when one is totally dependent on constant affirmation of others in order to have a sense of self-esteem. The essential difference as described there may be misunderstood to be quantitative rather than qualitative; i.e. that the psychologically healthy person needs external affirmation once or twice a day, whereas the psychologically unhealthy person requires it fifty times a day. This view is not correct and requires further clarification.

A psychologically healthy person desires the approval of others because he wishes them to *perceive* his value. The psychologically unhealthy person expects others to *create* his value. It is not that he has a sense of self-worth and because of his insecurity needs to be reminded more often, but rather that he does not have a sense of self-worth until someone gives it to him. He is much like a light bulb which lights up only if the electric current flows. As soon as the current ceases, the room is in darkness again. Likewise, individuals who lack self-esteem may have a momentary feeling of self-worth, but it lasts only as long as the approval continues.

A man whom I saw on psychiatric consultation had been active in a leadership role in many community projects. "I have a wall full of plaques given to me as tributes," he said. "They don't mean a thing to me." The feeling of self-worth that he enjoyed when he was publicly recognized for his leadership lasted only for the few moments of the ceremony.

It is healthy to enjoy approval from others, but they should not be expected to create our identity.

NOTES

Today I shall . . .

. . . try to see if I have a sense of self-worth in the absence of other people's complimentary remarks.

May 29, 1993
May 19, 1994
June 7, 1995
May 27, 1996
June 14, 1997
June 3, 1998

From the Sages דְּאָכֵיל אַלְיָתָא טָשֵׁי בַּעֲלִיתָא דְּאָכֵיל קָקוּלֵי אַקִּיקְלֵי דְּמָתָא שָׁכֵיב

One who eats fat meat may need to hide in the attic, but one who eats vegetables may do so in an open field (*Pesachim* 114a).

Many people live beyond their means and sink into deep debt. Whether they must then "hide in the attic" to escape their creditors or whether they mortgage themselves so heavily that the debt burden crushes them is immaterial. The message in the quoted passage from the Talmud is clear: Live within your means, and you can be free. Live beyond your means, and you become a fugitive.

Rational people would not assume a crushing burden. The awareness that an extravagant expenditure will result in progressively consuming interest payments can more than negate any transitory pleasure. People do not take on these debts for the ephemeral pleasurable experience, but because of an ego unrestrained by rational thought; these people feel that they must have what others have. "Keeping up with the Joneses" may override all rational considerations.

Why do people "keep up with the Joneses"? They desperately need to give themselves an artificial sense of self-worth, and this dependence on external appearances indicates a feeling of personal bankruptcy.

They pay a steep price for this type of ego-gratification. A good sense of self-esteem would eliminate this need and preserve their health as well as their fortune.

NOTES

Today I shall . . .

. . . try to avoid living beyond my means, realizing that this is often merely an ego-satisfying drive which can be avoided by achieving a healthy sense of self-worth.

Building by youth may be destructive, while when elders dismantle, it is constructive (*Nedarim* 40a). מִבְּנְיַן יְלָדִים סְתִירָה וּסְתִירַת זְקֵנִים בִּנְיָן *From the Sages*

May 30, 1993
May 20, 1994
June 8, 1995
May 28, 1996
June 15, 1997
June 4, 1998

It seems paradoxical, but it is true. We make the most important decisions of our lives when we are young and inexperienced, and our maximum wisdom comes at an age when our lives are essentially behind us, and no decisions of great moment remain to be made.

While the solution to this mystery eludes us, the facts are evident, and we would be wise to adapt to them. When we are young and inexperienced, we can ask our elders for their opinion and then benefit from their wisdom. When their advice does not coincide with what we think is best, we would do ourselves a great service if we deferred to their counsel.

It may not be popular to champion this concept. Although we have emerged from the era of the '60s, when accepting the opinion of anyone over thirty was anathema, the attitude of dismissing older people as antiquated and obsolete has-beens who lack the omniscience of computerized intelligence still lingers on.

Those who refuse to learn from the mistakes of the past are doomed to repeat them. We would do well to swallow our youthful pride and benefit from the teachings of the school of experience.

NOTES

Today I shall. . .

. . . seek advice from my elders and give more serious consideration to deferring to their advice when it conflicts with my desires.

SIVAN

11

סיון

May 31, 1993
May 21, 1994
June 9, 1995
May 29, 1996
June 16, 1997
June 5, 1998

From the Scriptures

שָׁכְרוּ וְלֹא יַיִן נָעוּ וְלֹא שֵׁכָר

They were drunk although not with wine, they staggered although they drank no ale (*Isaiah* 29:9).

In the field of alcoholism treatment, there is a concept of a "dry drunk." This term describes those who have stopped drinking alcohol, but whose behavior remains essentially unchanged from their drinking days.

Just as a "dry drunk" phenomenon occurs with someone who has stopped drinking, it can occur in someone who never drank excessively. In the above verse, the Prophet describes such behavior occurring in the absence of alcohol intoxication.

Active alcoholics are generally oblivious to their self-centered behavior. Seeking to satisfy their own needs regardless of how this may affect others, they are likely to project blame for everything that goes wrong onto anyone and everyone — except themselves. They refuse to make any changes in the way they live; instead, they demand that others accommodate.

We often observe this same behavior in people who do not use intoxicants. In a way, alcoholics are more fortunate, for eventually the toxic effects of alcohol will force upon them the realization of their destructive behavior. People who do not drink and who are thus not likely to have any toxic disasters which precipitate a crisis must therefore exercise even greater scrutiny, lest they unknowingly indulge in behavior that is destructive to themselves and others.

NOTES

_____
_____
_____
_____
_____
_____
_____
_____
_____

Today I shall . . .

. . . find myself a competent, trusted friend to help me see if I might not be denying self-destructive behavior.

אִישׁ אֲשֶׁר יִתֵּן לַכֹּהֵן לוֹ יִהְיֶה *From the*
Whatever a person gives to the *Scriptures*
Kohen (priest) will be his (*Numbers*
5:10).

SIVAN
סיון

June 1, 1993
May 22, 1994
June 10, 1995
May 30, 1996
June 17, 1997
June 6, 1998

The Talmud relates that King Munbaz distributed his treasures in a year of famine. His family confronted him and said, "Your ancestors accumulated wealth, and you are dissipating it." Munbaz responded, "My ancestors accumulated wealth in this world, and I am accumulating it in a higher world. They stored their wealth where human hands could reach it, and I am storing it beyond anyone's reach."

The wise words of Munbaz take on special significance in an era such as ours, in which so many people suffer bitter disappointment when the savings they worked for all their lives disappear before their eyes. Major corporations that once appeared invincible have failed, and along with their failures went the pensions that thousands of workers had relied upon for their retirement years. Savings institutions that appeared eternally secure have gone bankrupt, and people who had invested in what they felt were safe securities were left penniless.

While no one disagrees with judicious savings, these economic upturns have proven the Psalmist's caution, not to trust in humans who may not be able to save themselves (*Psalms* 146:3).

The verse cited above is generally interpreted to mean that any of the tithes given to an individual *Kohen* belong to him exclusively. Another interpretation may be that whatever we give to *tzedakah* will be our own. That is something that, as Munbaz said, is beyond human capacity to steal or diminish.

NOTES

Today I shall . . .

. . . remember that the only wealth that I can truly claim as my own is that which I have given to *tzedakah*.

June 2, 1993
May 23, 1994
June 11, 1995
May 31, 1996
June 18, 1997
June 7, 1998

From the Sages

אֵין לְךָ כָּל עֵשֶׂב וְעֵשֶׂב שֶׁאֵין לוֹ מַזָּל בָּרָקִיעַ שֶׁמְּכָּה אוֹתוֹ וְאוֹמֵר לוֹ גְּדַל

Over every single blade of grass, there is a heavenly force that whips it and commands, "Grow!" (*Bereishis Rabbah* 10:7).

Every living thing in the world has potential, and it is the Divine will that everything achieve its maximum potential. We think of humans as the only beings that have a *yetzer hara* which causes them to resist growth. Certainly animals and plants, which do not have a *yetzer hara*, should achieve their maximum potential quite easily.

Not so, says the *Midrash*. Even plants, and in fact all living matter, have an inherent "laziness," a tendency towards inertia. Even the lowly blade of grass needs to be stimulated and urged to grow.

We can see from here that a human being thus has two inhibiting forces to overcome in order to achieve growth: (1) the *yetzer hara*, which is unique to us, and (2) the force of inertia, which is common to all matter.

The *Tanya* postulates the existence of absolutely righteous people who have totally eliminated the *yetzer hara* from within themselves. We may ask, in the absence of even a vestige of *yetzer hara*, how can they grow? The answer may be that they strive to overcome the inertia that is inherent in all matter, including themselves.

If a lowly blade of grass has both a tendency towards inertia and a spiritual "mentor" which demands that it fulfill itself, we human beings, with two adversaries, certainly have even more powerful forces urging us to achieve our full potential. We should be aware of what can hamper our achievement and make the effort to overcome it.

NOTES

Today I shall . . .

. . . bear in mind that there are numerous obstacles to spiritual growth, and that I must try to triumph over them.

זֶה לְעֻמַּת זֶה עָשָׂה הָאֱלֹקִים *From the* **Scriptures**

God created one force that is equivalent to its opposite (*Ecclesiastes* 7:14).

June 3, 1993
May 24, 1994
June 12, 1995
June 1, 1996
June 19, 1997
June 8, 1998

There is a principle that God created a universe that is in balance. For every force, there is a counterforce that is equal in magnitude. Because of this delicate balance, people are truly free to choose among alternatives.

Yesterday, we discussed the inhibiting force inherent in all matter, the inertia that acts to maintain the status quo. Opposing it is an inherent force to remain alive and to grow. The operation of these two opposing forces can be seen in the plant world. In thick forests, where the foliage blocks the sunlight, it is fascinating to observe how branches from trees grow towards those spaces which are reached by the sun. The convoluted shapes of the branches are the result of this attempt to reach sunlight. If trees had intelligence, we would say that they realized that they could not receive the sunlight in their fixed places and therefore directed their offshoots to go to places where the sun's rays do reach. Since plants do not have intelligence, some force within them must be seeking to preserve their existence and to allow them to grow.

Because we are living matter, we have two opposing forces. However, unlike plants, we also have the capacities of reason and intelligence and thus can choose with which forces we wish to ally ourselves.

We should be aware that in our "forest" exist obstructions to the spiritual light that is essential for our growth. We should emulate plants in reaching out to those areas where that light is greatest.

NOTES

Today I shall . . .

. . . search for sources of spiritual illumination and reach out to them in order to absorb their light.

June 4, 1993
May 25, 1994
June 13, 1995
June 2, 1996
June 20, 1997
June 9, 1998

From the Scriptures

אַשְׁרֵי שֶׁקֵל יַעֲקֹב בְּעֶזְרוֹ שִׂבְרוֹ עַל ה' אֱלֹקָיו

Fortunate is the person who has the God of Jacob as his help; his hope is in his God (*Psalms* 146:5).

We may see ourselves as dependent for survival on those means that we employ to earn our livelihood. We often tend to forget that our true dependence is on God. Consequently, if anything should occur that appears to jeopardize our means of earning a living, we may panic. A firm trust in God would allow us to approach such situations with constructive rational thought rather than with panic, which is likely to be destructive.

Rabbi Schneur Zalman once lodged at an inn and asked the innkeeper where he could find a *minyan* (quorum of ten) for morning services. The innkeeper explained that he was the only Jew in this tiny hamlet. "Then how do you pray all year round without a *minyan*?" the rabbi asked.

"What can I do?" the innkeeper said. "This is my *parnasah* (livelihood)."

"Do you think that God has provided a *parnasah* for all the Jews in the city, but has none for you?" the rabbi asked. The following morning, Rabbi Schneur Zalman awoke to find that the innkeeper had packed all his belongings on wagons. Upon inquiring, he was told that the innkeeper was moving to the city. Rabbi Schneur Zalman would always relate this story as an example of the unwavering trust in God which simple folk were able to achieve.

A group of blind men asked a sighted person to lead them. Each put his hand on the shoulder of the one in front of him. They all knew that although they were being immediately led by the man in front of them, the ultimate leader of the entire procession, who made their safe progress possible, was the sighted person on whom all were ultimately dependent.

The things we work with and the people with whom we transact are but the means or the vehicles with which the Ultimate Provider tends to our needs.

NOTES

_____
_____
_____
_____
_____
_____
_____
_____
_____
_____

Today I shall . . .

. . . remember that my Ultimate Provider is God, Who has limitless ways to provide for my needs.

הָאָב זוֹכֶה לְבֵן בְּנוֹי וּבְכֹחַ וּבְעוֹשֶׁר וּבְחָכְמָה *From* **the** ***Sages***

A **father transmits to his son beauty, strength, wealth, wisdom, and longevity** (*Eidiyos* 2:9).

June 5, 1993
May 26, 1994
June 14, 1995
June 3, 1996
June 21, 1997
June 10, 1998

While some character traits, or at least tendencies to certain traits, appear to have a genetic factor, the lion's share of attitudes are learned. Undoubtedly the most significant influence on a child is his parents' attitudes, rather than their genetic composition.

One psychologist said, "If you have given your child self-confidence, you have given him everything. If you have not given your child self-confidence, then regardless of whatever else you have given, you have given nothing."

The crucial question is: What should parents do to help their child develop self-confidence? While many fine books suggest techniques to avoid common practices that depress a child's self-esteem, one factor overrides all else: *self-esteem is contagious*. Parents who feel secure about themselves will convey an attitude of security and self-confidence to their children. Parents who are insecure and anxiety-ridden are not likely to foster self-confidence in their children, regardless of how many books on parenting they may have absorbed.

As with so much else, the place to begin is with ourselves. By far the most effective way to instill a positive sense of self-awareness in our children is by developing our own self-awareness which will both lead to the discovery of our strengths and skills, and will reveal existing deficits that may then be corrected. Not only will the parents then transmit their self-esteem, the children may also benefit by observing the methods that their parents use to achieve positive feelings about themselves.

NOTES

Today I shall . . .

. . . try to enhance my self-esteem and overcome my anxieties and insecurities.

June 6, 1993
May 27, 1994
June 15, 1995
June 4, 1996
June 22, 1997
June 11, 1998

From the Sages

הָעוֹשִׂים גּוּפָם עִיקָר וְנַפְשָׁם טְפֵלָה אִי אֶפְשָׁר לִהְיוֹת אַהֲבָה וְאַחֲוָה אֲמִיתִית בֵּינֵיהֶם

Those who give priority to their physical selves and make the soul subordinate cannot achieve sincere brotherhood (*Tanya*, chapter 32).

Rabbi Schneur Zalman states that a thorough unity is achieved between friends when their *neshamos* (souls) are permitted to fuse. Since all *neshamos* are part of God Himself, and inasmuch as God is the Absolute One, all souls can similarly be one. Separation and divisiveness among humans do not derive from the soul, but from the physical self.

The needs and desires of the physical self—the quest to satisfy one's earthly drives — are the causes of divisiveness. The *neshamah* does not seek pride nor wealth, is not offended, and does not seek to berate others. All these are traits of the physical self. To the degree that one recognizes the *neshamah* as one's true essence and subordinates the physical self thereto, to that degree one can eliminate the divisive factors and achieve true unity and brotherhood.

We thus see why spirituality is of such overwhelming importance. Hillel said that the essence of the Torah is "love your neighbor as you would yourself." To achieve such love, one must eliminate the impediments to sincere love of another, and as Rabbi Schneur Zalman stated, these impediments are the non-spiritual aspects of life. The greater the degree of spirituality one achieves, the more perfect can one's love of another person be.

NOTES

_____
_____
_____
_____
_____
_____
_____
_____
_____
_____

Today I shall. . .

. . .seek to establish the primacy of spirituality in my life.

כָּל אַהֲבָה שֶׁהִיא תְלוּיָה בְדָבָר, בָּטֵל דָּבָר, *From*
בָּטְלָה אַהֲבָה *the*

Any love that is contingent upon a *Sages*
specific factor is lost when that factor is
gone (*Ethics of the Fathers* 5:19).

June 7, 1993
May 28, 1994
June 16, 1995
June 5, 1996
June 23, 1997
June 12, 1998

We may not be aware of some of our own faults,
although we may easily detect them in others. We may
observe a scene of a powerful dictator standing on a
balcony, greeting the throngs who are shouting his praises
and wildly waving banners bearing his likeness. Watching
how the dictator basks in his glory and in the adoration of
the populace, we wonder, "What kind of fool is he?
Doesn't he realize that most of those people who are so
enthusiastically cheering him actually despise him with a
passion? They are there only because they fear his wrath,
knowing that they forfeit their lives if they fail to acclaim
him. Why, these very people will dance with exuberance in
the streets when he is overthrown! How strange, that a
person can delude himself to think that people who hate
him actually love him!"

We know all this, yet in our own lives it is not unusual for
us to "buy affection" in one way or another. Sometimes we
do things for people in order to make them beholden to us,
and when they then go through the motions that would
indicate that they do indeed favor us, we interpret it as
sincere affection or admiration, rather than what it really is
— an affected attitude, beneath which there may be
smoldering resentment, quite like that of the dictator's
"admirers."

Certainly, we should do favors for friends, and we should
extend ourselves to strangers as well, but we should not
expect, nor even have a need to expect, that our action
alone will earn us their love or respect.

NOTES

_____
_____
_____
_____
_____
_____
_____
_____
_____

Today I shall. . .

. . . avoid trying to buy my way into people's affection and
admiration.

June 8, 1993
May 29, 1994
June 17, 1995
June 6, 1996
June 24, 1997
June 13, 1998

From the Sages אִם לָמַדְתָּ תּוֹרָה הַרְבֵּה אַל תַּחֲזִיק טוֹבָה לְעַצְמְךָ

If you have learned much Torah, do not take credit for yourself (*Ethics of the Fathers* 2:9).

The Talmud does not hesitate to reveal shortcomings of great sages, so that we learn that we are all susceptible to err and that our greatest scholars accepted reprimand even from their inferiors and did *teshuvah*.

On returning from a successful term at the academy, Rabbi Eliezer ben Shimon allowed his ego to soar because of his great progress in learning. On the way, he encountered a man who was exceedingly ugly and said to him, "Are all the people in your city as ugly as you?" The man responded, "Why don't you go and complain to the One Who fashioned me?"

Rabbi Eliezer realized what a terrible thing he had said. He begged the man's forgiveness, but the latter refused. When they entered the town, and Rabbi Eliezer was greeted by the townsfolk, the man said to them, "He does not deserve to be called a rabbi." Only after the people pleaded with the man did he forgive Rabbi Eliezer, cautioning him never to allow his achievements to go to his head again.

How could Rabbi Eliezer have made such a gross remark? The Talmud cites this incident to tell us that vanity is so degenerating a trait that it can cause even a highly spiritual person like him to sink so low as to insult someone in this manner. Once a person feels superior to another, the arrogance that is likely to follow can bring in its wake the most vulgar attitudes.

We must be extremely cautious that we do not allow our successes to go to our heads.

NOTES

Today I shall . . .

. . . try to acquire and retain humility. Even when I make outstanding achievements, I must never consider myself superior to others.

For I know my transgressions, and my sins are forever before me (Psalms 51:5).

כִּי פְשָׁעַי אֲנִי אֵדָע וְחַטָּאתִי נֶגְדִּי תָמִיד *From the Scriptures*

June 9, 1993
May 30, 1994
June 18, 1995
June 7, 1996
June 25, 1997
June 14, 1998

Since a person should believe that once he has repented properly, God has totally erased his sin, as the Prophet states, *I have erased your sin like a fog that cleared* (Isaiah 44:22), why does the Psalmist assert that his sin always remains before his eyes?

It sometimes happens that a parent wishes to do something for a child's benefit, but in spite of the parent's best intentions, the act causes the child to be harmed. Although there was certainly no hostile intent and no negligence — to the contrary, the parent was trying to help the child — the parent's pain over the incident may never disappear. Even if the child has completely forgiven the parent and knows that the parent's intentions were only for his good, the love of the parent for the child is so intense that the parent cannot make peace with what he or she has done. Furthermore, this distress may not be relieved by any logical argument.

I know of a mother who took her child for a recommended medical treatment which unfortunately resulted in an adverse reaction and very serious consequences. Although the child later recovered, there was no comforting the mother. Though she had done the right thing by any reasonable standard, she could not forgive herself for having brought distress upon her child.

King David's repentance was *teshuvah me'ahavah*, or repentance out of an intense love for God. David had complete trust that God had erased his sin, but like the mother in the above example, he could never be completely consoled knowing that he had offended the One Whom he so loved.

Today I shall . . .

. . . try to develop a relationship with God so that I would no more think of offending Him than doing harm to someone I love intensely.

NOTES

_____
_____
_____
_____
_____
_____
_____
_____
_____

June 10, 1993
May 31, 1994
June 19, 1995
June 8, 1996
June 26, 1997
June 15, 1998

From the Scriptures לֹא תַעֲמֹד עַל דַּם רֵעֶךָ

Do not stand on your neighbor's blood (*Leviticus* 19:16).

This *mitzvah* is one of a group which require a person to be considerate of others' rights and possessions. Examples include returning a lost object to its rightful owner, helping load and unload a beast of burden, lending money to the needy, etc. According to the Talmud, the above verse means that we should not stand idly by while someone else's possessions are being destroyed, if we can do something to save them. The uniqueness of this verse lies in the graphic image used: standing idly by while another's blood is being shed.

I often receive calls such as this: "A friend of mine is drinking far too much, and I see that he is in the process of ruining himself. What can be done for him?" When I explain to the caller that as a true friend, he should try to approach his friend and, in as gentle and non-judgmental terms as possible, inform him of his concern, the answer is usually, "I don't want to get involved. Isn't there something that you can do?"

Alcohol is not necessarily the only problem that may ruin us. We may observe a person entering into a business venture with someone known to be unscrupulous and opportunistic, or into a relationship which we believe is a serious mistake. It may not be pleasant to try to deter a person from whatever path he or she is taking, and we may indeed be told to mind our own business. Nevertheless, we should not shirk from making the effort. Even advice that is initially ignored may make an impression and lead to reconsideration.

If the Torah had used less forceful words, we might indeed take refuge and mind our own business. The metaphor of considering it equivalent to standing idly by and watching someone's blood being shed emphasizes the gravity of the responsibility to prevent others from harming themselves.

NOTES

Today I shall . . .

. . . not turn away if I am aware of someone doing something self-destructive, if there is any chance that I may be able to prevent this harm.

אָמַר רַב סָלָא . . . כָּל אָדָם שֶׁיֵּשׁ לוֹ עַזּוּת פָּנִים *From*
סוֹף נִכְשָׁל בַּעֲבֵירָה . . . רַב נַחְמָן אָמַר בְּיָדוּעַ *the*
שֶׁנִּכְשַׁל בַּעֲבֵירָה *Sages*

Rav Sala said, "Every arrogant person will
eventually sin .." Rav Nachman said,
"It is evident that an arrogant person is
one who has already sinned" (*Taanis* 7b).

June 11, 1993
June 1, 1994
June 20, 1995
June 9, 1996
June 27, 1997
June 16, 1998

Rav Sala states that arrogance causes wrongdoing, and
Rav Nachman asserts that wrongdoing causes arrogance.
As with so many other differences of opinion among
Talmudic authors, both positions are valid.

Rav Sala is pointing to a common phenomenon. Arrogance is an attitude of self-righteousness. Arrogant people
discount opinions of others and consider themselves
superior to everyone. They may go so far as to consider
themselves above the law; rules that apply to others simply
do not apply to them, only to those of lesser stature.
Obviously, such an attitude makes breaking the law an
available option, because to arrogant people, their actions
cannot be wrong.

Rav Nachman states that arrogance is a defensive
maneuver employed after the act in an effort to relieve the
sense of guilt. Tormented by the guilt of having done
something wrong, people may assume an attitude of
defiance and deny that what they did was wrong. Since
authority and/or prevailing opinion hold that the act was
indeed wrong, they defend themselves by both dismissing
those who hold that opinion as know-nothings and setting
themselves up as superior in wisdom.

Arrogance and sin thus do have a cause-effect relationship, which can go either way.

NOTES

Today I shall . . .

. . . be alert to any attitude or behavior of arrogance on my
part.

June 12, 1993
June 2, 1994
June 21, 1995
June 10, 1996
June 28, 1997
June 17, 1998

From the Sages

חָכָם . . . אֵינוֹ נִכְנָס לְתוֹךְ דִּבְרֵי חֲבֵרוֹ

"A wise person ... does not interrupt when another person is speaking"
(*Ethics of the Fathers* 5:9)

While it appears that the Talmud is prescribing rules of courtesy, this passage goes beyond the issue of propriety. Interrupting another person is not merely rude, but also unhealthy.

Cardiologists have described a "Type A" personality, which they find to be a significant cause of coronary heart disease. Among the characteristics of Type A people are the following: operating under pressure of time, doing multiple things at the same time (e.g. eating breakfast while talking on the phone and also reading the morning news), and *finishing other people's sentences.* The latter indicates not only impatience, which itself demonstrates the pressure under which they are operating, but also a presumptuousness, since they are taking for granted that they know what other people intend to say.

Teaching ourselves to allow other people to finish their sentences is a simple way to learn patience. Once we achieve it, it becomes easier to correct other Type A behaviors, such as making a mad dash to enter an elevator before the doors close completely, losing our composure in congested traffic, or feeling oppressed by the approach of a deadline. We may learn to take life in stride and even to relax, thereby eliminating the stress factor that has been implicated in heart disease.

No wonder that Solomon referred to the Torah as "a Torah of life." Adhering to its guidelines can actually prolong life.

NOTES

Today I shall ...

... try to control my impulse to finish other people's sentences for them.

K**now whence you derive** (*Ethics of the Fathers* 3:1). דַּע מֵאַיִן בָּאתָ *From the Sages*

June 13, 1993
June 3, 1994
June 22, 1995
June 11, 1996
June 29, 1997
June 18, 1998

This Talmudic statement is usually understood as giving a reason for humility. People who might be carried away by vanity should reflect on their humble beginnings and thereby stop any self-aggrandizement.

A scientist who studied the growth and development of the human being remarked, "As I stared through the microscope at the single-cell fertilized ovum, and I realized that this infinitesimally tiny bit of matter could compose the masterpieces of Beethoven and Michelangelo, I was momentarily breathless, overcome with awe. Except for the nutrients it would receive, nothing would be added to this single cell. It is absurd that it has within itself the potential to achieve such greatness. Neither the cell nor its nutrients, nor both together even in the most sophisticated of combinations, could make such a quantum leap, and the only logical conclusion is that some external power instills this intelligence within this bit of protoplasm. It was at that moment that I came to know God."

NOTES

Today I shall . . .

. . . think how the marvelous phenomenon of the human being originating from a microscopic bit of matter attests to the existence of God.

June 14, 1993
June 4, 1994
June 23, 1995
June 12, 1996
June 30, 1997
June 19, 1998

From the Sages

כְּשֶׁאֲנִי מְדַבֵּר הַדִּבּוּר מוֹשֵׁל בִּי וּכְשֶׁאֵינִי מְדַבֵּר אֲנִי מוֹשֵׁל מִלְאָמְרוֹ

When I speak, my words are master over me. When I do not speak, I am master in that I withhold them (*Orchos Tzaddikim*, Chapter 21).

Everyone has an inherent drive for power and control. We may use it for evil; for example, we may seek control over other people. On the other hand, we may use it for good and try to control our own drives and urges. In any case, it is often frustrating to discover that something is beyond our control.

Words are within our control until we have spoken them; then, we cannot control their effects. At the very best, we can retract what we have said, but that only sets up an opposing force to that which we have created. The original words can never be recalled. We often find ourselves powerless and subjected to the consequences of what we have said, in which case the words we have spoken have indeed become our masters.

How do we avoid this feeling of powerlessness? We have to take control of our speech and learn to keep silent when we have nothing constructive to say. If we do have to speak, we should choose our words very carefully.

If we had to choose a boss, we would certainly be very careful in our selection. We should be no less cautious with words.

NOTES

Today I shall . . .

. . . watch carefully what I say, realizing that once I have said something, I am powerless over those words.

אֶת ה׳ אֱלֹקֶיךָ תִּירָא – לְרַבּוֹת תַּלְמִידֵי חֲכָמִים *From* **Y**ou shall stand in awe of your God. This *the* includes Torah scholars as well (*Pe-* *Sages* sachim 22b).

SIVAN

26

סיון

June 15, 1993
June 5, 1994
June 24, 1995
June 13, 1996
July 1, 1997
June 20, 1998

On 16 Nissan, it was explained that the true fear of and reverence for God refers to the fear of doing anything that would estrange one from Him. Inasmuch as the commission of transgressions causes such estrangement, the fear of God thus refers to fear of sinning.

Since reverence for Torah scholars is derived from the verse referring to fear of God, it means that we should be afraid to behave in a manner that would alienate us from Torah scholars or them from us.

This is a commendable fear, because it fosters closeness to scholars. There is another type of fear that has the polar opposite effect, in that it leads to estrangement. This is the fear that because scholars are more learned or more spiritual, one feels so inferior that one withdraws from them. Or perhaps out of fear that scholars may reprimand one for one's dereliction, one may shrink from being close to them.

The Talmud states that a shy person does not make a good student, because he will be hesitant to assert himself to ask when he does not understand something. He may be afraid that asking will expose his ignorance.

Feelings of inferiority can cause people to be strangers to one another. Ironically, sometimes each person may withdraw from the other because each one considers himself inferior. A healthy self-esteem will enable one to be close to others, to be a good friend and a good student.

NOTES

Today I shall . . .

. . . avoid withdrawing from people more learned than myself.

June 16, 1993
June 6, 1994
June 25, 1995
June 14, 1996
July 2, 1997
June 21, 1998

*From the
Scriptures*

חֲנֹךְ לַנַּעַר עַל פִּי דַרְכּוֹ גַּם כִּי יַזְקִין לֹא יָסוּר
מִמֶּנָּה

Train a lad according to his manner;
even when he grows old he will not
deviate from it (*Proverbs* 22:6).

Parents have the primary responsibility for training their children, and most do their utmost to provide their children with the tools to carry them successfully through life. Generally, the emphasis in education is on skills that will enable children to earn a livelihood and be contributing members of society.

Parents also hope that their children will live to a ripe old age. When that wish comes true, the former child who is now a septuagenarian retiree cannot make much use of the livelihood skills the parents had provided. Diseases of old age may preclude many activities, including driving a car, and a housebound, bored retiree may find the "golden years" a burden. Parents should therefore provide their children with a training that will serve as a basis for adapting to all phases of life.

Yes, even when their children are the tender age of five, parents should be thinking about providing for their happiness sixty years later. As the Psalmist says, *They will blossom in their old age* (*Psalms* 92:15).

NOTES

Today I shall . . .

. . . prepare myself as well as my children with the means to make the later years of life enjoyable rather than monotonous.

דַּהֲיָה לִי דָרָא דְּלִבְנֵי אֲתִי כָּל חַד וְאַד שָׁקְלִי *From*
חֲדָא אָמַר לִי אֲנָא חֲדָא דִּשְׁקַלִי *the*

[I]n Sodom] when someone built a stone *Sages*
fence, people would walk by and take
one stone each, saying, "I am not really
harming him. I am taking only one stone"
(*Sanhedrin* 109b).

June 17, 1993
June 7, 1994
June 26, 1995
June 15, 1996
July 3, 1997
June 22, 1998

The Talmud elaborates on the social practices of Sodom,
some of which are uncomfortably reminiscent of some
current social customs.

Sodom was characterized by self-will run riot. Nothing
stood in the way of gratifying a Sodomite's desires,
regardless of what they were. Any barriers to gratification
that might arise from guilt were eliminated by two widely
practiced maneuvers: rationalization and legislation. If one
had no way to justify a particular immoral or unethical act,
a law was passed to legalize it. Sodom was the symbol of
justified and legalized social and moral corruption.

There is one example of Sodomite rationalization —
considering a particular improper act trivial and insignificant. Each Sodomite who took only one stone from the
neighbor's fence told him or herself that this infraction of
another person's property rights was so minor that it would
hardly be noticeable. In this way, the owner's entire fence
was demolished.

I once brought a letter to my grandfather which my father
had intended to mail to him. My grandfather opened up his
desk drawer and tore up a postage stamp saying, "We have
no right to withhold revenue from the postal service that is
due to them." To a person for whom pennies (and postage
was three cents back then) are negligible, misappropriation
of thousands of dollars may also be feasible.

NOTES

Today I shall . . .

. . . be cautious not to do any improper act, even in the
minutest quantity or degree.

SIVAN

סיון

Erev
Rosh Chodesh
[Eve of the
New Month]
June 18, 1993
June 8, 1994
June 27, 1995
June 16, 1996
July 4, 1997
June 23, 1998

*From
the* Theft of an object is theft, and theft of
Sages time is theft (*Mesilas Yesharim*, Chapter 11).

כִּי הֲרֵי גָזֵל חֵפֶץ גָזֵל וְגָזֵל זְמַן גָזֵל

Stealing is abhorrent to most people. They would never think of taking something which does not belong to them. Still, they may not be bothered in the least by making an appointment and keeping the other person waiting for a few minutes. Rabbi Luzzato points out that this double standard is a fallacy, because stealing others' time is no less a crime than stealing their possessions.

Moreover, stealing time is worse in one aspect: stolen objects can be returned, but stolen time can never be repaid.

Not every lateness is a theft. Sometimes, circumstances totally beyond our control can cause us to be delayed. Still, many realistic factors can be foreseen and should be taken into account. If the usual travel time between two points is fifteen minutes, we should provide an extra few minutes for a very likely possibility — congested traffic.

According to Jewish law, someone who stole an object from another cannot be forgiven by God until he or she has made restitution and received forgiveness from the owner. Without these two premises, even Yom Kippur does not atone one's sin. This rule also applies if one has caused another person a loss of time.

If someone has wrongfully infringed on our time, it is proper that we should call it to his or her attention. As with other offenses, we should try to sincerely forgive if the offender changes his or her ways. If we have infringed on someone else's time, we must be sure to ask forgiveness and to remember that *teshuvah* consists of a sincere resolution not to repeat the same act again.

NOTES

Today I shall . . .

. . . be extremely careful not to cause anyone a loss of time, and if I have done so, ask forgiveness.

אֵין הָעֵדִים נַעֲשִׂים זוֹמְמִין עַד שֶׁיָּזִמּוּ אֶת עַצְמָן *From* mpeached witnesses are not considered *the* guilty until they have impeached them- *Sages* selves (*Makkos* 5a, *Rabbeinu Chananel*).

First Day of Rosh Chodesh Tammuz
June 19, 1993
June 9, 1994
June 28, 1995
June 17, 1996
July 5, 1997
June 24, 1998

When someone says something uncomplimentary to us, we are of course displeased. The intensity of our reaction to an unkind remark, however, depends upon ourselves.

A former patient called me one day, sobbing hysterically because her husband had told her that she was a poor wife and a failure as a mother. When she finally calmed down, I asked her to listen carefully to me.

"I think that the scar on your face is very ugly," I said. There was a moment of silence. "Pardon me?" she said.

"I spoke very distinctly, but I will repeat what I said. 'The scar on your face is repulsive.' "

"I don't understand, doctor," the woman said. "I don't have a scar on my face."

"Then what did you think of my remark?" I asked.

"I couldn't understand what you were talking about," she said.

"You see," I pointed out, "when I say something insulting to you, and you know that it is not true, you do not become hysterical. You just wonder what in the world it is that I am talking about. That should also have been your reaction to your husband's offensive remarks. Instead of losing your composure, you should have told him that he is delusional. The reason you reacted as extremely as you did is because you have doubts about yourself as to your adequacy as a wife and mother."

A good self-esteem will not make offensive comments pleasant to hear, but it can greatly diminish their impact upon us.

NOTES

Today I shall . . .

. . . be alert to my reactions and remember that no one can make me feel inferior without my consent.

**Second Day of
Rosh Chodesh**

June 20, 1993
June 10, 1994
June 29, 1995
June 18, 1996
July 6, 1997
June 25, 1998

*From
the
Sages*

עֲבֵירוֹת שֶׁבֵּין אָדָם לַחֲבֵירוֹ אֵין יוֹם הַכִּפּוּרִים
מְכַפֵּר עַד שֶׁיְרַצֶּה אֶת חֲבֵירוֹ

Transgressions against a fellow man are not forgiven by Yom Kippur until one makes amends (*Yoma* 85b).

Prior to the High Holidays, a man asked his rabbi for guidance in doing proper *teshuvah*. Among other things, the rabbi instructed him to make a list of all the people he had harmed, because unless one obtains forgiveness from those whom one offended, *teshuvah* is incomplete.

Before Yom Kippur, the man returned and showed the rabbi the list he had made of people he had harmed. "Your list is incomplete," the rabbi said. "Go back and finish it."

The man was bewildered. How could the rabbi know whether the list he had made was complete or not? Nevertheless, he gave it greater consideration and indeed added several names to the list. To his surprise, the rabbi again rejected the list as being incomplete.

"What is it that you want of me?" the man asked. "You forgot to put *yourself* at the top of the list," the rabbi said. "When you do improper things, you harm yourself. Not until you realize that improper behavior is self-destructive can your *teshuvah* be complete."

This is an extremely important point. Indeed, Moses stressed this in his final message to the Israelites. *I have placed before you life and death, blessing and curse . . . to love your God, obey him and cleave unto him, that is your life* (Deuteronomy 30:19-20). Moses made it clear that fulfilling the Divine will is life, and deviating therefrom is self-destructive.

Just as we might be considerate of others not to harm them, we should also show the same consideration for ourselves.

NOTES

Today I shall . . .

. . . realize that transgressing the Divine will is self-destructive, and make a commitment to preserve my life.

מֶה אָנוּ מֶה חַיֵּינוּ . . . מֶה נֹּאמַר לְפָנֶיךָ *From* **What are we? What are our lives? ...** *our* **What can we say before You?** *(Siddur). Prayers*

TAMMUZ

תמוז

June 21, 1993
June 11, 1994
June 30, 1995
June 19, 1996
July 7, 1997
June 26, 1998

One way to read this prayer is to see the last phrase as an answer to the series of questions posed earlier. Read it: "What are we, and what are our lives and traits? Only that which we say before God." In other words, I can only know that much about myself which I have the courage to reveal to God. That which I cannot own up to, that which I keep so concealed that I cannot verbalize when I communicate with God, remains alien to me.

The Rabbi of Kotzk interpreted the verse, *There shall not be a foreign god among you (Psalms 81:10)*, to mean, "Do not let God be foreign to you." To the degree that we alienate ourselves from God, we also alienate ourselves from ourselves.

Tachanun, the practice of daily soul-searching and *teshuvah*, is more than a ritual. By disclosing ourselves before God, we become aware of ourselves. While *tachanun* does contain prescribed prayers of confession, it is highly commendable that following them, we enter into a spontaneous conversation with God, telling Him all our innermost thoughts. In this way, we remove the barriers of denial and repression that both cause us to disown part of ourselves and put our correctable character defects out of reach.

Today I shall ...

. . . try to confide in God, and tell him, both in silent and verbal expression, all my innermost thoughts and feelings.

NOTES

_____

June 22, 1993
June 12, 1994
July 1, 1995
June 20, 1996
July 8, 1997
June 27, 1998

From the Scriptures Do not curse God (*Exodus* 22:27).

אֱלֹקִים לֹא תְקַלֵּל

I frequently heard my father quote this verse and interpret it to mean, "A person with Godliness does not curse."

Few things were as absolutely forbidden in our home as uttering a curse. I know that my father was severely provoked many times, but even when angry, no malediction ever crossed his lips. He would tell us that when someone would provoke his mother beyond tolerance, she would say, "May he have soft bread and hard butter." That was the strongest curse Grandmother could utter, but from my father I never heard even that.

How often have we regretted harsh words that were spoken in rage? Such remarks may cause as much pain to the speaker as to the one to whom they are said.

Since we are vulnerable to rage, perhaps we would be wise to provide ourselves with an array of expressions that we can draw upon so that when we are provoked to fury, we will be able to discharge our emotions without being malevolent. One tried-and-true example? "May he have soft bread and hard butter."

NOTES

_____
_____
_____
_____
_____
_____
_____
_____
_____
_____

Today I shall . . .

. . . scrupulously avoid pronouncing a curse in anger, regardless of how furious I may be.

דִּבְרֵי חֲכָמִים בְּנַחַת נִשְׁמָעִים *From the* **T**he words of the wise are heard with *Scriptures* pleasantness (*Ecclesiastes* 9:17).

The Talmud states that on Friday afternoon, a person must alert his household to prepare the necessities for Shabbos. However, he must do so in a soft voice, so that his words will be obeyed.

Many late Friday afternoons, people feel themselves under pressure while rushing to prepare for Shabbos. If one sees that some things have not yet been done, it is easy to lose composure and scream at other members of the household. The Talmud cautions against doing so and implies that shouted instructions are less likely to be carried out.

A politician who had concluded an address inadvertently left a copy of his speech on the lectern. In the margins were comments indicating manners of delivery, e.g. "gesture," "clap hands," "slow and emphatically," etc. At one point he had written, "Argument awfully weak here. Scream loudly."

If we have something of substance to say, the message will be adequately conveyed in a soft tone, because the content alone will carry it. Only when our words have little substance do we seek to make an impression by delivering them with many decibels.

Even in situations of great urgency, we have no need to lose our composure. I can attest that when life-threatening emergencies presented themselves in the hospital, greater efficiency and more rapid response ensued when everyone kept a cool head.

The words of Solomon are correct. The wise speak pleasantly, and those who shout may not be wise.

June 23, 1993
June 13, 1994
July 2, 1995
June 21, 1996
July 9, 1997
June 28, 1998

NOTES

Today I shall . . .

. . . keep my voice soft and pleasant at all times, especially when I have something urgent to communicate.

TAMMUZ

5

תמוז

June 24, 1993
June 14, 1994
July 3, 1995
June 22, 1996
July 10, 1997
June 29, 1998

From the Sages

יְהִי בֵיתְךָ פָּתוּחַ לִרְוָחָה

Let your home be open to all (*Ethics of the Father* 1:5).

I have traveled to many communities to lecture on various subjects. I have also attended other guest speakers' lectures. Invariably, after the lecture, the speaker is invited to a home where a small group of people gather for an informal chat, while hors d'oeuvres are served.

It has been very distressing to me that even when my audience appears to receive my talk well, no one may invite me to a post-lecture gathering. Why? I keep kosher, many of these people do not, and they find it awkward that the guest would not partake of their refreshments.

This baffles me. If my lecture was not well received, I could understand people's reluctance to invite me. But when the response is virtually ecstatic, and I receive immediate requests for repeat performances, why, then, am I shunned? If I were a person of any other faith or nationality, I would be welcomed in everyone's home. Why are the doors of my own people closed to me? The abundance of kosher foods available no longer makes keeping kosher an inconvenience.

Observant Jews adhere to kosher laws as a matter of conviction. Even if someone is not of that mindset, he or she can at least maintain a home where every Jew can be welcomed (or at least have a cup of coffee!).

So many doors are closed to Jews. We should not be closing our doors to our own.

NOTES

Today I shall . . .

. . . try and make my home a place where every Jew can feel welcome and comfortable.

וּכְתַבְתָּם עַל מְזֻזֹת בֵּיתֶךָ וּבִשְׁעָרֶיךָ *From the*
Ａnd you shall inscribe them on the *Scriptures*
doorposts of your home and gates
(*Deuteronomy* 6:9).

June 25, 1993
June 15, 1994
July 4, 1995
June 23, 1996
July 11, 1997
June 30, 1998

Some people seem to have two personalities. Some are very gentle, polite, and accommodating during the workday to clients and customers, but when they come home they become demanding and unyielding tyrants. On the other hand, others are loving, considerate, and patient at home, but in business affairs are ruthless, letting nothing stand in the way of gaining profit.

Neither behavior pattern is acceptable. Our lives must be governed by principles that apply everywhere, and we must practice them in all our affairs. For the Jew, these principles are found in the Torah, which includes not only the Scriptures, but also the Talmud and the various works compiled by Torah scholars throughout the ages.

In the portion of the Torah inscribed on the *mezuzah*, we read that one should converse in Torah while in the home, on the road, when one arises, and when one retires. This message is to be inscribed on the doorposts of our homes. In other words, from awakening until bedtime, both within the home and outside the home, the words of the Torah are to direct us in our actions. There can be no dichotomy.

The *mezuzah* is affixed to the doorpost so that it should be noticed both when we leave the house to enter the world of commerce and when we return home after the workday. While it is a beautiful custom to kiss the *mezuzah* as a sign of endearment, this gesture should not be perfunctory. The words of the *mezuzah* should influence our behavior everywhere.

NOTES

_____
_____
_____
_____
_____
_____

Today I shall . . .

. . . observe the *mezuzah* as I enter and leave my house, and remember what it is meant to teach me.

June 26, 1993
June 16, 1994
July 5, 1995
June 24, 1996
July 12, 1997
July 1, 1998

From the **A**ccept truth from whomever speaks it
Sages (*Rambam Introduction to Avos* 19).

קַבֵּל הָאֱמֶת מִמִּי שֶׁאֲמָרוֹ

Some extremely choosy people will accept guidance or teaching only from an acknowledged authority, because they consider accepting anything from anyone of lesser stature a demeaning affront to their ego.

Among my physician colleagues, I have observed this phenomenon when a patient requests consultation. Those doctors who have self-esteem and know that they are competent have no problem accepting consultation, but those who are less self-confident may interpret the request for consultation as an insinuation that they are inadequate. They may be insulted by this request, and if they do comply with it, they will accept as a consultant only the chief of the department at a university medical school or some other renowned personage. Any other consultant constitutes a threat to their ego, an admission that "he may know more than I do."

Physicians are not the only guilty party; professionals and artisans of all types can also show a lack of self-confidence by displaying this intellectual snobbery.

The Talmud states that truly wise people can learn from everyone, even from people who may be far beneath them. Limiting ourselves to learning only from outstanding experts is not only vain, but it also severely restricts our education. Humility is essential for learning, and we should accept the truth because it is the truth, regardless of who speaks it.

NOTES

Today I shall . . .

. . . try to learn from everyone, even from someone whom I may consider inferior to me in knowledge.

שִׂנְאָה תְּעוֹרֵר מְדָנִים וְעַל כָּל פְּשָׁעִים תְּכַסֶּה אַהֲבָה *From the Scriptures*

Hatred arouses strife, whereas love can cover up for all sins (*Proverbs* 10:12).

June 27, 1993
June 17, 1994
July 6, 1995
June 25, 1996
July 13, 1997
July 2, 1998

What are facts? What is reality? Often they are what we think they are, much like an optical illusion, such as a diagram that can look like the upper or lower surface of a staircase, depending on how we view it.

We often demonstrate our subjectivity when we make evaluations of other people. For example, if we do not like someone with a personality trait of rigidity, we may consider him "as stubborn as a mule." If, however, we admire him, he becomes "a person with great integrity who will never yield on a principle." In both cases, we sincerely believe that we are being thoroughly objective.

How we feel towards others can profoundly affect how we interpret their behavior, yet our true feelings may be repressed and hidden even from ourselves. This phenomenon is most likely to occur with people who are closest to us. Although parents, children, spouses, and siblings may feel profound affection for their family members, they may be unaware of some repressed negative feelings which may manifest themselves with their finding fault with these family members. They may be unaware that what they are critical of (which they assume to be "fact") is actually a distorted conclusion due to a misperception, which is itself brought about by repressed negative feelings towards their loved ones. In fact, their love itself may cause them to repress negative feelings, which then find circuitous ways of expressing themselves.

Today I shall . . .

. . . be hesitant in criticizing faults in others and be aware that the fault that I see in others may be due to my misperceptions.

NOTES

_____
_____
_____
_____
_____
_____
_____
_____

June 28, 1993
June 18, 1994
July 7, 1995
June 26, 1996
July 14, 1997
July 3, 1998

From the Scriptures

בְּצֶלֶם אֱלֹקִים בָּרָא אֹתוֹ

He created him [Adam] in the image of God (*Genesis* 1:27).

Since God is not corporeal, the term "image of God" obviously refers to humanity's capacity for Godliness, i.e. to share in the Divine attributes of rational thinking, spirituality, sanctity, creativity — attributes that distinguish us from all other living things.

The serpent seduced Adam and Eve to eat of the forbidden Tree of Knowledge by convincing them that doing so would enable them to become God-like (ibid. 3:5). Why did they succumb to this argument, since they already knew that they were created *betzelem Elokim*, with the capacity to be God-like? Today, sadly, we have found one answer.

Misguided proponents of drugs claimed that certain drugs would create new senses of perception, and that users would thereby be able to perceive the "real truth" of the universe. As a result, millions of people, many of them young people with minds still in the delicate formative stage, have had their brains poisoned and their thinking distorted.

The tragic mistake of the Sixties bears great resemblance to the first sin. God bestowed humanity with a mind fully capable of participating in Godliness in its most comprehensive sense. Artificial substitutes proffered were treacherously deceptive; far from granting new vistas of truth, the forbidden fruit was described by God as something that would bring only death and destruction. We have witnessed an analogue of Adam and Eve's sin.

We are fully endowed to be able to know the truth. All we must do is make the effort. Chemicals are not a shortcut to truth, but a sure road to destruction.

NOTES

Today I shall . . .

. . . utilize my God-given mental capacities to search for truth and not be misled by false promises for instant spirituality.

חֲבָּה יְתֵרָה נוֹדַעַת לוֹ שֶׁנִּבְרָא בְצֶלֶם . . . חֲבָּה *From*
יְתֵרָה נוֹדַעַת לָהֶם שֶׁנִּקְרְאוּ בָנִים לַמָּקוֹם *the*
[Man was created in God's image, and *Sages*
the Israelites are children unto God.]
It is an extra measure of love that man was
informed that he was created in God's
image . . . it is an extra measure of love
that they [the Israelites] were informed
that they were called children unto God
(*Ethics of the Fathers* 3:18).

TAMMUZ

תמוז

June 29, 1993
June 19, 1994
July 8, 1995
June 27, 1996
July 15, 1997
July 4, 1998

It is one thing to be gifted, and another thing to know that one is gifted.

A woman who was admitted for treatment for alcoholism insisted on test after test to determine whether she had suffered brain damage because of her use of alcohol. When she could not be reassured, I became suspicious that something was preventing her from accepting this reassurance.

A long psychiatric interview revealed the reason for her reluctance. This young woman wanted the test to prove that she indeed *had* sustained brain damage.

Why would anyone wish to have such a terrible diagnosis? The answer is that this young woman feared taking on the challenges of life, and brain damage would have provided her with a lifetime of excellent excuses: "Stop trying to help me stay sober. It's too late. Sobriety is difficult enough to achieve for people who have a properly intact brain. I am beyond recovery — I am brain damaged! You expect me to go to school or hold a job? I am too brain damaged for that."

As horrible a diagnosis as brain damage may be, for this young woman it had a redeeming feature: it would absolve her of responsibility. Knowing that one has talents and abilities makes one responsible to use them.

We have been informed that we have God-like attributes and that we are the children of God. It may be more comfortable for us to make believe this is not so, but we should not deny the truth.

NOTES

Today I shall . . .

. . . confront myself with the realities of my abilities and avoid taking refuge in a delusion of inadequacy.

TAMMUZ

תמוז

June 30, 1993
June 20, 1994
July 9, 1995
June 28, 1996
July 16, 1997
July 5, 1998

From the אֲלַמְּדָה פֹשְׁעִים דְּרָכֶיךָ וְחַטָּאִים אֵלֶיךָ
Scriptures יָשׁוּבוּ

I will teach the defiant Your ways, and the sinful will return to You (*Psalms* 51:15).

Every human being craves happiness. People are more than willing to spend great sums of money in the hope of achieving happiness. Unfortunately, their efforts are usually in vain, because happiness cannot be bought. Luxurious homes, sumptuous feasts, and lavish occasions may provide transitory pleasures, but never true happiness.

Living with faith and trust in God can deliver the sought-for happiness. The reason more people do not achieve happiness is because they fall short of the requisite degree of faith and trust in God. We may worry about our financial future and the ability to provide for our families the way we would like, especially during economic downturns. When adversities occur, we are likely to become deeply dejected. A profound and unquestioning faith and trust in Divine benevolence will provide the serenity, security, and convictions that could eliminate these worries and sadness.

People have varying degrees of faith and trust. The higher their level, the lesser are their worries and sadness. If we were able to achieve complete faith and trust, our dispositions would be such that happiness would radiate from us.

NOTES

Today I shall . . .

. . . seek to strengthen my faith and trust in God so that I may achieve true happiness and be an example for others.

הֱוֵי עַז כַּנָּמֵר וְקַל כַּנֶּשֶׁר רָץ כַּצְּבִי וְגִבּוֹר כָּאֲרִי *From* לַעֲשׂוֹת רְצוֹן אָבִיךְ שֶׁבַּשָּׁמָיִם *the*

Be courageous as a leopard, light as an *Sages* eagle, swift as a deer, and strong as a lion to do the will of your Heavenly Father (*Ethics of the Fathers* 5:23).

July 1, 1993
June 21, 1994
July 10, 1995
June 29, 1996
July 17, 1997
July 6, 1998

Numerous traits comprise the character of a human being. We tend to consider some traits as commendable and others as undesirable.

Traits *per se* are neither good nor bad. They acquire a value according to the way they are applied. Hate is generally assumed to be a very loathsome trait, but when one despises evil and injustice and seeks to eradicate them, it becomes a constructive and admirable trait. Love, on the other hand, is generally looked upon as a very positive trait. Yet, when misapplied, love can transgress the boundaries of decency and result in grossly immoral behavior.

Rather than seek to eradicate an undesirable trait, we might consciously redirect it so that it serves a useful function. While redirection can happen with some drives at an unconscious level (which constitutes the psychological defense mechanism of *sublimation*), we have no control over what happens in the unconscious. Preferably, we should avoid dismissing a trait which is generally considered unacceptable and *consciously* redirect it into a positive channel. It is obviously to our advantage to redirect energy, rather to have to repress it, since maintaining that repression requires expenditure of energy.

NOTES

_____
_____
_____
_____
_____
_____
_____
_____
_____

Today I shall . . .

. . . try to direct all my traits in a way that will serve a constructive purpose.

July 2, 1993
June 22, 1994
July 11, 1995
June 30, 1996
July 18, 1997
July 7, 1998

From the Scriptures וְהָיָה אִם שָׁמֹעַ תִּשְׁמְעוּ אֶל מִצְוֹתַי אֲשֶׁר אָנֹכִי מְצַוֶּה אֶתְכֶם

And it shall be if you will heed the commandments that I command you (*Deuteronomy* 11:13).

The Talmud teaches that the evil inclination — the insatiable desire within each of us to experiment with the forbidden — is not so foolish as to entice a person to commit a major transgression. It does not tell an honest person to shoplift; that would certainly meet with fierce resistance. Rather, "First the evil inclination tells you, 'Do this,' then 'Do this,' until it gradually works its way up to the point where you may entirely reject God" (*Shabbos* 108b).

The usual interpretation is that the first "Do this" is a seduction to commit a *minor* transgression, and then it gradually works its way up to more serious ones. The armed robber began by stealing a chocolate bar. Rabbi Yosef Schneersohn said that the *yetzer hara* is even more wily than that. He may begin by recommending "perform this commandment, because it is a perfectly reasonable thing to do," by urging the person to *perform commandments because they are logical*. "Observe the Sabbath because you need a day of rest after six days of hard work. Give charity because it is only right to help the needy. Keep kosher because kosher foods are healthier." A person thus trains himself to follow the dictates of his reasoning, rather than to do something because it is the will of God. The evil inclination's next step is, "This particular commandment is obsolete. It no longer has any logical validity."

The only way to avoid this trap is to avoid its first piece of advice. We do the right thing because it is *right*, not because it accords with our personal likes and desires. Therefore, we preface the performance of a commandment with a blessing that states, "I am doing this in order to fulfill the Divine command." While we should try to understand the commandments, to the best of our ability, our understanding of them should not be our main motivation for performing them.

NOTES

_____
_____
_____
_____
_____
_____
_____
_____
_____

Today I shall . . .

. . . observe all commandments because they are the Divine will, rather than only because I understand their purpose.

אֵיזוֹ הִיא דֶרֶךְ טוֹבָה שֶׁיִּדְבַּק בָּהּ הָאָדָם. רַבִּי אֱלִיעֶזֶר אוֹמֵר: עַיִן טוֹבָה.

From the Sages

Which is the good way of life to which a person should adhere? Rabbi Eliezer says: A benevolent eye (*Ethics of the Fathers* 2:13).

July 3, 1993
June 23, 1994
July 12, 1995
July 1, 1996
July 19, 1997
July 8, 1998

"A benevolent eye" or "a good eye" is the Hebrew expression for not begrudging people that which they have. The corollary is that the way of life to avoid is having "a malevolent eye," i.e. begrudging people what they have.

In Yiddish, the equivalent of "a benevolent eye" is "to *fargin*," as in the expression "I *fargin* him with all my heart." There is no equivalent word in English for *fargin*, and it can only be translated in the negative, i.e. to *fargin* is to not begrudge. As noted in 23 Adar, the absence of a word in a language may be a clue about something in that particular culture. Is it possible that much of the English-speaking world knows only how to begrudge, but does not know how to *fargin*?

Be that as it may, Rabbi Eliezer considers "a benevolent eye" much more than just a desirable trait. He considers it an all-encompassing feature that constitutes *the* optimum adjustment to life. Other people may possess more material wealth. Their children may have achieved more. They may enjoy better health. In whatever way other people may be more fortunate, Rabbi Eliezer sees *farginning* them as the character trait that will make all other traits fall into line. Conversely, not *farginning* is a trait that so permeates one's personality that everything one thinks, feels, or does will be negatively affected.

Perhaps not everyone can rejoice in what others have, but we can all *fargin*.

NOTES

Today I shall . . .

. . .try to *fargin* everyone what they have and avoid begrudging anything to anyone.

July 4, 1993
June 24, 1994
July 13, 1995
July 2, 1996
July 20, 1997
July 9, 1998

From our Prayers

בָּרוּךְ אַתָּה ה' אֱלֹקֵינוּ מֶלֶךְ הָעוֹלָם שֶׁהַכֹּל בָּרָא לִכְבוֹדוֹ

Blessed are You, O God, King of the Universe, Who created everything for His glory (*The Marriage Ritual*).

The surging divorce rate in recent years is appalling. While the Torah indeed provides for dissolving a relationship, there has never been in Jewish history anything like the current number of failed marriages.

Perhaps the problem stems from the partners' primary goals as they enter marriage. In Western civilization, what is called "love" has been accepted as the cornerstone of marriage. Unfortunately, this "love" too often refers to an attraction for the partner because of how he or she can gratify the other's physical and emotional needs. If this primary goal is not adequately met, the cement of the relationship disintegrates, and secondary factors alone cannot maintain it.

In the past, the primary focus of a marriage was the establishment of a family. [The first *mitzvah* found in the Torah is *be fruitful and multiply* (*Genesis* 1:28).] While physical and emotional needs were important, they were not primary, but secondary. Hence, when problems of this nature did develop, the relationship was still held together by the primary binding forces, and these secondary problems could be rectified and resolved.

NOTES

Today I shall . . .

. . . try to realize what the true primary goals of my relationship with others should be.

עֲבָדַי הֵם וְלֹא עֲבָדִים לַעֲבָדִים *From* **The Jewish people are My servants, and** *the* **not servants to servants** (*Bava Metzia* 10a). *Sages*

July 5, 1993
June 25, 1994
July 14, 1995
July 3, 1996
July 21, 1997
July 10, 1998

As a host and his guest left the apartment building, the doorman greeted them in a belligerent tone of voice. The host responded in a gentle tone of voice and with a very pleasant smile.

"Is he that grouchy all the time?" the guest asked.

"Sometimes even worse," the host answered.

"Then why are you so pleasant in your response to him?" the guest asked.

"Because," the host answered, "I am not about to let him dictate how I am going to act."

If we react to others' provocation, we are essentially allowing them to control our behavior. A sign of slavery is being deprived of the ability to think for oneself, so here, if we react reflexively rather than rationally, we are at least temporarily in involuntary servitude. How foolish to allow ourselves to become enslaved, even momentarily.

The antidote is to avoid reflex reactions. We can make it a point never to respond when provoked until we have stopped and allowed ourselves ample time to think rationally about what has happened and to plan what would be a rational, well-calculated response.

One might think that delaying a response to provocation is out of consideration for the other person, to protect others from one's own wrath. This is true, but secondary. The primary reason is that we maintain our own freedom and do not become puppets manipulated by others.

NOTES

Today I shall . . .

. . . avoid reflex responses, and maintain my freedom and dignity as a rational person.

**Fast of Shivah
Asar B'Tammuz**

*[When 17
Tammuz
falls on the
Sabbath, the
fast is observed
on Sunday.]*

*July 6, 1993
June 26, 1994
July 15, 1995
July 4, 1996
July 22, 1997
July 11, 1998*

NOTES

_____
_____
_____
_____
_____
_____
_____
_____
_____
_____

*From
the
Sages*

בְּשִׁבְעָה עָשָׂר בְּתַמּוּז נִשְׁתַּבְּרוּ הַלּוּחוֹת

On the seventeenth day of Tammuz, the Tablets [of the Ten Commandments] were broken [by Moses] (*Taanis* 26b).

Today the Jews worshiped the Golden Calf and on this day, therefore, Moses broke the Tablets of the Law. Jews initiate a three-week period of mourning which ends on the Ninth of Av, the day on which spies sent by Moses to scout Canaan returned with a report so pessimistic that the Israelites wept all night. (Both days also become days of mourning for other tragedies that have befallen the Jewish people, e.g. both Sanctuaries were destroyed on the Ninth of Av.)

The two events — the worship of the Golden Calf and the despair of the Israelites — are closely related. The Torah relates that the Israelites despaired of entering the Promised Land because they lacked faith that God would enable them to conquer it. Their worship of the Golden Calf and their despair of entering the Promised Land both came from a lack of faith in God.

Some people would be horrified to think of themselves as idolaters, yet their behavior may manifest a lack of faith and trust in God. For example, Torah law requires that a certain percentage of one's income be given as *tzedakah*. Reluctance to do so shows a lack of faith in the Divine promise that those who give *tzedakah* will be rewarded manyfold. Failure to refrain from conducting one's business on the Sabbath displays a lack of trust in God, Who decreed that the Sabbath be a day of rest and has promised that those who observe it will gain much more by obeying him than they could through human effort.

The mindset of those who worshiped the Golden Calf and thereby repudiated the true God led directly to the disastrous reaction to the libel of the spies, which caused the loss of an entire generation in the desert and delayed the acquisition of the Promised Land for forty years.

Thanking God requires more than lip service; it must be made manifest in our daily lives.

Today I shall . . .

. . . strengthen my faith and trust in God, and not allow any doubt in Him to affect my actions.

כָּל אֶחָד יֹאמַר שֶׁזֶּהוּ הָעִיקָר הַגָּדוֹל ... אַךְ *From* מַה שֶׁלֹּא יִרְבּוּ לְעַיֵּין עָלָיו הוּא מִפְּנֵי רוֹב פִּרְסוּם *the* הַדְּבָרִים וּפְשִׁיטוּתָם *Sages*

Everyone will say that [piety] is a major principle ... but why they do not study it is because it is so obvious and certain (*Introduction to Path of the Just*).

July 7, 1993
June 27, 1994
July 16, 1995
July 5, 1996
July 23, 1997
July 12, 1998

We take many things for granted. Is justice important? Of course! Is morality vital? Without a doubt! Are honesty and decency essential character traits? How can one even pose a question when the answer is so obvious?

In *Path of the Just,* a monumental work on ethics, Luzzato points out that some people exert a great deal of effort in order to try to gain greater understanding in various subjects, some of which are abstract and have little practical application, but they neglect investigating concepts which are important in everyday life. These people don't minimize the value of the latter; to the contrary, because these subjects *are* so important, everyone takes for granted that they understand them as well as they can figure two plus two equals four.

What is justice? What constitutes morality? What does it mean to be honest and decent? Who determines desirable values? To what degree is a particular trait commendable? In Luzzato's time, like today, these subjects were relegated to pundits in ivory towers who had nothing better to do than spend time analyzing and deliberating these "intangibles." People who were occupied in business, homemaking, labor, and professions had little time for such luxuries. Too many still think they don't.

Luzzato points out that unless we make a concerted effort to understand the values that we espouse, we may be grossly derelict without being aware of it.

NOTES

Today I shall ...

... turn my attention to understanding those values that I consider important in proper living.

July 8, 1993
June 28, 1994
July 17, 1995
July 6, 1996
July 24, 1997
July 13, 1998

From the Sages

אֵלּוּ דְבָרִים שֶׁאֵין לָהֶם שִׁעוּר הַפֵּאָה וְהַבִּכּוּרִים וְכוּ׳

These are the precepts that have no prescribed measure: the corner of a field [which must be left for the poor], the first-fruit offering, etc. (*Peah* 1:1).

This portion of the Talmud is recited in the introductory prayers of the morning service, in order that a person begin the day with a portion of the Oral Law. Of the hundreds of thousands of passages of the Talmud, why was this one selected?

This passage lists five items that have no prescribed measure. The implication is that other than these five, *everything* has a limit. With this important concept, we should begin our day.

Some people know no limits. Many behavioral excesses have joined the category of "olics," so that we now have not only alcoholics, but workaholics, foodaholics, chocoholics, sportaholics, worryaholics, etc. Any activity can be overdone.

More of a good thing is not necessarily better, as people with obesity, for example, have discovered. Unfortunately, many people who do something to excess are not aware of their error. They believe that they are still acting within the normal range.

As with alcoholics, people who are affected by any excessive behavior are generally unable to set limits for themselves. Outsiders must make objective observations to recognize if reasonable limits have been exceeded. We would be wise to seek the appraisal of competent and interested people to help us determine whether we are functioning within the range of accepted norms.

NOTES

_____
_____
_____
_____
_____
_____
_____
_____
_____
_____

Today I shall . . .

. . . be aware that I may be exceeding limits in some aspects of my behavior and seek a competent outside evaluation of myself.

דְּאָזֵיל מִבֵּי דִינָא שְׁקַל גְּלִימָא לֵיזְמַר זְמַר *From*
וְלֵיזִיל בְּאוֹרְחָא *the*

If the court awards the garment to your *Sages*
adversary, sing a happy tune as you leave
(*Sanhedrin* 7a).

July 9, 1993
June 29, 1994
July 18, 1995
July 7, 1996
July 25, 1997
July 14, 1998

Someone who loses even a substantial amount of money as a result of a drop in the value of the stocks that he or she owns will not be upset as intensely or for as long a time as if he or she had lost a much smaller amount of money in a court. The reason? In the first instance, although he lost, no one else won. In the latter case, his loss resulted in his adversary's triumph, and that hurts more.

Here, two plus two does not equal four, but much more. If one's loss and the other's gain had occurred independently of one another, the reaction would not have been as great. The fact that another person gains something should not be distressful, since one should be able to *fargin* (see 14 Tammuz). The fact that one has lost, while unpleasant, usually does not provoke so extreme a reaction. But if the two come together, and the other person's gain comes as the result of one's loss, two plus two suddenly equal a million.

Competition exists in law, business, sports, and many other events. Life is full of situations where one wins and the other loses. Unless we learn to restore the equation to its arithmetical equivalent, so that the whole should not be greater than the sum of its parts, we are in for trouble. Inability to gracefully accept a loss in competition may result in severe emotional stress and cause not only interpersonal and behavioral consequences, but may also take a severe toll on one's health.

The Talmud is right. If you lose at competition, walk away singing.

NOTES

Today I shall . . .

. . . try to develop an attitude of acceptance when I lose in competition.

July 10, 1993
June 30, 1994
July 19, 1995
July 8, 1996
July 26, 1997
July 15, 1998

בָּרָאתִי יֵצֶר הָרָע וּבָרָאתִי לוֹ תּוֹרָה תַּבְלִין

I created the yetzer hara, and I created the Torah as its antidote (*Kiddushin* 30b).

Many commercial products that we use both at home and in industry are toxic. We use them because they serve a particular constructive purpose, but we are also aware that they are dangerous chemicals. Indeed, they usually contain a warning, such as "not for internal use" or "avoid contact with eyes," followed by an antidote with instructions of what to do in case the precautions were not heeded.

Rational people will be very cautious with these chemicals, using them only as directed. If someone accidentally swallowed one of them, he or she will immediately use the specific antidote recommended by the manufacturer. Trying something else instead would be foolish at best and suicidal at worst. The manufacturer obviously knows best what the most effective antidote is.

So it is with the *yetzer hara*. Our appetites and other physiologic drives have their source in the *yetzer hara*, so they must be used only as directed. Misuse can be dangerous and even lethal. Fortunately, the manufacturer issued precautionary instructions (to be found in books of *mussar*) and provided an effective antidote: Torah. How foolish would it be to ignore the manufacturer's instructions or to try to find an antidote other than the one prescribed!

Our physical bodies are very dear to us, and we scrupulously follow instructions on products to avoid physical harm. If there are no instructions on the product package, we will immediately call a poison control center for instructions from the experts on how to avoid harm. Our spiritual selves should be treated with equal respect. We should follow instructions and whenever in doubt, promptly ask the experts.

NOTES

_____
_____
_____
_____
_____
_____
_____
_____
_____
_____

Today I shall . . .

. . . give my spiritual life serious consideration and protect it as I do my physical self.

אֹזֶן שֹׁמַעַת תּוֹכַחַת חַיִּים בְּקֶרֶב חֲכָמִים *From the*
תָּלִין *Scriptures*

The ear that listens to the admoni-
tions of life will rest among the
wise (*Proverbs* 15:31).

July 11, 1993
July 1, 1994
July 20, 1995
July 9, 1996
July 27, 1997
July 16, 1998

An actor once approached the gates of heaven and asked for admission. "What worthy deeds have you done in your lifetime?" the angel asked.

"Why, I portrayed the futility of materialism and the tragedies that result from dishonesty. People would cry and become remorseful while watching my acting."

"Very well," said the angel. "You sit here at the gate, and as soon as the first person who did *teshuvah* as a result of your acting will appear, you may enter."

People who are interested in refining their characters must ask themselves what they are doing to bring it about. To what sources are they turning to derive teachings on correct values and how to achieve them? Clearly, they are not available on television; those who spend their after-work hours glued to the television screen can hardly claim to be working on self-improvement. Nor are the variety of pastimes, in which many people indulge, sources for character betterment.

Those who truly wish to improve themselves will seek the company of the spiritually wise who are able to teach them.

NOTES

Today I shall . . .

. . . examine myself to see which steps I have taken to bring about the character improvement that I desire.

July 12, 1993
July 2, 1994
July 21, 1995
July 10, 1996
July 28, 1997
July 17, 1998

From the Sages כָּל מִי שֶׁצָּרִיךְ לִטוֹל וְאֵינוֹ נוֹטֵל הֲרֵי זֶה שׁוֹפֵךְ דָּמִים

One who is needy and refuses to accept help, it is as though he shed innocent blood (*Jerusalem Talmud, Peah* 8:8).

Maimonides extols what he calls the golden path, the middle way which a person should follow in life. He states that every trait has two opposite but equally undesirable extremes. The proper degree of any trait is not necessarily the median; it may be more toward one of the two poles, but it is never the extreme.

Self-sufficiency is certainly a desirable goal, and striving for independence is commendable. Some indolent people do not even try to carry their own weight. Their parasitism may be so reprehensible to other people that the latter may react by going to the opposite extreme and refusing to accept help when they need it. They may sustain physical injury by starvation or exposure, rather than accept a helping hand.

While accounts of great *tzaddikim* who subjected themselves to extreme degrees of deprivation do exist, these people had reached a level of spirituality so high that this deprivation would not harm them. For the average person, Solomon's caution, "Do not attempt to be too much of a *tzaddik*" (*Ecclesiastes* 7:16), should prevail. To do so may simply be an "ego trip." Some bridges can support vehicles of any tonnage; other bridges have a limit on the tonnage, lest they collapse under excess weight.

In this trait, like so many others, people may not be the best judge of their own capacities. Their best move is to seek competent spiritual guidance.

NOTES

Today I shall . . .

. . . allow myself to accept legitimate help and be cautious of over-reacting in any extreme.

וְכִבַּדְתּוֹ מֵעֲשׂוֹת דְּרָכֶיךָ מִמְּצוֹא חֶפְצְךָ וְדַבֵּר *From the*
דָּבָר *Scriptures*

You shall honor it [Shabbos] by refraining from your usual weekday practices, nor pursuing your business, nor speaking thereof (*Isaiah* 58:13).

July 13, 1993
July 3, 1994
July 22, 1995
July 11, 1996
July 29, 1997
July 18, 1998

The observance of Shabbos and the festivals is characterized by not only abstinence from work, but also from all types of "weekday" activities, including even how one converses. "Your conversation on Shabbos should not be similar to your weekday conversation" (*Shabbos* 113b).

A personal incident illustrates that by properly honoring the Shabbos and festivals, one achieves the respect of others.

As a resident in psychiatric training, I explained to the program director that I was unable to work on the festival days, and that these should be considered vacation days and deducted from my allotted vacation time.

The director shook his head. "No need for that," he said. "Non-Jewish people can do anything they wish on their holidays. If they can wash the car, paint the garage, or go to the theater, then they can just as well come to work. In your case, you are not permitted to do anything, so obviously you cannot come to work, and this need not affect your vacation time."

It has been said, "Even more than Israel has kept the Shabbos, the Shabbos has kept Israel." If we honor the Shabbos properly, the Shabbos will honor us.

NOTES

Today I shall . . .

. . . dedicate myself to a full observance of Shabbos and the festivals.

July 14, 1993
July 4, 1994
July 23, 1995
July 12, 1996
July 30, 1997
July 19, 1998

From the Sages

לְשׁוֹן הָרַע מַהוּ? הַמְסַפֵּר בִּגְנוּתוֹ שֶׁל חֲבֵרוֹ אַף
עַל פִּי שֶׁאוֹמֵר אֱמֶת

What is lashon hara? One who speaks disparagingly of another person, even though he may speak the truth (*Orchos Tzaddikim,* Chapter 25).

One *mussar* spokesman said that there should never be any need to speak about another person. "If you wish to speak of someone's praises, praise God instead. If you wish to find fault with someone, you would do better to focus on your own defects."

The second statement takes on additional significance in light of what psychologists have learned about lack of self-awareness. Some have suggested that when people talk about other people, they turn the conversation away from themselves and, by focusing on other's shortcomings, they avoid the need to focus on their own. Slandering other people thus sets back the struggle for self-awareness, which is essential for optimum emotional and psychological health, because it directs one's attention away from oneself and onto the defects in others. One thereby does not have the information necessary to improve.

The Talmud states that *lashon hara* adversely affects three people: the one who speaks, the one who listens, and the subject of the conversation (*Arachin* 15b). We can easily understand how it hurts the last two, and we now have another insight into how gossips actually hurt themselves.

NOTES

Today I shall . . .

. . . assiduously avoid talking about other people's faults, and instead try to find my own, so that I can improve upon them.

וְעָשׂוּ לִי מִקְדָּשׁ וְשָׁכַנְתִּי בְּתוֹכָם *From the*
They shall make for Me a Sanctuary *Scriptures*
and I shall dwell among them (*Exodus* 25:8).

July 15, 1993
July 5, 1994
July 24, 1995
July 13, 1996
July 31, 1997
July 20, 1998

The Midrash notes that God did not say, "I shall dwell within it" (the Sanctuary), but "I shall dwell among *them*" (the Israelites), i.e. the Divine Presence will be within each person.

There are two types of possible relationships. A person may relate to an object, which is a one-way relationship, since the object cannot reciprocate, or a person may react to God and to people, which should be a two-way relationship. Another difference between relating to objects and to beings is that things should be *used*, whereas God and people should be *loved*. Unfortunately, the reverse may occur, wherein people fall in love with things but they use God and people. People who behave this way perceive God and people as if they were objects. Inasmuch as the love of oneself is an inevitable fact, love of God and people can occur only when they are permitted to become part of oneself, because then one loves them as one does one's own eyes and ears.

If my relationship to God is limited to going to the Sanctuary and praying for my needs, then I am merely *using* Him, and God becomes an external object. But when I make His will mine, then His will resides within me and He becomes part of me. This is undoubtedly what the *Zohar* means by, "Israel, the Torah, and God are one unit," because the Torah, which is the Divine will, is inseparable from God, and when one incorporates the Torah with one's own code of conduct and values, one unites with God.

NOTES

_____
_____
_____
_____
_____
_____
_____

Today I shall . . .

. . . try to make my relationship with God more than an object relationship, by incorporating the Torah to be my will.

July 16, 1993
July 6, 1994
July 25, 1995
July 14, 1996
Aug. 1, 1997
July 21, 1998

From the Scriptures

מֹנֵעַ בָּר יִקְּבֻהוּ לְאוֹם

One who withholds grain will be cursed by the nation (*Proverbs* 11:26).

This verse refers to people who have knowledge and refuse to share it with others. Our Sages strongly criticize these people. The Talmud states that prophets who did not convey their prophecies to the people committed a grave sin. The Sages extend this principle to one who has gained insights into the Torah and does not make them available to others.

This principle applies to skills and talents. In the Sanctuary, those *Kohanim* (priests) who possessed certain talents were soundly condemned if they guarded them as family secrets.

Exclusive economic rights such as patents and copyrights pose no problem; inventors and authors should enjoy the profits of their labor. However, when the question is not one of income, but merely one of pride in being the sole person to possess information that others could use and enjoy, the Talmud spares no words in its condemnation.

We pray to God to grant us wisdom, and if we possess a particular skill, we should recognize it as a Divine gift. We should be grateful for having been chosen as the recipient of this gift, and so we should never be selfish and claim this gift as our exclusive property. Rather, we should make our talents and knowledge available to everyone.

To the degree that people can teach, they are obligated to do so, regardless of their status in life. If others fail to take advantage of what a teacher has to offer, that is their misfortune.

NOTES

Today I shall . . .

. . . refrain from keeping to myself any knowledge or information that can be helpful to others.

כָּל עָרוּם יַעֲשֶׂה בְדָעַת וּכְסִיל יִפְרֹשׂ אִוֶּלֶת *From the*
Every clever person will act with good *Scriptures*
sense, whereas a fool will declare
his folly (*Proverbs* 13:16).

July 17, 1993
July 7, 1994
July 26, 1995
July 15, 1996
Aug. 2, 1997
July 22, 1998

The Malbim interprets this verse to mean that the clever person will find ways to resolve doubts, but the fool will create new ones.

The doubts to which the Malbim is referring are those that relate to Torah and *mitzvos*. A person who feels that observance of the *mitzvos* is an imposition may look for ways to justify non-compliance, and may do so by casting doubts on their validity. He may find what he feels to be inconsistencies, or argue that science challenges Torah principles. However, he succeeds in deceiving no one other than himself. Everyone else knows that he is not motivated by a search for truth, but merely by a desire to avoid any inconveniences.

A clever person, who may be subject to the same arguments, will realize that all of the objections of which he can think were known to greater minds than his. Our history is replete with intellectual giants and philosophical geniuses, whose absolute dedication to Torah and *mitzvos* was not affected in the least by all the challenges which may appear so cogent. One can safely rely on their conclusion that after considering all arguments, they concluded that the teachings of Torah were correct.

The person who uses arguments to evade Torah observance is placing his mind above that of the intellectual giants of our heritage. Only a fool would do that.

NOTES

Today I shall . . .

. . . rest assured that the teachings of the Torah are the correct way of life.

Erev
Rosh Chodesh
[Eve of the
New Month]
July 18, 1993
July 8, 1994
July 27, 1995
July 16, 1996
Aug. 3, 1997
July 23, 1998

From the וַיָּמָת מֶלֶךְ מִצְרַיִם וַיֵּאָנְחוּ בְנֵי יִשְׂרָאֵל מִן
Scriptures הָעֲבֹדָה וַיִּזְעָקוּ

he king of Egypt died, and the Israelites sighed in their enslavement, and they wailed (*Exodus* 2:23).

One commentary explains that the enslaved Israelites had feared to sigh or cry, because their ruthless taskmasters would punish them for "complaining." When the king of Egypt died, the entire country was in mourning, and the Israelites exploited this opportunity to cry, since at that point, crying was socially acceptable as a sign of mourning the death of the king.

There is a Yiddish idiom: "to look for a *badekens.*" A *badekens* is that part of the marriage ceremony where the parents cover the bride's face with a veil and give her their blessing. A highly emotional moment, it generally brings all present to cry. Therefore, if people are reluctant to cry for fear of revealing their emotional pain, they will "look for a *badekens*"; i.e. find an opportunity where crying is the norm, so that their crying will not indicate any personal pain.

Why should we need any subterfuge? What is wrong with showing our emotions? Why is crying equated with character weakness? Why should brave people not cry when they feel hurt? Where is the benefit in being an unemotional stone? We may read an account of a person who "cried unashamedly." Why should there be any shame in crying?

Our ancestors in Egypt suppressed their emotions because they feared their oppressors' retaliation. Whom do we fear when we suppress our emotions? Perhaps only our friends and peers, who are also suppressing their emotions because they fear what *we* will think of them. How foolish!

NOTES
_____
_____
_____
_____
_____
_____
_____
_____
_____
_____

Today I shall . . .

. . . feel free to express my emotions and not restrain myself for invalid reasons.

מִי שֶׁכַּעֲסוֹ וְרָגְזוֹ אַמִּיץ אֵינוֹ רָחוֹק מִן *From* המְשׁוּגָּעִים *the*

One whose anger and wrath are intense *Sages*
is not too far removed from insanity
(*Orchos Tzaddikim*, Chapter 12).

It is not unusual to observe a person explode at what
appears to be a minor provocation. When the response is
so disproportionate to the stimulus, most likely the anger is
not at all directed toward this provocation, but it has been
displaced from some other target.

For example, someone becomes angry at his employer,
but knows that to express this anger would jeopardize his
job. His suppressed anger continues to churn within him
and intensify precisely because it is being suppressed,
because the frustration of not being able to discharge it
adds to its fury. Upon coming home, someone in the
household says or does something trivial, and our em-
ployee erupts with a violent outburst of rage.

Irrationality borders on insanity, since both essentially
deny reality. In the above case, reality did not warrant so
extreme a reaction; hence, the inappropriate reaction can
be considered akin to insanity.

Granted that one cannot safely discharge his anger at his
boss, but suppressing the anger is not the only alternative.
A few moments of rational thought might help him get a
handle on his anger. He might ask himself, "Why did the
boss's comment affect me so deeply? Is it because I resent
the superior-inferior relationship we have? Is it because I
am insecure and I am interpreting his remark as a threat to
my livelihood? Is it because his comment aroused self-
doubts which I have been harboring?"

Analysis of an emotion can help dissipate it and prevent
us from developing a short fuse which will result in an
explosive reaction.

Rosh Chodesh
July 19, 1993
July 9, 1994
July 28, 1995
July 17, 1996
Aug. 4, 1997
July 24, 1998

NOTES

Today I shall . . .

. . . try to analyze my anger and avoid developing an
inappropriate response.

2

אב

July 20, 1993
July 10, 1994
July 29, 1995
July 18, 1996
Aug. 5, 1997
July 25, 1998

From **אַתָּה יוֹדֵעַ רָזֵי עוֹלָם וְתַעֲלוּמוֹת סִתְרֵי כָּל חָי**
our **Y**ou know the secrets of the world and
Prayers that which is concealed in the recesses
of every living thing (*Yom Kippur Machzor*).

In this prayer, we acknowledge that God knows all our
hidden, innermost thoughts. We then come to *vidui*
(confession) and verbalize all our misdeeds and faults. This
process seems a bit contradictory. Since we have just
stated that God knows all that we do, feel, and think, why
do we relate everything verbally to Him?

We have many thoughts and feelings which we would
like to disown. We may consider them so reprehensible
that we hate to admit that we harbor them. We therefore
repress them, keep them out of our awareness, and make
believe that they do not exist.

A make-believe world is not real. Telling ourselves that
these unacceptable thoughts and feelings do not exist will
get us nowhere. From the depths of our unconscious
minds, they will continue to clamor for recognition and
expression. They either succeed in coming to the fore, or
they drain our energies as we force them back down.

Our Sages suggested a solution. There is no point in
concealing our thoughts or feelings anywhere, for regardless of where they may be hidden, God knows them. We
shouldn't worry, for His love is unconditional, and He loves
us in spite of our shortcomings. Since God knows that we
have these thoughts and feelings, then at least as far as He
is concerned, the secret is out. If so, we might as well be
aware of them ourselves. And now, the need for repression
disappears.

Therefore, we acknowledge our shortcomings verbally,
not in order to tell God, but to tell ourselves that which He
already knows.

NOTES

Today I shall . . .

. . . try to eliminate the need for repression by realizing that
God knows what I have kept secret even from myself.

גְּדוֹלָה גְּמִילוּת חֲסָדִים *From* the *Sages*

Gemilus chassadim is very great (*Succah* 49b).

July 21, 1993
July 11, 1994
July 30, 1995
July 19, 1996
Aug. 6, 1997
July 26, 1998

Some people do favors for other people to get approval. This behavior pattern is based on the assumption that if they do not help others, they will not be liked. This assumption in turn derives from a basic feeling that they are unlikable, and that they must do something positive to overcome this unlikability.

Such behavior is fraught with serious consequences. If the object of their kindness fails to show approval, they are likely to feel angry, because in their eyes he or she took advantage of them by accepting the favor and not paying out the expected approval. In general, people who feel that they are unlikable do not manage anger well, for they feel that showing anger and resentment will alienate people from them. Their only solution then is to do more for people to overcome this new threat of alienation. This process sets up a vicious cycle that drains their energies as they continue to exhaust themselves in both doing for others and suppressing their increasing anger, resentment, and unhappiness.

Therefore, we should not do acts of kindness to incur the favor of others. Instead, we should concentrate on doing kindness because it is right, and we can then show kindness even to our sworn enemies, who will never like us regardless of what we may do for them.

NOTES

Today I shall . . .

. . . do good deeds because they are the right thing to do, rather than to ingratiate myself.

AV

4

אב

July 22, 1993
July 12, 1994
July 31, 1995
July 20, 1996
Aug. 7, 1997
July 27, 1998

From the Sages אֵין הַיִּרְאָה גּוֹרֶמֶת שֶׁיִּתְעַצֵּל אֶלָּא עַצְלָה גּוֹרֶמֶת לוֹ שֶׁיִּתְיָרֵא

It is not that fear causes indolence, but rather that indolence causes fear (*Mesilas Yesharim*, Chapter 9).

With this statement, Rabbi Luzzato makes a very important psychological point: we often deceive ourselves by reversing cause and effect. How many times have we heard (and said): "I am afraid to do so and so because . . ."? We convince ourselves that this thought is the truth, while the real reason is that we are lazy. However, since we do not wish to admit laziness, we rationalize that the fear of some danger is keeping us from taking action.

I have seen many young people, who are reluctant to go on with their education or undertake any constructive course, become "drifters." They attribute their problem to indecisiveness or anxiety. Analytical oriented therapists may spend many fruitless hours trying to discover the psychological roots for their indecisiveness and anxiety. Cognitive psychotherapists, who urge them into action first and deal with the underlying factors later, have much better success. Why? The indecisiveness or anxiety is not the cause, but merely an excuse these young people give themselves to cover up their indolence.

Luzzato's *Path of the Just* is both a great work of ethics and a treasury of psychological wisdom. As the author says in the introduction, it is a book that should not only be studied and thoroughly digested, but re-read many times. Group study and discussion of this great work are particularly enlightening.

Nothing can be so misleading and hence destructive to our lives as self-deception. Serious study of *Path of the Just* accomplishes two things: (1) the *mitzvah* of Torah study, and (2) invaluable lessons about how to avoid self-deception.

NOTES

_____
_____
_____
_____
_____
_____
_____
_____
_____

Today I shall . . .

. . . realize that I may be cleverly deceiving myself. Therefore, I will try to find ways to discover such self-deception.

מִזְמוֹר לְתוֹדָה . . . עִבְדוּ אֶת ה' בְּשִׂמְחָה *From the*
A song of gratitude . . . Serve God *Scriptures* with joy (*Psalms* 100:1-2).

AV

5

אב

July 23, 1993
July 13, 1994
Aug. 1, 1995
July 21, 1996
Aug. 8, 1997
July 28, 1998

People who have sustained adversity often feel very grateful for having been personally spared. When they walk away unscathed from a severe automobile accident, they may be thankful that they did not suffer serious injury. This gratitude may be so overwhelming that it utterly obscures the financial loss of the ruined car.

One might think that victims of automobile accidents or burnt houses would be bitter and defiant, expressing anger at God for the grave loss they had sustained. Instead, it appears to be within human nature to react differently. If we are alive and whole, and our children are safe, our gratitude may be so dominant that anger does not even appear.

Strangely, when lesser reversals occur, anger and bitterness do appear. The reason must be that we are not aware of any great danger from which we were spared. The Talmud states that the verse, *He does great works alone* (*Psalms* 136:4), means that God alone is aware of the wondrous acts that occur, and that humans who benefit from them are unaware of them.

A person would be wise to always be grateful, even when adversities occur, and apply the same attitude as when one walks away without a scratch from a serious automobile accident saying, "Thank God, I'm safe."

NOTES

Today I shall . . .

. . . make it a point to be grateful to God under all circumstances.

July 24, 1993
July 14, 1994
Aug. 2, 1995
July 22, 1996
Aug. 9, 1997
July 29, 1998

From the Scriptures

טוֹב פַּת חֲרֵבָה וְשַׁלְוָה בָהּ מִבַּיִת מָלֵא זִבְחֵי רִיב

A piece of dry bread with peace is better than an abundant house with strife (*Proverbs* 17:1).

One young man whom I treated for drug addiction expressed what must be on the minds of many young people who have either used drugs or resorted to other unhealthy types of behavior.

"I wanted the kicks and I wanted them now," he said. "I didn't see any reason to wait for anything because I had no dreams of a happy future. Why should I exert myself? To achieve success and wealth? I could go to law school, and if I were lucky, become a successful lawyer and make a great deal of money. I could then have a house in the suburbs with a huge garden and a swimming pool. I could have a luxury car and a summer home with a speedboat. Well, that is exactly what my home looks like, and our home must be one of the most miserable places in the world. My parents have always been bickering, and they are now in the middle of divorce proceedings. If knocking myself out to achieve success will bring me that kind of happiness, forget it!"

For some young people, the worst thing that happened to them was that the American dream came true — and proved itself to be a nightmare. Money alone cannot create a pleasant, peaceful household; only when the family's goals are spiritual can the household be a happy one. If this household is not rich, the absence of luxuries can be tolerated; if it is rich, the luxuries can be truly enjoyed.

NOTES

_____
_____
_____
_____
_____
_____
_____
_____
_____

Today I shall . . .

. . . re-examine my values with the realization that material success alone never produces happiness.

מְכַסֶּה פְשָׁעָיו לֹא יַצְלִיחַ *From the*

Oｎｅ who conceals his sins will not *Scriptures*
succeed (*Proverbs* 28:13).

July 25, 1993
July 15, 1994
Aug. 3, 1995
July 23, 1996
Aug. 10, 1997
July 30, 1998

Another verse states, *Fortunate is one who conceals his faults* (*Psalms* 32:1). How are these two verses to be reconciled?

There are two types of concealment. People who realize that they have done wrong and now feel badly about it are obviously not likely to make a public declaration. Rather, they will be remorseful and resolve not to make the same mistake again. They do not deceive themselves and think they have done no wrong. The Psalmist speaks of these people and says, *Fortunate is he whose sins God will not consider, and there is no deceit in his spirit* (ibid. 32:2). This honesty leads to forgiveness, and the concealment referred to is in contrast to those who flaunt their wrongful behavior, thereby indicating that they believe it to be correct.

Proverbs is referring to those who conceal their sins from themselves, either by repression or by any of the many distortions that people use to justify their errant behavior. These people are dishonest with themselves, and they stand in contrast to the person who "has no deceit in his spirit."

Obviously, people who deceive themselves cannot be honest with others, even if they try to do so. The unlucky prospector, for instance, who actually believes that his fool's gold is genuine, will think he is being honest when he sells it as genuine. If his "innocent" dishonesty is exposed, his loss of trustworthiness will preclude his being successful in anything else.

Honesty is certainly commendable, but we must first make certain that we are honest with ourselves.

NOTES

Today I shall . . .

. . . examine myself, my emotions, and my motivations, to avoid self-deception.

AV

8

אב

July 26, 1993
July 16, 1994
Aug. 4, 1995
July 24, 1996
Aug. 11, 1997
July 31, 1998

From the Sages כֵּיוָן שֶׁעָבַר אָדָם עֲבֵירָה וְשָׁנָה בָּהּ . . . נַעֲשֵׂית לוֹ כְּהֶיתֵּר

If a person commits a sin and repeats it, it appears to him as permissible (*Yoma* 86b).

As every scientist knows, different substances have different properties. Some liquids freeze at 0 degrees C; others at minus 60 degrees C. Some materials burn at higher temperatures than others, and some metals have greater resilience than others. In order to know how to work with any substance, we must know what its particular properties are. Ignorance of a substance's properties results in failure of the project at best and disaster at worst, as in the case of an engineer who overestimates the strength of the cables that suspend a bridge.

What are the properties of a human being? Physically, we know that we can survive only within a certain range of temperatures. But what about the guidelines for our spiritual survival? It would be foolish to think that there are no limits. Excellent guidelines do exist, and these are available in Jewish works on ethics.

The above Talmudic passage is an example. A person knows that doing something is wrong, but submits to temptation and does it anyway. He or she is likely to feel guilty, do *teshuvah* and thereby avoid repeating the act. However, if he or she fails to do so and repeats the forbidden act, the stimulus necessary for *teshuvah* may be lost. The Talmudic authors were astute students of human behavior, and they tell us that two consecutive commissions of a wrong act may cause people to totally lose their perspective; they are now apt to develop an attitude whereby what was once wrong is now perfectly permissible.

We do not have much leeway. If we do not promptly try to amend a wrong act, we may lose the opportunity to do so, because if we repeat it a second time, we may no longer realize that it is wrong.

NOTES

Today I shall . . .

. . . resolve to promptly do *teshuvah* at the first awareness that I have done something wrong.

Fast of Tishah B'Av
[When 9 Av falls on the Sabbath, the fast is observed on Sunday.]
July 27, 1993
July 17, 1994
Aug. 5, 1995
July 25, 1996
Aug. 12, 1997
Aug. 1, 1998

אֵיכָה יָשְׁבָה בָדָד *From the*
Scriptures

H ow she [Jerusalem] sits in isolation!
(*Lamentations* 1:1).

The opening verse of the book of Scriptures that depicts the fall of Jerusalem cites a state of isolation. *Badad* connotes loneliness, abandonment, and the state of being shunned by others. This term also appears in the Torah in regard to the expulsion of a *metzora* (someone who suffers from a disease called *tzaraas*), who is to be isolated from the community (*Leviticus* 13:46).

The Talmud states that the affliction of the *metzora* is in retribution for the sin of *lashon hara*. Indulging in harmful talk brings about enmity and divisiveness. Gossip and slander can turn people against one another and sow suspicion where once there had been trust and friendship.

The Talmud states that when Jews were united, and when there was no *lashon hara* among them, they were triumphant, even though they were far from perfect in other respects. On the other hand, when *lashon hara* causes dissension, all other merits may not suffice to tip the scales.

On the ninth day of Av, Jerusalem became *badad*, shunned by its neighbors, shunned by its former friends, and to all outward appearances, even shunned by God. Why? Like the *metzora,* the Israelites had been guilty of behavior that brought about divisiveness. By bringing about the state of *badad* within their ranks, they themselves became *badad*, isolated from God.

We must jettison all personal whims and desires that stand in the way of Jewish unity, for in unity lies our salvation.

NOTES

Today I shall . . .

. . . try to find ways in which I can bring myself closer to other Jews and fastidiously avoid any behavior that can cause divisiveness.

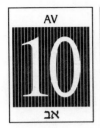

July 28, 1993
July 18, 1994
Aug. 6, 1995
July 26, 1996
Aug. 13, 1997
Aug. 2, 1998

From the Scriptures

וְהָדַרְתָּ פְּנֵי זָקֵן וְיָרֵאתָ מֵאֱלֹקֶיךָ אֲנִי ה'

You shall honor an elderly person, and you shall fear your God, for I am God (*Leviticus* 19:32).

This *mitzvah* is of particular importance in our times, when many people are living to an older age.

Living longer does not always bring the joys of the golden years that some people expect. The "fifty-two weeks of vacation a year" after retirement are often not a blessing; finding themselves with much time on their hands, many retired people are extremely bored.

Not all couples age together; as our life spans increase, so does the possibility of losing our partner and remaining alone for many years. Children may live far away, and even when close, they may lead busy lives with little time to devote to their aging parents. The wear and tear diseases — emphysema, arthritis, osteoporosis — may make many people housebound. Failing sight and hearing make the radio and television useless companions. While we pray for long life, the "golden years" may be very, very lonely.

In a society which prizes productivity, the elderly do not have much value, and although society may pay its debt to them (albeit in inadequate payments), it may be done with an attitude that is characteristic of a debtor to a creditor: resentment.

As is evident in the construction of the verse cited above, the Torah equates honoring the elderly with honoring God Himself.

NOTES

Today I shall . . .

. . . do something to make the life of an elderly person a bit more pleasant.

כְּרָחֹק מִזְרָח מִמַּעֲרָב הִרְחִיק מִמֶּנּוּ אֶת *From the*
פְּשָׁעֵינוּ *Scriptures*

As far as east is from west, that is how far God has removed our sins from us (*Psalms* 103:12).

July 29, 1993
July 19, 1994
Aug. 7, 1995
July 27, 1996
Aug. 14, 1997
Aug. 3, 1998

The usual interpretation is that when one does complete *teshuvah*, one's sins are removed. According to this interpretation, east and west are understood as extremely remote from each other. Another interpretation is based on the exact opposite; namely, that east and west are not far from each other at all. If we face east and make a 180-degree turn, we are now facing west, even though we remain in the very same place. Applying this concept to *teshuvah*, we do not have to travel to great lengths to achieve *teshuvah* and to have our sins removed. All we need to do is turn around and face another direction.

The word *teshuvah*, which means "to turn back," contains this very principle. If we travel on the highway and discover that we have been heading in the wrong direction, progress begins the very moment we turn the car around and head in the right direction. That there may be a delay in reaching the destination should be of little concern, because in the journey of life, the Judge awards merits according to effort rather than according to reaching any one fixed endpoint.

More than one person has made the mistake of making a left turn where a right turn was called for, and only obstinate, opinionated, "I am never wrong" people will refuse to stop at the first opportunity available to inquire and make sure that they are headed in the right direction.

We are all fallible. We may inadvertently make wrong turns in life. How are we to know if we are heading in the right direction unless we stop and ask?

NOTES

Today I shall . . .

. . . try to avail myself of a competent spiritual mentor to help me in following the correct path in life.

July 30, 1993
July 20, 1994
Aug. 8, 1995
July 28, 1996
Aug. 15, 1997
Aug. 4, 1998

From the Scriptures

כִּי הַמִּשְׁפָּט לֵאלֹקִים הוּא

For the judgment belongs to God (*Deuteronomy* 1:17).

When the *Tzaddik* of Sanz assumed his first rabbinic position, he was approached by someone who wished to sue in the rabbinical court the wealthiest, most powerful person in the community. The *Tzaddik* sent a court summons to this man, but the *shammash* (bailiff) returned saying that the man had very rudely turned him away.

The *Tzaddik* sent a second summons. The defendant responded with a message, "You are new here and very young. You may not be aware that I am the one who supports all religious activities in the community. To be a rabbi in the community requires my approval. Be aware of this and retract your summons."

The *Tzaddik* sent a third summons, warning that failure to honor it would result in dire consequences. The rich man then came and surprisingly brought the plaintiff with him. He explained that the entire thing had been a sham that he had staged simply to test whether the new rabbi would have the courage to implement the law, even when his own position was in jeopardy.

The community's number one citizen welcomed the rabbi, stating, "You are the kind of rabbi we need."

Not everyone feels this way. Some people try to use "pull" to receive preferential treatment. They should realize that when justice is the issue, it is corrupt to seek preferential treatment and corrupt to give it.

The judgment belongs to God, and when litigants and judges are engaged in a *din Torah*, they are in the immediate Divine Presence, and there can be no favoritism.

NOTES

Today I shall . . .

. . . remember not to show favoritism, even when under pressure.

וְעָשִׂיתָ מַעֲקֶה לְגַגֶּךָ . . . כִּי יִפֹּל הַנֹּפֵל מִמֶּנּוּ *From the*
You shall make a fence to your roof *Scriptures*
. . . so that the falling person should
not fall therefrom (*Deuteronomy* 22:8).

July 31, 1993
July 21, 1994
Aug. 9, 1995
July 29, 1996
Aug. 16, 1997
Aug. 5, 1998

Rashi notes the unusual term *the falling person should not fall* and explains that even though the person who may be injured may be "a falling person," i.e. someone who merited punishment for wrongs he or she had committed, nevertheless, you should not be the vehicle for punishment.

Some people act in a hostile manner toward a certain person, even going so far as to condemn him and cause him harm. They may justify their behavior by saying, "Why, that no good . . . do you know what he did? He did this and that, and so he deserves to be tarred and feathered."

The Talmud states that God uses good people to deliver rewards, but when punishment is warranted, He chooses people who themselves deserve punishment. Hence, it is not good to be a punitive instrument. The Torah cautions us not to intervene in Divine judgment. God's system is adequate. We should take reasonable actions to protect our interests so that they are not harmed by others, but we should not take upon ourselves to mete out punishment.

The principle of fencing in a roof applies to every situation where someone else might come to harm as a result of something we did or did not do. Being a responsible person requires using reason. As the Talmud says, "A wise person is one who can foresee the future" (*Tamid* 32a). We don't necessarily need prophetic foresight, just the ability to calculate what might result from our actions.

NOTES

Today I shall . . .

. . . be cautious to behave in such a manner that no one can come to harm as a result of my actions.

Aug. 1, 1993
July 22, 1994
Aug. 10, 1995
July 30, 1996
Aug. 17, 1997
Aug. 6, 1998

*From the
Scriptures*

הוֹד וְהָדָר פָּעֳלוֹ וְצִדְקָתוֹ עֹמֶדֶת לָעַד

His deeds are glory and beauty, and His righteousness remains forever
(*Psalms* 111:3).

The Hebrew phrase, *His righteousness remains forever*, can also be read as "His *tzedakah* remains forever."

The Talmud relates that Rabbi Akiva was once collecting funds for a worthy cause. As he approached the home of a regular contributor, he heard him tell his son, "Go to the market and buy leftover vegetables because they are cheaper." Rabbi Akiva then turned away and returned only after most of the needed money had been collected.

"Why did you not come to me first?" the man asked.

Rabbi Akiva told him of the conversation he had overheard, and that he did not wish to impose upon him for a larger donation when he was in financial straits.

"You heard only the communication with my son, but you were not privy to my communication with God," the man said. "When I economize, I do so on my household expenses. The *tzedakah* remains unchanged."

When budget cuts must be made, everyone has their particular priorities. Some people may cut their *tzedakah* while retaining the scheduled trade-in for a new-model car. Some people will bargain hard for a reduction in their children's tuition, while they accept other prices without bickering.

The Psalmist tells us that the measure of a person's action is that his or her *tzedakah* remains forever; i.e. *tzedakah* is the last budget item to be cut.

NOTES

Today I shall . . .

. . . rethink my priorities. The values I place on things may be reflected by which items I am willing to do without.

D o not put a stumbling block before the blind וְלִפְנֵי עִוֵּר לֹא תִתֵּן מִכְשֹׁל *From the Scriptures* (*Leviticus* 19:14).

AV

15

אב

Aug. 2, 1993
July 23, 1994
Aug. 11, 1995
July 31, 1996
Aug. 18, 1997
Aug. 7, 1998

The Talmud extends this concept to include giving anyone wrong advice. Clearly, no rational person would knowingly put an obstacle in front of a blind person. Similarly, no one with a conscience would knowingly give anyone bad advice, but sometimes people inadvertently do so because they fail to think things through.

While good intentions are laudable, they are not always enough. "Here, take some of these pills (for sleep, headache, anxiety, joint pains). My doctor gave them to me, and they are excellent." It is well to remember that "one person's meat is another's poison." This principle cannot be more true than when it comes to medications.

Amateur psychology is a popular field; so many people like to offer advice to husbands, wives, and parents as to what to do about their school troubles, marital problems, and children's discipline. Less than amateur legal advice is also available in abundance.

Our egos may feel good when we offer advice, and we may sincerely believe that the advice we are giving is sound, but great caution is necessary to avoid unintentionally misleading someone. If any of our advice is wrong, we have in fact "put a stumbling block before the blind."

NOTES

Today I shall . . .

. . . be cautious when offering advice and moreover avoid recommending something unless I am absolutely certain that it is the right thing to do.

AV

16

אב

Aug. 3, 1993
July 24, 1994
Aug. 12, 1995
Aug. 1, 1996
Aug. 19, 1997
Aug. 8, 1998

From the אֹתִי עָזְבוּ מְקוֹר מַיִם חַיִּים לַחְצֹב לָהֶם
Scriptures בֹּארֹת בֹּארֹת נִשְׁבָּרִים אֲשֶׁר לֹא יָכִלוּ
הַמָּיִם

They have forsaken Me, the source of life-giving waters, to dig wells that cannot give water *(Jeremiah 2:13)*.

In a world filled with nationalistic pride, where nations, ethnic groups, and individuals are all searching for their historic roots, it is nothing less than mind-boggling that a people who has an unparalleled wealth of recorded and documented history and literature would so ignore its rich heritage. What do most Jewish children know about their people? Only a fraction receive more than a fragmentary awareness of Jewish history. All can identify Twain and Poe, but few know Maimonides or Yehudah HaLevi. They are likely to know much about Nathan Hale and even Simon Bolivar but have never heard of Rabbi Akiva and Bar Kochba. They may remember the Alamo, but not Massada.

Why do we so despise ourselves? Where is our pride? How can we expect our youth to develop a sense of self-esteem if by our own dereliction we fail to convey to them a justified sense of pride in who they are?

We do not need to drink at others' wells. Our own is filled with sweet, life-sustaining water.

NOTES

Today I shall . . .

. . . do whatever I can to further Jewish education both among adults and children.

לֹא תָלִין נִבְלָתוֹ עַל הָעֵץ . . . כִּי קִלְלַת *From the*
אֱלֹקִים תָּלוּי *Scriptures*

[If a criminal has been executed by hanging] his body may not remain suspended overnight . . . because it is an insult to God (*Deuteronomy* 21:23).

Aug. 4, 1993
July 25, 1994
Aug. 13, 1995
Aug. 2, 1996
Aug. 20, 1997
Aug. 9, 1998

Rashi explains that since man was created in the image of God, anything that disparages man is disparaging God as well.

Chilul Hashem, bringing disgrace to the Divine Name, is one of the greatest sins in the Torah. The opposite of *chilul Hashem* is *kiddush Hashem*, sanctifying the Divine Name. While this topic has several dimensions to it, there is a living *kiddush Hashem* which occurs when a Jew behaves in a manner that merits the respect and admiration of other people, who thereby respect the Torah of Israel.

What is *chilul Hashem*? One Talmudic author stated, "It is when I buy meat from the butcher and delay paying him" (*Yoma* 86a). To cause someone to say that a Torah scholar is anything less than scrupulous in meeting his obligations is to cause people to lose respect for the Torah.

Suppose someone offers us a business deal of questionable legality. Is the personal gain worth the possible dishonor that we bring not only upon ourselves, but on our nation? If our personal reputation is ours to handle in whatever way we please, shouldn't we handle the reputation of our nation and the God we represent with maximum care?

Jews have given so much, even their lives, for *kiddush Hashem*. Can we not forego a few dollars to avoid *chilul Hashem*?

NOTES

Today I shall . . .

. . . be scrupulous in all my transactions and relationships to avoid the possibility of bringing dishonor to my God and people.

AV

18

אב

Aug. 5, 1993
July 26, 1994
Aug. 14, 1995
Aug. 3, 1996
Aug. 21, 1997
Aug. 10, 1998

From the **V**anity is a sign of ignorance of Torah
Sages (*Kiddushin* 49b).

סִימָן לְגַסּוּת עֲנִיּוּת הַתּוֹרָה

The Talmud and the ethical works condemn vanity as the worst of all character traits. Whereas the Divine Presence is infinite, and God does not abandon even the worst sinner, He cannot countenance a vain person: *Haughty eyes [vanity] . . . him I cannot tolerate* (*Psalms* 101:5).

It is not difficult to understand the Divine intolerance, since we ourselves also are uncomfortable in the presence of those who boast of their achievements, try to impress everyone with name dropping, and have an attitude of superiority and condescension. While we may be unable to avoid these people's company, we certainly do not try to cultivate friendships with them. The irony is that while we may despise this attitude in others, we may sometimes fall into the trap of harboring it ourselves.

Luzzato states that the magnitude of one's vanity is directly proportional to the magnitude of one's folly (*Path of the Just*, Chapter 23). Truly wise people are not vain.

Imagine yourself speaking to an audience through a computerized public address system which has been so programmed that anytime you say something to impress other people with your greatness, the words that come out of the loudspeaker are, "I am a fool." How careful you would be to avoid making a spectacle of yourself!

Such a computerized speaker system actually exists within each of us, says Luzzato. Anytime people boast about themselves, they are announcing to the whole world, "I am a fool." Any self-respecting person would be cautious not to make such a declaration.

NOTES

_____
_____
_____
_____
_____
_____
_____
_____
_____
_____

Today I shall . . .

. . . be careful not to humiliate myself by trying to impress others with how great I am.

316 / GROWING EACH DAY

כִּי הָאֱלֹקִים בַּשָּׁמַיִם וְאַתָּה עַל הָאָרֶץ עַל כֵּן *From the*
יִהְיוּ דְבָרֶיךָ מְעַטִּים *Scriptures*

AV

19

אב

Because God is in Heaven and you are on the earth, therefore let your **words be few** (*Ecclesiastes* 5:1).

Aug. 6, 1993
July 27, 1994
Aug. 15, 1995
Aug. 4, 1996
Aug. 22, 1997
Aug. 11, 1998

I remember reading that every person is born with an allotted number of words that one may speak during one's lifetime. When this allotment is exhausted, one's life comes to an end. This idea would explain the above verse: God is infinite, but people live in a finite world where everything has its limitations. Some things may be greater, other things may be less, but nothing on earth is infinite. Since the number of words a person may speak must also be finite, we should speak as little as possible simply to extend our lives.

Even if one does not accept this concept as factual, it is an excellent guideline. People on a fixed income will budget themselves carefully, since any unwise expenditures may deprive them of the means to obtain necessities. If we think of our words as being limited, then those squandered in non-essential conversation have become unavailable to us for more important things.

When we discover that we have wasted money, we are likely to become very upset with ourselves. We usually then resolve to be more cautious and discriminating in our future purchases. Let us now think back on how many words we have wasted, and even if they were not outright lies or slander, nevertheless, they were simply useless. We would be wise to make a reckoning of our words as well as our money and similarly resolve not to be wasteful of them in the future.

NOTES

Today I shall . . .

. . . consider my words as valuable assets which, while in sufficient supply, are nonetheless limited; I will therefore try to act accordingly.

Aug. 7, 1993
July 28, 1994
Aug. 16, 1995
Aug. 5, 1996
Aug. 23, 1997
Aug. 12, 1998

From the Sages

אַרְבַּע מִדּוֹת בְּנוֹתְנֵי צְדָקָה . . . לֹא יִתֵּן וְלֹא יִתְּנוּ אֲחֵרִים רָשָׁע

There are four categories of people who give tzedakah ... [the fourth of which is] one who does not give and discourages others from giving; he is wicked (*Ethics of the Fathers* 5:16).

Since this passage is listing varieties of those who *give* tzedakah, why does it include a category of someone who does *not* give? Not giving is not a sub-type of giving.

In the effort to streamline everything and make life less complicated, we have centralized many things, including tzedakah. Communities often have one organization that has one major fund drive a year. Those people who wish to operate in this manner are certainly at liberty to do so, but when they insist that this unified drive be the only one in the community, and they discourage all other tzedakah collections or campaigns, they are actually infringing on the privilege of others to dispense their tzedakah as they see fit.

I have the right to invest in mutual funds and allow others to diversify my investments for me, but I also have the right to choose for myself which stocks I wish to own. No one has the authority to deprive me of the right to make my own selections.

The passage cited is indeed considering only those who give, but among them there is a sub-type of those who give only once to a centralized drive and refuse to give to any other collection. While they certainly have the right to do so, when they try to exert their authority to prevent other collections in the community, while insisting that everyone must give only as they do, their behavior is unacceptable.

If you give tzedakah once, you have done one *mitzvah*. If you give tzedakah twenty times (even if you give a smaller amount each time), you have done twenty *mitzvos*.

NOTES

_____
_____
_____
_____
_____
_____
_____
_____
_____

Today I shall . . .

. . . retain my right to give tzedakah as I see fit.

חֲכָמֵנוּ כָּלְלוּ הַחֲלָקִים הָאֵלֶה בְּסֵדֶר . . . לְפִי *From* הַהַדְרָגָה הַמִּצְטָרֶכֶת *the*

Our Sages gathered these sections in an *Sages* order . . . according to the requisite steps (Introduction to *Path of the Just*).

Aug. 8, 1993
July 29, 1994
Aug. 17, 1995
Aug. 6, 1996
Aug. 24, 1997
Aug. 13, 1998

While character refinement is an important and desirable goal, we must be careful to stride toward it in a reasonable and orderly manner. Overreaching ourselves may be counterproductive.

Physical growth is a gradual process. In fact, it is not even uniform; the first two decades are a sequence of growth spurts and latency periods. Generally, the body does not adjust well to sudden changes, even when they are favorable. For instance, obese people who lose weight too rapidly may experience a variety of unpleasant symptoms. Although the weight loss is certainly in the interest of health, the body needs time to adjust to the change.

If we are convinced, as we should be, that spirituality is desirable, we might be tempted to make radical changes in our lives. We may drop everything and set out on a crash course that we think will lead to rapid attainment of the goal. This plan is most unwise, because psychologically as well as physically, our systems need time to consume new information, digest it, and prepare ourselves for the next level.

Luzzato's monumental work on ethics, *The Path of the Just*, is based on a Talmudic passage which lists ten consecutive steps toward spirituality. Luzzato cautions: "A person should not desire to leap to the opposite extreme in one moment, because this will simply not succeed, but should continue bit by bit" (Chapter 15).

NOTES

Today I shall . . .

. . . resolve to work on my spirituality gradually and be patient in its attainment.

AV

אב

Aug. 9, 1993
July 30, 1994
Aug. 18, 1995
Aug. 7, 1996
Aug. 25, 1997
Aug. 14, 1998

From the חֲזַק וְנִתְחַזַּק בְּעַד עַמֵּנוּ וּבְעַד עָרֵי אֱלֹקֵינוּ
Scriptures Let us strengthen ourselves for our nation and in behalf of the cities of our God (*II Samuel* 10:12).

At our rehabilitation center, we used to call the weekly meeting of all the residents and staff "Bus Stop." A great many people may be congregated at a bus station, but each person is going his or her own way. Everyone at the bus stop is detached from everyone else, and there is no common goal. Nothing ties these people together, except that all are making use of the bus station for their individual purposes. Yet, it is not a place of anarchy, chaos, or unruly behavior. All is orderly and peaceful.

Our "Bus Stop" was intended to focus on whether each person was pursuing a private goal, or whether he or she had a sense of community, where people could have a broader perspective and join together in achieving common goals that could not be reached individually.

We have various types of communities where we work together: cities, neighborhood organizations, unions, religious and educational institutions, cultural groups, and various other special interest groups. In some, our membership is merely perfunctory, and while we pay lip service to the sense of community, essentially we proceed on our own. If conflict arises, we choose the individual good over the good of the community.

A true sense of community among all participants would avoid such conflict, and all could benefit from it.

NOTES

Today I shall . . .

. . . examine my commitment to the various communities of which I am a part, and work toward a sense of community that will be mutually beneficial.

יַעֲשֶׂה [אָדָם] אֶת כָּל דְּבָרָיו בְּסֵדֶר *From the Sages*

A person should do everything in an orderly manner (*Rabbi Yisrael of Salant*).

Aug. 10, 1993
July 31, 1994
Aug. 19, 1995
Aug. 8, 1996
Aug. 26, 1997
Aug. 15, 1998

Rabbi Yisrael of Salant founded the *mussar* movement, a formal and programmed study of ethics. All his writings deal with ways to achieve spirituality. How can orderliness and organization be a method to achieve spirituality?

People on vacation use their time haphazardly. They arise at any time of the day and let their whim determine their activities. They feel no accountability and no purpose in what they are doing.

The essence of Judaism is the concept that each person has a mission on this earth. There are no "after-work" hours, and one is never really on vacation from working toward an ultimate goal. While judicious rest and relaxation are necessary for optimum health, they are in fact part of the "workday." One cannot do things according to whim. Within reasonable parameters, a person's life should be orderly and scheduled.

Employees are held accountable for time while they are on the job. Schedules allow for lunch and for coffee breaks, but they are not free to do whatever they wish, whenever they wish.

A person should know that we are on earth "on a job," and since we are accountable for every minute, it is essential that we have order in our lives.

NOTES

Today I shall . . .

. . . try to bring greater order into my life, knowing that I am here for a specific mission.

Aug. 11, 1993
Aug. 1, 1994
Aug. 20, 1995
Aug. 9, 1996
Aug. 27, 1997
Aug. 16, 1998

From the Scriptures כִּי נָפַלְתִּי קָמְתִּי

For after I fell, I have arisen (*Michah* 7:8).

The *Midrash* comments: "Had I not fallen, I would not have arisen," and so indicates that some heights are not attainable without an antecedent fall.

Obviously, no one designs a fall in the hope that it may lead to a greater elevation. Michah's message, however, is that if a person should suffer a reversal, he or she should not despair, because it may be a necessary prelude to achieving a higher level than would have been possible otherwise.

We can find many analogies to this concept. When we swing a pickaxe, we first lower it behind ourselves in order to deliver a blow with maximum force. Runners often back up behind the starting line to get a "running start." In many things, starting from a "minus" position provides a momentum that would otherwise not be attainable.

When things are going well, most people let well enough alone. The result? Mediocrity has become acceptable. Changing might involve some risk, and even if we could achieve greater things, we might not wish to take a chance when things are proceeding quite satisfactorily. However, when we are in an intolerable situation, we are compelled to do something, and this impetus may bring about creativity and progress.

We even see this concept in the account of creation in *Genesis*. First there was darkness, then came light.

NOTES

Today I shall . . .

. . . realize that a reversal may be the seed of future growth, and I must never despair.

כִּי אָדָם אֵין צַדִּיק בָּאָרֶץ אֲשֶׁר יַעֲשֶׂה טּוֹב *From the*
וְלֹא יֶחֱטָא *Scriptures*

There is no person on earth so righteous, who does only good and does not sin (*Ecclesiastes* 7:20).

Aug. 12, 1993
Aug. 2, 1994
Aug. 21, 1995
Aug. 10, 1996
Aug. 28, 1997
Aug. 17, 1998

Reading the suggestions for ridding oneself of character defects, someone might say, "These are all very helpful for someone who has character defects, but I do not see anything about myself that is defective."

In the above-cited verse, Solomon states what we should all know: no one is perfect. People who cannot easily find imperfections within themselves must have a perception so grossly distorted that they may not even be aware of major defects. By analogy, if a person cannot hear anything, it is not that the whole world has become absolutely silent, but that he or she has lost all sense of hearing and may thus not be able to hear even the loudest thunder.

In his monumental work, *Duties of the Heart,* Rabbeinu Bachaye quotes a wise man who told his disciples, "If you do not find defects within yourself, I am afraid you have the greatest defect of all: vanity." In other words, people who see everything from an "I am great/right" perspective will of course believe that they do no wrong.

When people can see no faults in themselves, it is generally because they feel so inadequate that the awareness of any personal defects would be devastating. Ironically, vanity is a defense against low self-esteem. If we accept ourselves as fallible human beings and also have a sense of self-worth, we can become even better than we are.

NOTES

Today I shall . . .

. . . be aware that if I do not find things within myself to correct, it may be because I am threatened by such discoveries.

Aug. 13, 1993
Aug. 3, 1994
Aug. 22, 1995
Aug. 11, 1996
Aug. 29, 1997
Aug. 18, 1998

*From
the
Sages*

וֶהֱוֵי מְקַבֵּל אֶת כָּל הָאָדָם בְּסֵבֶר פָּנִים יָפוֹת

Greet every person in a pleasant manner
(*Ethics of the Fathers* 1:15).

Occasionally, when I walk into an office, the receptionist greets me rudely. Granted, I came to see someone else, and a receptionist's disposition is immaterial to me. Yet, an unpleasant reception may cast a pall.

A smile costs nothing. Greeting someone with a smile even when one does not feel like smiling is not duplicity. It is simply providing a pleasant atmosphere, such as we might do with flowers or attractive pictures.

As a rule, "How are you?" is not a question to which we expect an answer. However, when someone with whom I have some kind of relationship poses this question, I may respond, "Not all that great. Would you like to listen?" We may then spend a few minutes, in which I unburden myself and invariably begin to feel better. This favor is usually reciprocated, and we are both thus beneficiaries of free psychotherapy.

This, too, complies with the Talmudic requirement to greet a person in a pleasant manner. An exchange of feelings that can alleviate someone's emotional stress is even more pleasant than an exchange of smiles.

It takes so little effort to be a real *mentsch*.

NOTES

_____
_____
_____
_____
_____
_____
_____
_____
_____

Today I shall ...

... try to greet everyone in a pleasant manner, and where appropriate offer a listening ear.

אַל תּאֹמַר מֶה הָיָה שֶׁהַיָּמִים הָרִאשֹׁנִים הָיוּ *From the*
טוֹבִים מֵאֵלֶּה כִּי לֹא מֵחָכְמָה שָׁאַלְתָּ עַל זֶה *Scriptures*

Do not say that the earlier days were
better than these, because this is
not a quest that comes from wisdom
(*Ecclesiastes* 7:10).

Aug. 14, 1993
Aug. 4, 1994
Aug. 23, 1995
Aug. 12, 1996
Aug. 30, 1997
Aug. 19, 1998

I have been in the practice of relaxing myself each day with self-hypnosis, which allows me to go back in time and relive some very pleasant childhood experiences.

One time, I was relaxing (after having just emerged from the whirlpool treatment in a spa), and I used the opportunity to go back in time to enjoy a fun-filled day in a summer camp, some forty years earlier. Only later did it occur to me that at the spa I was *also* having a wonderful time! Why could I not enjoy this present moment? Why did I have to go back in time to an experience of the past?

The reason, I think, is because that enjoyable day at camp had closure; it had ended having indeed been a great day. While the spa was equally pleasant, there was still an uncertainty as to whether this spirit would be maintained. At any moment, there might have been a call from the office with some disturbing news. The subconscious expectation that something upsetting might happen did not (and still does not) allow me to fully enjoy the present.

King Solomon says that it is not wise to reflect upon the past as idyllic. Why? When circumstances are favorable, wisdom allows us to actually enjoy the present. As the Psalmist says, *He will not fear bad tidings, his heart being firm in trust in God* (*Psalms* 112:7). There is no reason to have an attitude of foreboding. While it is foolish to build castles in the sky, it is equally foolish to build dungeons in the cellar.

NOTES

Today I shall . . .

. . . try to enjoy whatever I can to the utmost, and trust in God for the future.

Aug. 15, 1993
Aug. 5, 1994
Aug. 24, 1995
Aug. 13, 1996
Aug. 31, 1997
Aug. 20, 1998

From the Scriptures חָכְמַת עָרוּם הָבִין דַּרְכּוֹ

A clever wise person will understand his way (*Proverbs* 14:8).

This verse can be applied to understanding the ways and tactics of the *yetzer hara*. The *yetzer hara* has one mission: to cause a person to self-destruct. However, the *yetzer hara* is very wily. Realizing that a person will defend against his evil seductions, it seeks first to disarm the person.

Suppose that I was your sworn enemy, determined to destroy you. It would be foolish for me to make a frontal attack, since you would undoubtedly defend yourself. I must therefore seek to first disarm you.

Each time I meet you, I greet you pleasantly and inquire as to your welfare. I try to find occasions where I may be of actual help to you. Although you may have initially been wary that I might be hostile to you, my repeated benevolent behavior eventually leads you not only to drop your suspicions, but even to believe that I am your friend and have your best interests at heart. Once I have achieved this, I am then free to do whatever I wish to destroy you, since your assumption of my good intentions has caused you to relinquish your guard.

The *yetzer hara* operates in the exact same way. It may tell you to do things for yourself that seem innocent enough. "How can you go to *shul* in such a snowstorm? You may catch cold. You can pray at home, because God is everywhere." Strange, this same argument does not keep you from going to the office.

A truly wise person will think, "If I were the *yetzer hara*, what measures might I use to mislead someone?" And then use the very same cleverness to outwit the *yetzer hara*.

NOTES

Today I shall . . .

. . . be on the alert for any suggestions that might be the work of the *yetzer hara*.

There is nothing **new** under the sun וְאֵין כָּל חָדָשׁ תַּחַת הַשָּׁמֶשׁ *From the* *Scriptures*
(*Ecclesiastes* 1:9).

America was always there, long before Columbus discovered it. Penicillin killed bacteria long before Fleming discovered it. We could go on to list numerous discoveries which could have benefited mankind long before they came to our attention.

It has been said that when the student is ready, the teacher appears. We can say the same thing about discoveries: they become evident to us when we are ready for them.

Just what constitutes this state of readiness is still a mystery. While technological advances are usually contingent upon earlier progress, many other discoveries were right before our eyes, but we did not see them.

This concept is as true of ideas and concepts in our lives as it is true of scientific discoveries. The truth is out there, but we may fail to see it.

In psychotherapy, a therapist often points out something to a patient numerous times to no avail, until one day, "Eureka!" — a breakthrough. The patient may then complain, "Doctor, I have been coming to you for almost two years. Why did you never point this out to me before?" At this point, many therapists want to tear out their hair.

Just as patients have resistances to insights in psychotherapy, we may also resist awareness of important ideas and concepts in our lives. If we could sweep out these resistances, we could see ourselves with much more clarity. We must try to keep our minds open, particularly to those ideas we may not be too fond of.

Erev Rosh Chodesh
[Eve of the New Month]
Aug. 16, 1993
Aug. 6, 1994
Aug. 25, 1995
Aug. 14, 1996
Sept. 1, 1997
Aug. 21, 1998

NOTES

Today I shall . . .

. . . try to keep an open mind so that I may discover ideas that can be advantageous to myself and others.

First Day of
Rosh Chodesh
Elul
Aug. 17, 1993
Aug. 7, 1994
Aug. 26, 1995
Aug. 15, 1996
Sept. 2, 1997
Aug. 22, 1998

From the
Scriptures **W**alk in modesty before your God
(*Michah* 6:8).

וְהַצְנֵעַ לֶכֶת עִם אֱלֹקֶיךָ

Good things can be accomplished with either a great deal of pomp and ceremony, or with a great deal of quiet and modesty. Some people like to call attention to themselves, while others go about their business without being noticed.

While both may have the same result, there is much to be said in favor of the latter method. Ostentatious performances are likely to arouse envy, and those who begrudge one's good works may attempt to undermine them or to upstage them. Critics seem to come out of the woodwork. Things that are accomplished in a manner that does not provoke attention are more likely to take shape and establish themselves firmly.

The Talmud uses the Ten Commandments as an example. The first Tablets, given at the Revelation at Sinai with thunder, lightning, and much fanfare, did not survive. The second Tablets, given to Moses in virtual silence, remained with the Israelites for centuries and exist to this day in the Ark which was hidden prior to the destruction of the First Temple.

We may feel an urge to make a public declaration of some worthy deed, but when we do it primarily to serve our ego, it is as unwise as it is unnecessary. When we do good deeds, the feeling of achievement that they bring should be reward enough. We should not need the acclaim of others to tell us that what we have done is good. We would do well to leave the noisemaking to the proverbial empty kettles.

NOTES

_____
_____
_____
_____
_____
_____
_____
_____
_____

Today I shall . . .

. . . do whatever I feel is necessary for the good of the community without any fanfare.

אִם תָּשׁוּב יִשְׂרָאֵל . . . אֵלַי תָּשׁוּב *From the* **I**f you return, O Israel ... you shall *Scriptures* **return unto Me** (*Jeremiah* 4:1).

Today is the first day of Elul, a period of time which is particularly propitious for *teshuvah,* for it precedes Rosh Hashanah, the Day of Judgment.

The Sages say that the Hebrew letters of the word אֱלוּל, *Elul,* form an acrostic for the verse in *Song of Songs*: אֲנִי לְדוֹדִי וְדוֹדִי לִי, *I am devoted to my Lover and He is devoted to me* (6:3). *Song of Songs* utilizes the relationship between a bridegroom and his betrothed to depict the relationship between God and Israel. Any separation between the two causes an intense longing for one another, an actual "lovesickness" (ibid. 2:5).

Second Day of Rosh Chodesh
Aug. 30, 1992
Aug. 18, 1993
Aug. 8, 1994
Aug. 27, 1995
Aug. 16, 1996
Sept. 3, 1997
Aug. 23, 1998

The love between God and Israel is unconditional. Even when Israel behaves in a manner that results in estrangement, that love is not diminished. Israel does not have to restore God's love, because it is eternal, and His longing for Israel to return to Him is so intense that at the first sign that Israel is ready to abandon its errant ways that led to the estrangement, God will promptly embrace it.

Song of Songs depicts the suffering Israel has sustained at the hands of its enemies, and we can conclude that the Divine distress at this suffering of His beloved Israel is great. *Teshuvah* is a long process, but all that is needed for the restoration of the ultimate relationship is a beginning: a sincere regret for having deviated from His will, and a resolve to return.

NOTES

Today I shall . . .

. . . seek to restore my personal relationship with God by dedicating myself to *teshuvah.*

Aug. 31, 1992
Aug. 19, 1993
Aug. 9, 1994
Aug. 28, 1995
Aug. 17, 1996
Sept. 4, 1997
Aug. 24, 1998

From the Scriptures

וִהְיִיתֶם נְקִיִּם מֵה' וּמִיִשְׂרָאֵל

You will be above suspicion both before God and before Israel (*Numbers* 32:22).

Although we should not try to impress other people, we should take their opinions into consideration, for we should not do anything that can arouse unwarranted accusations of wrongdoing.

Accusing an innocent person of wrongdoing is wrong itself, and it is wrong for us to cause other people to do wrong, even if we cause it very indirectly. Secondly, if observers who do not know all the circumstances surrounding our behavior see a respectable person doing something which they had believed to be wrong, they may use this incident as an example for themselves that it is indeed right.

The Talmud states that the proper way to live is that which is honorable in one's own mind and will also appear honorable to others (*Ethics of the Fathers* 2:1). Attitudes are contagious, and how we behave does influence others.

This principle applies especially in the case of children. We all know the saying, "Most kids hear what you say, some kids do what you say, but all kids do what you do."

Although we cannot use what other people think as the sole criterion for our behavior, we must nevertheless consider that while God may know what is in our heart, other people do not, and we should therefore not cause others to come to erroneous conclusions.

NOTES

Today I shall . . .

. . . act in keeping with the Divine will, but in a manner that will be manifestly honorable.

A simpleton will believe everything פֶּתִי יַאֲמִין לְכָל דָּבָר *From the Scriptures* (*Proverbs* 14:15).

Faith and belief are both defined as accepting as true something which transcends logic and which may not be subject to proof by rational argument. Yet, belief in God is not the "blind faith" of a simpleton.

A simpleton does not think, either because he lacks the capacity or does not wish to make the effort. Therefore, he is gullible and can be easily swayed in any direction. Being credulous is not the same as having faith.

When we reflect on the concept of a Supreme Being, Who is in every way infinite, we are likely to feel bewilderment, because our finite minds cannot grasp the infinite. Since all of our experiences involve finite objects, we lack a point of reference for dealing with the infinite.

When this reflection brings us to realize that the question of the existence of an infinite Supreme Being cannot be logically resolved, we then turn to the unbroken *mesorah*, the teachings which have been transmitted from generation to generation, from the time when more than two million people witnessed the Revelation at Sinai. When we accept our faith on this basis, we do so as the culmination of a process of profound thought which is no way similar to the credulousness of a simpleton.

This process also helps us with other questions that we have about God. For instance, the fact that we cannot possibly logically understand God does not preclude our coming to a knowledge of His Presence.

Sept. 1, 1992
Aug. 20, 1993
Aug. 10, 1994
Aug. 29, 1995
Aug. 18, 1996
Sept. 5, 1997
Aug. 25, 1998

NOTES

Today I shall . . .

. . . strengthen my faith by reflecting on the unbroken chain of tradition since Sinai.

ELUL

אלול

Sept. 2, 1992
Aug. 21, 1993
Aug. 11, 1994
Aug. 30, 1995
Aug. 19, 1996
Sept. 6, 1997
Aug. 26, 1998

From the Sages

נוֹהֲגִים . . . לוֹמַר סְלִיחוֹת וְתַחֲנוּנִים מֵרֹאשׁ
חֹדֶשׁ אֱלוּל וָאֵילָךְ

It is customary... to say prayers for forgiveness and mercy from the beginning of Elul and onward (*Shulchan Aruch, Orach Chaim* 581:1).

In secular society, the new year is frequently ushered in with levity and drinking, whereas in Judaism, the beginning of a new year is a solemn occasion preceded by a month of soul-searching and *teshuvah*.

The first day of the new year is an undeniable indication that another year of life has receded into the past. If one looks back on the bygone year and sees nothing of real achievement, one is likely to become quite dejected. People who must face the realization that a year of their lives has essentially been wasted cannot celebrate the arrival of a new year unless they drink to the point they become oblivious to this reality. Only then can they exclaim, "Happy New Year!"

In Judaism we prepare for the advent of a new year with reflection and *teshuvah*. Whereas making a personal inventory should be done all year long, it takes on special significance during the month before Rosh Hashanah. A comprehensive reflection on the events of the past year enables us to see what we have done right, so that we may enhance our efforts in those directions, and to see where we have gone wrong, so that we can avoid repeating the same mistakes.

Such an analysis enables us to use the lessons of the bygone year to better ourselves in the coming one.

This is why we do not drink or behave raucously on Rosh Hashanah. If the past year has value as a lesson for the future, there is no need to drown it from our consciousness.

NOTES

_____
_____
_____
_____
_____
_____
_____
_____

Today I shall. . .

. . .intensify my personal inventory of the past year, so that I may greet the new year with joy and serenity.

הָרוֹצֶה לְהַחְמִיר יַחְמִיר לְעַצְמוֹ אֲבָל לֹא *From*
לַאֲחֵרִים *the*

If one wishes to add on more restrictions *Sages*
than the law requires, one may do so for
oneself, but not [make such demands] of
others (*Shulchan Aruch*).

Sept. 3, 1992
Aug. 22, 1993
Aug. 12, 1994
Aug. 31, 1995
Aug. 20, 1996
Sept. 7, 1997
Aug. 27, 1998

Some people employ a double standard. One set of rules applies to themselves, and another to everyone else. The *Shulchan Aruch,* the standard authoritative compilation of Jewish law, accepts this policy — but on one condition: the more restrictive set of rules must apply to oneself, and the more lenient apply to other people.

Guidelines exist for many things, such as the percentage of income that one should give for *tzedakah.* Many *tzaddikim,* righteous people, retained only the barest minimum of their income for themselves, just enough to provide for their families, and gave everything else to the poor. However, they would never expect anyone else to follow their example, and some even forbade it.

Our minds are ingenious in concocting self-serving rationalizations. Sometimes we may have excellent reasons not to give more liberally to *tzedakah,* even if it is within the required amount. We may project into the future, worry about our economic security, and conclude that we should put more money away for a rainy day. Yet we often criticize people who we feel do not give enough to *tzedakah.*

We should be aware of such rationalizations and remember that the more demanding rules should apply to ourselves. If we are going to rationalize, let us rationalize in a way that gives the benefit of doubt to others.

NOTES

Today I shall . . .

. . . remember to be more demanding of myself than I am of others.

Sept. 4, 1992
Aug. 23, 1993
Aug. 13, 1994
Sept. 1, 1995
Aug. 21, 1996
Sept. 8, 1997
Aug. 28, 1998

From the Scriptures

פֶּן יֵשׁ בָּכֶם שֹׁרֶשׁ פֹּרֶה רֹאשׁ וְלַעֲנָה

Lest there be among you [someone with] a root that will produce bitter herbs (*Deuteronomy* 29:17).

A person who is diagnosed with, God forbid, a cancer, will submit to that treatment which has the highest degree of certainty of cure. If surgery promises a 50% chance, but the likelihood of cure increases to 70% with the addition of radiation and up to 85% with chemotherapy, a reasonable person will submit to all three treatments, in order to maximize his or her chances of survival. People also know that just removing most of the malignant cells is inadequate, because a single surviving cancerous cell can reproduce itself and be lethal. Furthermore, a malignant growth does not remain localized, but can spread beyond its place of origin to other vital organs.

This approach is also how we must deal with those character traits that endanger our spiritual life. Greed, envy, hatred, selfishness, vanity, and arrogance are all negative traits which must be totally eliminated. Allowing even the smallest remnant of any of these traits to remain is like harboring a single cancerous cell. If we value our spiritual life as much as we do our physical life, we will do everything possible to attain total elimination of negative traits.

Moses speaks of the "root" that will multiply and bear bitter fruit. Any negative trait will not only reproduce itself but, like a malignant cancer cell, may spread and affect other components of one's character.

If we value spiritual life, we will do whatever is necessary to preserve it.

NOTES

_____
_____
_____
_____
_____
_____
_____
_____
_____

Today I shall . . .

. . . think about how important spirituality is to me, and what I am ready to do to preserve it.

From the Scriptures

הַשְׁלֵךְ עַל ה' יְהָבְךָ

Throw your burden upon God (*Psalms* 55:23).

Sept. 5, 1992
Aug. 24, 1993
Aug. 14, 1994
Sept. 2, 1995
Aug. 22, 1996
Sept. 9, 1997
Aug. 29, 1998

Imagine driving a car along the road and suddenly realizing that the brakes have been detached from the brake pedal and the wheels from the steering wheel. In panic, you stamp on the pedal and turn the steering wheel frantically, all to no avail. With the car out of control, your best chance may be to open the door and jump out. However, if you haven't realized that in fact you have lost control, you still try to maintain it, and your life is in danger.

While such dramatic happenings fortunately do not occur every day, we should realize we actually do not have control over many things in life. Trying to exert control where no control is possible is worse than futile, for just as in the above example, it precludes taking whatever other action may be possible.

Many people perform an action that they consider to be proper and accompany it with a prayer for success; others consider prayer only as a last resort. God listens to everyone's prayer, regardless of the circumstances in which it is said. However, even those who use prayer as a last resort should realize when it is indeed a last resort, i.e. when they can do no more, because the conditions are beyond their control. This realization may help them avoid futile behavior.

We may not like to face reality, but denying it is hazardous.

NOTES

_____
_____
_____
_____
_____
_____
_____
_____
_____

Today I shall . . .

. . . realize that many things I think I can control may actually be beyond my control, and I must turn them over to God.

ELUL

אלול

Sept. 6, 1992
Aug. 25, 1993
Aug. 15, 1994
Sept. 3, 1995
Aug. 23, 1996
Sept. 10, 1997
Aug. 30, 1998

From our Prayers

וְעַל נִסֶּיךָ שֶׁבְּכָל יוֹם עִמָּנוּ

[I thank You] for Your miracles that are with us each day (*Siddur*).

I once heard it said, "Coincidences are miracles in which God prefers to remain anonymous."

If we were to carefully scrutinize everything that occurs in our daily lives, we would find many such "coincidences." Sometimes we may not be aware of the significance of a particular occurrence until much later, when we may have forgotten how or why we think it occurred, and so we just write it off to chance. Other times, we notice that things seem to "just happen at the right time." And in some instances, the likelihood of the desired occurrence being chance is statistically so remote that it may penetrate the skepticism of even the most confirmed non-believer.

Why don't people see the Divine hand in so many things? Could it be that being aware would require them to be thankful to God, because it is unconscionable to be an ingrate (and if one has difficulty with feelings of gratitude, it is simply easier to deny the awareness of the Divine favor)? Could it be that the awareness that God is looking after them would obligate them to live according to the Divine will, and since that might entail some inconveniences and restrictions on their behavior, it is more comfortable to believe that "God does not care"?

Psychologists have great respect for the human capacity to rationalize, to convince oneself of the absolute truth of whatever it is that one wishes to believe or not believe. How much wiser we would be to divest ourselves of such self-deceptions.

NOTES

Today I shall . . .

. . . scrutinize my daily happenings with an alertness to how many favorable "coincidences" have occurred in my life.

וְאֶעֶשְׂךָ לְגוֹי גָּדוֹל . . . וֶהְיֵה בְּרָכָה *From the*
Scriptures

I shall make you into a great nation
... and you will be a blessing
(*Genesis* 12:2).

ELUL
9
אלול

Sept. 7, 1992
Aug. 26, 1993
Aug. 16, 1994
Sept. 4, 1995
Aug. 24, 1996
Sept. 11, 1997
Aug. 31, 1998

This verse is part of the first recorded Divine communication to the Patriarch Abraham, in which God promised him various rewards if he left his homeland and went to Canaan. One of the rewards was "you will be a blessing," meaning that he would be given the power to bestow blessings on others (*Rashi*).

The same Hebrew phrase can also be read: "*you shall* be a blessing," in the imperative. In other words, God commanded Abraham to lead the kind of life that would make his very presence a blessing to everyone in his environment.

In *Generation to Generation* (CIS 1986), I related that my mother told me how excited and elated everyone was when I took my first steps. An itinerant rabbi who collected funds for a *yeshivah* was also there. He sadly commented, "When I first walked, my parents were delighted too, but now no one is delighted when they see me walk in." My mother related this comment to me many times, and one of my goals in life has been to fulfill my mother's prayer that people should not be displeased when I walk in.

Abraham received many Divine blessings, but along with them came an assignment: he was to make *himself* into a blessing. If we read on, we can then understand the continuation of the above chapter, *Abraham went as God had commanded him* (ibid. 12:4); i.e. he conducted his life in such a manner that he was indeed a blessing. The commandment to Abraham was intended for all of his descendants. By living a spiritual life, we can both endear ourselves to everyone and be a blessing to our environment.

Today I shall . . .

. . . try to behave in such a manner that I will be an asset to my community.

NOTES

ELUL

10

אלול

Sept. 8, 1992
Aug. 27, 1993
Aug. 17, 1994
Sept. 5, 1995
Aug. 25, 1996
Sept. 12, 1997
Sept. 1, 1998

From the Scriptures The memory of a righteous person is a blessing (*Proverbs* 10:7).

זֵכֶר צַדִּיק לִבְרָכָה

At a family therapy session, one family member said something totally uncalled for, provocative, and insulting to another person. The remark was extremely irritating to me, even as an observer, and I anticipated an explosive outburst of outrage from the recipient. To my great surprise, the latter remained quiet and merely gestured to indicate that he was dismissing the comment as being unworthy of a response.

After the session, I complimented the man on his self-restraint. He explained, "A friend of mine once had a very angry outburst. During his rage he suffered a stroke from which he never regained consciousness.

"I am not afraid that if I become angry I would also suffer a stroke. However, what I and everyone else remember of my friend are the last words of his life, which were full of bitterness and hostility. That is not the way I wish to be remembered. Since no person can know exactly when one's time is up, I made up my mind never to act in such a manner, so that if what I was doing was to be my last action on earth, I would not be remembered that way."

The Talmud tells us that when Rabbi Eliezer told his disciples that a person should do *teshuvah* one day before his death, they asked, "How is a person to know when one will die?" Rabbi Eliezer answered, "Precisely! Therefore one should do *teshuvah* every day, since tomorrow may be one's last day."

The verse cited above may be explained in the same way. People should behave in a way that they would wish others to remember them, for that can indeed be a blessing.

NOTES

Today I shall . . .

. . . behave as though this day is the one by which I shall be remembered.

Each day we hope for Your salvation *our* (*Shemoneh Esrei*). *From our Prayers*

כִּי לִישׁוּעָתְךָ קִוִּינוּ כָּל הַיּוֹם

Sept. 9, 1992
Aug. 28, 1993
Aug. 18, 1994
Sept. 6, 1995
Aug. 26, 1996
Sept. 13, 1997
Sept. 2, 1998

The Talmud states that one of the questions that will be posed to each person on his or her day of judgment is, "Did you look forward to salvation?" While the question refers to anticipating the ultimate Redemption, it can also refer to the salvation of the individual.

Positive attitudes beget positive results, and negative attitudes beget negative results. Books have been written about people who have recovered from hopeless illnesses because, contrary to medical opinion, they did not give up hope. On the contrary, they maintained a positive attitude. While this phenomenon may be controversial (for many people are skeptical that cheerful outlooks can cure), people certainly can and have killed themselves by depression. With a negative attitude, a person suffering from an illness may even abandon those practices that can give strength and prolong life, such as the treatment itself.

I have seen a poster that displays birds in flight. Its caption comments, "They fly because they think they can." We could do so much if we did not despair of our capacity to do it.

Looking forward to Divine salvation is one such positive attitude. The Talmud states that even when the blade of an enemy's sword is at our throat, we have no right to abandon hope of help.

No one can ever take hope from us, but we can surrender it voluntarily. How foolish to do so.

NOTES

Today I shall . . .

. . . try to always maintain a positive attitude and to hope for Divine salvation.

Sept. 10, 1992
Aug. 29, 1993
Aug. 19, 1994
Sept. 7, 1995
Aug. 27, 1996
Sept. 14, 1997
Sept. 3, 1998

גָּדוֹל כְּבוֹד הַבְּרִיּוֹת

*From
the
Sages*
The dignity of a human being is extremely important (*Berachos* 19b).

The Talmud refers many times to the importance of preserving human dignity.

In *Generation to Generation* (CIS 1986), I related how my father used to discipline me when I was a child. When I did something wrong, he would shake his head and say, *"Es passt nisht* (This does not become you)." In other words, I was not bad for having done something wrong; I was too good to do something that was beneath my dignity. This method is an excellent way to discipline children without making them feel they are bad.

People share certain biological behaviors with animals, but our mental life is unique to us. Clearly, human dignity does not reside in that part which is animal, but in that part which is distinctly human: the rational mind, the creative mind, the capacity to be spiritual.

Isn't it simply beneath our dignity to indulge in those behaviors which are primarily animal, rather than uniquely human? As I observe the enormous efforts made and expenditures invested in catering to taste buds, I wonder, "Where is our self-respect?" Granted, we must eat to stay alive, and eating tasty foods may indeed enhance digestion. Still, is it not beneath our dignity to indulge in gustatory delights to the extent that we appear to be more concerned about stimulating our tongues and stomachs than our brains? People who honestly value the truly human part of themselves — their rational and volitional minds — have other priorities.

NOTES

_____
_____
_____
_____
_____
_____
_____
_____
_____

Today I shall . . .

. . . rethink my priorities and behave with the dignity that I owe to myself as a human being.

קְנֵה לְךָ חָבֵר *From the Sages*

A cquire for yourself a friend (*Ethics of the Fathers* 1:6).

ELUL

13

אלול

Sept. 11, 1992
Aug. 30, 1993
Aug. 20, 1994
Sept. 8, 1995
Aug. 28, 1996
Sept. 15, 1997
Sept. 4, 1998

What is so important about "acquiring" a friend? Don't friendships occur spontaneously?

Many people think they have friends, and some people think they have many friends. However, let's reflect: "Is there anyone with whom I am so close and whom I would trust so completely that I would confide in him or her and tell everything and anything that is on my mind?" Many of us would find that such friends are few in number, and some of us may totally lack this type of relationship.

In his work on *Ethics of the Fathers*, Rabbeinu Yonah states that if a person tries to achieve perfection in all character traits at one time, he or she is likely to achieve nothing, but if the effort is concentrated upon improving one trait, success in that one area will facilitate improving many other traits. Similarly, trying to achieve a great number of friendships at once will likely create superficial friends. However, if a person will cultivate one friendship and so achieve the desired intimacy and trust, he or she may thereafter find it much easier to develop more profound and meaningful relationships with many people.

The teaching of the above Talmudical passage is now evident. Acquire *"a"* friend, i.e. try to develop a single relationship that grows beyond a superficial skin-deep level. Not only is that friendship important in its own right, but it will also enhance the quality of all the other relationships.

NOTES

_____
_____
_____
_____
_____

Today I shall . . .

_____
_____

. . . try to cultivate a single friendship into one of complete trust and intimacy.

Sept. 12, 1992
Aug. 31, 1993
Aug. 21, 1994
Sept. 9, 1995
Aug. 29, 1996
Sept. 16, 1997
Sept. 5, 1998

*From the
Scriptures*

וְאָכְלוּ אֹתָם אֲשֶׁר כֻּפַּר בָּהֶם

They will eat them [the offerings] and will be forgiven (*Exodus* 29:33).

How can eating serve as an atonement?

My father used to tell of a *tzaddik* who was staying at an inn. One morning when they served the breakfast cereal, he said, "This is unusually good. Is there any more?" After being served a second portion, he again asked for more, ate it, and continued to request more cereal until he was told that it was all gone.

The *tzaddik's* disciples were bewildered. Their teacher usually ate barely enough for survival. When they asked him why he had deviated from his usual practice, he explained:

"When I first tasted the cereal, I realized that the cook must have by mistake poured kerosene into the pot instead of oil. I know that she is a poor widow, and that this innkeeper happens to be a very irascible person. If this mistake had been discovered, she would surely have been dismissed. I therefore wished to avoid anyone else tasting the cereal and exposing the problem."

Eating only to satisfy one's appetite obviously cannot constitute forgiveness, but it is possible to eat with other motivations, which can make it an act of Divine service. We may not all be capable of an act such as that of the *tzaddik,* but if we can bring ourselves to the point where we truly eat for nutrition, in order that we have the strength to function optimally, so that we may do with our lives that which God wants of us, then our eating, too, can be a Divine service.

NOTES

_____
_____
_____
_____
_____
_____
_____
_____
_____
_____

Today I shall . . .

. . . try to make eating an act of Divine service, dedicating myself to do the will of God.

"וְאָהַבְתָּ אֵת ה' אֱלֹקֶיךָ'' שֶׁיְּהֵא שֵׁם שָׁמַיִם מִתְאַהֵב עַל יָדְךָ *From the Sages*

"**Y**ou shall love your God" means that you should make the Divine Name beloved (*Yoma* 86a).

Sept. 13, 1992
Sept. 1, 1993
Aug. 22, 1994
Sept. 10, 1995
Aug. 30, 1996
Sept. 17, 1997
Sept. 6, 1998

Rabbi Shimon ben Shatach once bought a donkey and found a gem in the carrying case which came with it. The rabbis congratulated him on the windfall with which he had been blessed. "No," said Rabbi Shimon, "I bought a donkey, but I didn't buy a diamond." He proceeded to return the diamond to the donkey's owner, an Arab, who remarked, "Blessed be the God of Shimon ben Shatach."

A non-Jew once approached Rabbi Safra and offered him a sum of money to purchase an item. Since Rabbi Safra was in the midst of prayer at the time, he could not respond to the man, who interpreted the silence as a rejection of his offer and therefore told him that he would increase the price. When Rabbi Safra again did not respond, the man continued to raise his offer. When Rabbi Safra finished, he explained that he had been unable to interrupt his prayer, but had heard the initial amount offered and had silently consented to it in his heart. Therefore, the man could have the item for that first price. Here too, the astounded customer praised the God of Israel.

We have so many opportunities to demonstrate the beauty of the Torah's ethics. We accomplish three *mitzvos* by doing so: (1) practicing honesty, (2) *kiddush Hashem* (sanctifying the Divine Name), and (3) making the Divine Name beloved, according to the above Talmudic interpretation of the Scripture.

NOTES

Today I shall . . .

. . . try to act in a manner that will make the Divine Name beloved and respected.

Sept. 14, 1992
Sept. 2, 1993
Aug. 23, 1994
Sept. 11, 1995
Aug. 31, 1996
Sept. 18, 1997
Sept. 7, 1998

From the Sages

הָעַיִן רוֹאָה וְהַלֵּב חוֹמֵד

The eye sees, and the heart desires (*Rashi*, *Numbers* 15:39).

People cannot help when an improper impulse comes to mind, but they certainly can stop themselves from harboring the thought and allowing it to dominate their thinking. Yet, sometimes one may be responsible even for the impulse itself.

While some impulses are completely spontaneous, others arise out of stimulation. If a person reads, hears, or sees things which can provoke improper thoughts and feelings, he or she is then responsible for the impulses that are the consequences of that reading, listening, or observing.

This concept is especially important in our era, when not even a semblance of a code of decency exists as to what may or may not be publicly displayed. All varieties of media exploit our basest biological drives.

Given the interpretation of the right of free speech under which such provocative displays occur, the government has no way to restrain them. However, each person has not only a right, but also an obligation to be his or her own censor. No one has to look at everything that is displayed or printed, nor hear everything that is broadcast. Those who fail to exert their own personal censorship are tacitly stimulating immoral impulses, and for that alone they are liable.

NOTES

_____
_____
_____
_____
_____
_____
_____
_____

Today I shall . . .

. . . try to avoid looking, hearing, and reading things which can have a degenerating effect.

קְדֵרָא דְּבֵי שׁוּתְּפֵי לֹא חֲמִימָא וְלֹא קְרִירָא *From* **A** pot belonging to two partners is neither *the* hot nor cold (*Eruvin* 3a). *Sages*

If two people who partly own a pot of food disagree — one prefers it hot, and the other prefers it cold — the compromise of "lukewarm" displeases both.

One of the most frequent maladjustments in life comes as a result of trying to please everyone. Invariably, other people have conflicting opinions, so that if one satisfies A, one displeases B, and vice versa. Yet some people consistently try to accomplish this feat, and the result is nothing but frustration, since the compromise not only comes at great personal cost, but satisfies no one.

The desire to please everyone often stems from a lack of confidence in one's own convictions. If I know what I want and believe it to be right, I will pursue my path. While I know full well that some people may disagree with me, I must accept it as inevitable; if others are displeased because I do not defer to their wishes, that is their problem, not mine.

It is true that responsible people have the obligation to consider conflicting opinions and avail themselves of competent guidance, and that flexibility and compromise do have their place (it is appropriate to rethink one's position on controversial issues and not be obstinate in maintaining one's position, no matter what). Still, people cannot satisfy everyone while maintaining their own integrity.

Sept. 15, 1992
Sept. 3, 1993
Aug. 24, 1994
Sept. 12, 1995
Sept. 1, 1996
Sept. 19, 1997
Sept. 8, 1998

NOTES

Today I shall . . .

. . . try to think through what it is that I really want and not try to satisfy everyone.

Sept. 16, 1992
Sept. 4, 1993
Aug. 25, 1994
Sept. 13, 1995
Sept. 2, 1996
Sept. 20, 1997
Sept. 9, 1998

From the Sages

יְהִי כְבוֹד חֲבֵרְךָ חָבִיב עָלֶיךָ כְּשֶׁלָּךְ

Let the honor of your friend be as dear to you as your own *(Ethics of the Fathers* 2:15).

Pride, honor, and acclaim have an attraction all their own, but our Sages warn us that these may be destructive (ibid. 4:28). The frustration people may experience when they feel they did not receive due recognition may be extremely distressing.

People who crave honor may sometimes attempt to achieve it by deflating others, thinking that their own image is enhanced when others are disparaged. The truth, however, is just the reverse: when one deflates another, one's own image is diminished.

Rabbi Nechunya's students asked him, "By what merits did you achieve long life?" He answered, "I never accepted any honor that was at another person's expense." As an example the Talmud tells that when Rav Chana Bar Chanilai visited Rabbi Huna, he wanted to relieve the latter of carrying a shovel on his shoulder. Rabbi Huna objected, saying, "Since it is not your custom to be seen carrying a shovel, you should not do so now" *(Megillah* 28a). Rav Chana was willing to forgo his own honor for Rabbi Huna's sake, but Rabbi Huna would not hear of it.

Why does such an attitude merit long life? A person who is not preoccupied with his image, and is not obsessed with receiving honor and public recognition, is free of the emotional stress and frustration that plague those whose cravings for acclaim are bottomless pits. These stresses can be psychologically and physically devastating, and dispensing with them can indeed prolong life.

Aptly did Rabbi Elazar HaKappar say that honor drives a man out of this world *(Ethics of the Fathers* 4:28). One who pursues honors in this world mortally harms his chance for happiness.

NOTES

_____
_____
_____
_____
_____
_____
_____
_____
_____

Today I shall. . .

. . .concentrate on being respectful to others, and avoid pursuing recognition from others.

כִּי רְחִימְתִּין הֲוָה עַזִיזָא אֲפּוּתְיָא דְסַפְסִירָא *From*
שְׁכִיבֵן הָשְׁתָּא דְּלֹא עַזִיזָא רְחִימְתִּין פּוּרְיָא בַּר *the*
שִׁיתִּין גַּרְמִידֵי לֹא סַגֵּי לָן *Sages*

When our love was intense, we could live on the edge of a sword. Now that our love has faded, even a spacious home is not enough for us (*Sanhedrin* 7a).

Sept. 17, 1992
Sept. 5, 1993
Aug. 26, 1994
Sept. 14, 1995
Sept. 3, 1996
Sept. 21, 1997
Sept. 10, 1998

In my book, *Like Yourselves and Others Will Too* (Prentice-Hall 1978), I described a phenomenon called "New House Disease." When a couple, whose children have all married and moved out, acquire a beautiful new home or condominium and move into it, the marriage is in danger of falling apart.

What happened? Differences that had arisen between the couple were never confronted and resolved. Rather, they were glossed over and covered up, much as one might conceal a defect in the wall with wallpaper. Unresolved conflicts may give rise to resentments, which feed upon themselves and increase in intensity. (It is even possible that a particular resentment persists after the incident that caused it has been forgotten, and now the spouse retains the resentment without knowing why.) Since resentment is likely to result in guilt, the psychological defense mechanism now justifies the resentment by projecting it onto something else — the house. They reassure each other: "Nothing is really wrong between the two of us. We are having difficulties because we are living in this inadequate house. If we had a more spacious house with the necessary conveniences, everything would be O.K."

If after moving into the new house, the couple discovers that things are not O.K., they now have lost their last excuse to explain away their unhappiness and must come face to face with the unresolved conflict. This shock alone may terminate the relationship.

NOTES

Today I shall ...

... try to detect any existing conflicts and resolve them, instead of projecting them on reasonable but untrue causes.

Sept. 18, 1992
Sept. 6, 1993
Aug. 27, 1994
Sept. 15, 1995
Sept. 4, 1996
Sept. 22, 1997
Sept. 11, 1998

From the Sages

גּנְבָא אַפּוּם מַחְתַּרְתָּא רַחֲמָנָא קָרֵי

A thief about to break in may pray to God [**that he not be caught**] (*Berachos* 63a, *Ein Yaakov*).

Believing in God alone is not enough. Even praying to God may not be enough. Some people think that prayer means telling God what He is supposed to do for them. This attitude can result in the absurd situation described above.

We should pray for God to make His will known, and to help and guide us in fulfilling that will.

A recovered alcoholic told me that during his years of drinking, he frequently got into trouble and would then pray to God, "Just help me this once, and I will never drink again." Relief from his distress was invariably followed by relapse, and when he finally reached a crisis, he surrendered, praying, "Show me what You want of me."

His first type of prayer, he realized, was not really a prayer at all, just bargaining. Real prayer did not occur until he stopped asking God for what he wanted, and instead asked to be shown what God wanted.

Study of the *siddur* itself should enable us to reach a concept of genuine prayer without having to reach such a crisis. We declare our belief in the existence of God in the *Shema* which we promptly follow with a portion of the Torah that instructs us to fulfill His *mitzvos*. With this background, we proceed to the *Amidah,* where we pray for God to give us our needs, so that we may be able to fulfill His will.

NOTES

Today I shall . . .

. . . think of prayer as being directed to my achievement of what God wants, instead of demanding that God deliver what I want.

הֲרֵינִי מוֹחֵל לְכָל מִי שֶׁהִכְעִיס וְהִקְנִיט אוֹתִי אוֹ שֶׁחָטָא כְּנֶגְדִּי *From our Prayers*

I hereby forgive everyone who offended or angered me, or sinned against me (*Prayer on Retiring*).

Sept. 19, 1992
Sept. 7, 1993
Aug. 28, 1994
Sept. 16, 1995
Sept. 5, 1996
Sept. 23, 1997
Sept. 12, 1998

Since we pray to God to forgive our mistakes, certainly we should be willing to forgive others who have offended us.

Forgiveness must be more than perfunctory. A man once heard his rabbi state that Yom Kippur would not achieve forgiveness from God unless one has forgiven others. This fellow then went over to someone he disliked and said, "I forgive you today, but I want you to know that as soon as Yom Kippur is over, I will despise you as much as before."

When we pray to God for forgiveness, we cite the verse, *I have erased your sins like a thick cloud* (Isaiah 44:22), which tells us how we should grant forgiveness to others — by removing all traces of resentment.

What good comes from harboring resentments? We cannot act on them, for the Torah explicitly forbids taking revenge. Since resentments have no practical purpose, and since they are obviously very negative feelings, they can do nothing more than wear down our emotions. When we find a smelly item in the refrigerator, we quickly get rid of it so that it does not contaminate the other foods. We should view negative feelings in the same light, for they can infect all our other emotions with negativity.

Forgiving others and thereby ridding ourselves of resentments is in itself not only a virtuous character trait, for it is considerate of others; more importantly, it works to our own advantage.

NOTES

Today I shall . . .

. . . try to completely forgive others and realize that failure to do so will leave me with useless negative emotions.

Sept. 20, 1992
Sept. 8, 1993
Aug. 29, 1994
Sept. 17, 1995
Sept. 6, 1996
Sept. 24, 1997
Sept. 13, 1998

From the Sages

לָאו עַכְבְּרָא גַּנָּב אֶלָּא חוֹרָא גַּנָּב

The mouse [that steals a morsel of food] is not the thief, but rather the hole [through which the mouse escapes] is the thief *(Gittin* 45a).

In this picturesque statement, the Talmud explains that the hole in the wall is the culprit, because without a breach in the wall, the mouse would not be able to steal the food.

In the treatment of alcoholism, there is a concept called "enabling." "Enablers" are the people who essentially make it possible for the alcoholic to continue drinking. By analogy, although oxygen does not cause a fire, it is impossible for fire to burn in its absence, so one extinguishes a blaze by dousing it with water or smothering it, to prevent oxygen from reaching it. Similarly, an alcoholic could not continue to drink very long in the absence of enablers. It is sometimes more difficult to convince people to stop their enabling than the alcoholic to stop drinking.

We claim that we are intolerant of crime and injustice, but the fact is that these exist only because we *do* tolerate them. For example, many arguments are given for protecting the rights of those who violate the law, but the price we pay for this is that we allow these violations to continue.

In every society, community, or family, there may be enablers. Sometimes those who are most vehement in their condemnation are actually the enablers. We should do careful soul-searching to see whether we may not actually be enabling behavior of which we disapprove.

NOTES

_____
_____
_____
_____
_____
_____
_____
_____
_____

Today I shall. . .

. . .try to stop "enabling" those things that I know to be wrong.

נוֹחַ לוֹ לָאָדָם שֶׁלֹּא נִבְרָא יוֹתֵר מִשֶּׁנִּבְרָא עַכְשָׁיו *From* שֶׁנִּבְרָא יְפַשְׁפֵּשׁ בְּמַעֲשָׂיו *the*

It would have been better for man had he *Sages* not been created, but now that he has been created, he must carefully examine his actions (*Eruvin* 13b).

Sept. 21, 1992
Sept. 9, 1993
Aug. 30, 1994
Sept. 18, 1995
Sept. 7, 1996
Sept. 25, 1997
Sept. 14, 1998

Some people have made themselves modern disciples of Epicurus. After noting the prevalence of suffering and distress in the world, they conclude that humans are innocent victims of unjustified misery. Therefore, they find no reason to further restrict the few pleasures that people can have, and they say, "Let people do whatever their hearts desire."

These people act as though they were the first to discover the plight of mankind. The above Talmudic passage should teach them that several thousand years ago, some very wise people had already thoroughly analyzed human life. Although they too concluded that it would have been better for humanity not to have been created, we still do not have *carte blanche* to do whatever we please.

Our emotions profoundly influence our thought processes. People may come to conclusions that are completely false, but they will believe them to be correct because they want to believe them. This fallacy is dangerous; if someone indulges himself and knows that he is doing wrong, there is a possibility of *teshuvah,* but if he deceives himself and believes that he is just in his behavior, there is no possibility of *teshuvah.*

Try an experiment. Take an opinion you have about any issue. Now, consult the works of Torah literature. You will find, without exception, that every issue you raise has been thoroughly discussed centuries ago.

NOTES

Today I shall . . .

. . . be aware that challenges to Torah teachings are invariably rationalizations and try to control my pleasures instead of letting them control me.

Sept. 22, 1992
Sept. 10, 1993
Aug. 31, 1994
Sept. 19, 1995
Sept. 8, 1996
Sept. 26, 1997
Sept. 15, 1998

From the
Scriptures [Man and wife] shall be one body
(*Genesis* 2:24).

וְהָיוּ לְבָשָׂר אֶחָד

In recent times, we have witnessed an unprecedented tidal wave of divorce. This phenomenon appears to be directly linked to modern attitudes towards marriage. Let's look at the Torah's concept of marriage, which has produced much marital happiness for over three thousand years.

An analogy is a good start. Table salt is a chemical compound called sodium chloride; it consists of two elements, sodium and chlorine, in combination.

Pure sodium is very volatile. If dropped into water, it will explode into fire. No one would ever want to eat it. Chlorine is a corrosive gas, which can cause severe irritation and a choking sensation. When sodium and chlorine combine, however, each loses its individual properties; the fusion is a totally new compound which bears no resemblance to either component.

When the Torah states that husband and wife should become one, it means that two unique people should fuse into a new being. In forming this new being, each "element" must be ready and willing to divest itself of its own identity, so that this new "compound" may be that which is most desirable and most constructive.

Clearly, the sharing of oneself in a marriage relationship cannot be as dramatic and radical as in the example of sodium and chlorine fusing into table salt. Nevertheless, much of the incompatibility that has resulted in divorce is due to the refusal of partners to yield of themselves.

NOTES

_____
_____
_____
_____
_____
_____
_____
_____

Today I shall . . .

. . . try to realize that in marriage, I must be willing to relinquish some of my own individuality to permit the emergence of a family unit.

From the Scriptures

וַיָּקֶם מֹשֶׁה אֶת הַמִּשְׁכָּן . . . וּכְבוֹד ה'
מָלֵא אֶת הַמִּשְׁכָּן

Moses assembled the Sanctuary (Exodus 40:18) . . . The Glory of God filled the Sanctuary (*Exodus* 40:34).

Sept. 23, 1992
Sept. 11, 1993
Sept. 1, 1994
Sept. 20, 1995
Sept. 9, 1996
Sept. 27, 1997
Sept. 16, 1998

The Talmud describes in great detail how each component of the Sanctuary was fashioned, and that the completion of each component was a *mitzvah*. Nevertheless, the Divine Glory did not descend until the component parts were assembled into the whole.

The 613 *mitzvos* of the Torah are indeed the essential parts, without which the structure of a Torah life is impossible. However, they must be assembled into the ultimate whole, which is even greater than the sum of its parts.

In the past two centuries, the study of Torah works of *mussar* and *chassidus* were promoted by the great luminaries, Rabbi Yisroel of Salant and the Baal Shem Tov. Both met with resistance by many Torah scholars, who argued that the study of the Scriptures and Talmud alone was an adequate guide to living a Torah life.

These two great sages realized that while previous generations could assemble the component parts of the Torah into the desired whole, later generations required additional help in doing so. Formal study of *mussar* and *chassidus* is essential if people are to live a life that attests to the Glory of God.

Sometimes we may be disappointed in observing some people who are apparently observant of Torah and yet do not lead exemplary lives. Invariably, these people do not implement the teachings of *mussar* and *chassidus,* so that while they possess the building blocks, they fail to assemble the structure of a Jewish life.

NOTES

Today I shall . . .

. . . devote myself to the study of the ethics of Jewish living.

Sept. 24, 1992
Sept. 12, 1993
Sept. 2, 1994
Sept. 21, 1995
Sept. 10, 1996
Sept. 28, 1997
Sept. 17, 1998

From the אִם יִתָּקַע שׁוֹפָר בְּעִיר וְעָם לֹא יֶחֱרָדוּ
Scriptures If the shofar is sounded in the city, will the populace not tremble? (*Amos* 3:6).

The blow of a *shofar* is a call to arouse us from the lethargy of routine in which we have been immersed and to stimulate us to *teshuvah*. But what if someone hears the *shofar* and is not moved by it?

A village blacksmith's assistant once visited a large city and sought out the local smithy. He observed that the workers there used a bellows to fan the flames in the forge. The bellows were much more efficient than the exhausting manual fanning which he did back in his master's shop. He promptly bought a bellows, returned with great enthusiasm to his master, and informed him that there was no longer any need for them to exhaust themselves fanning the flames. He then set out to demonstrate the magic of the bellows, but alas, regardless of how vigorously he pumped, no flame appeared.

"I can't understand it," he said. "In the city, I saw with my own eyes the huge flame produced by the bellows."

"Did you first light a small fire?" the master asked.

"No," the assistant replied. "I just pumped the bellows."

"You fool!" the blacksmith said. "The bellows can only increase the size of the flame when you begin it with a spark. When you have no spark or fire, all the pumping of the bellows is of no use."

Like the bellows, the *shofar* can only arouse us if we have in us a *spark* of *teshuvah*, just a rudiment of desire. If we feel ourselves unmoved by the *shofar*, we had better try to light a spark of *teshuvah* within ourselves.

NOTES

Today I shall . . .

. . . try to begin *teshuvah*, so that the service of the approaching High Holidays will have the desired effect on me.

עֲשֵׂה . . . עֲשֵׂה לְמַעַן אַבְרָהָם יִצְחָק וְיַעֲקֹב *From*
לְמַעַן יוֹנְקֵי שָׁדַיִם שֶׁלֹּא חָטְאוּ *our*

Do [for Israel] for the sake of Abraham, *Prayers*
Isaac, and Jacob . . . Do [for Israel] for
the sake of nursing infants, who have not
sinned (*Siddur, Selichos*).

Sept. 25, 1992
Sept. 13, 1993
Sept. 3, 1994
Sept. 22, 1995
Sept. 11, 1996
Sept. 29, 1997
Sept. 18, 1998

In praying for salvation, we invoke the merits of our ancestors, and we also pray that we be helped for the sake of our future generations. The Talmud tells us that God acts towards us as we act towards other people. If we wish Him to judge us because of the merits of the past and the promise of the future, then we must take the past and the future into account in our own actions.

Today's generation is very much a "now" generation, considering only the thrills of the moment. Much of today's society turns its back on the traditions and values of the past, and behaves recklessly in exploiting the world for the pleasures of today, even though it pollutes the environment and depletes natural resources needed for the future.

Is it coincidence that our generation is infatuated with digital watches and clocks? Old-fashioned timepieces told time by a pointer, which had the past behind it and the future in front of it. These timepieces symbolized an awareness of both, but a digital display focuses exclusively on the present moment and gives no recognition to the existence of either the past or the future.

While we should not allow the burdens of the past nor the anxieties of the future to exert a destructive effect on our living, the constructive lessons of the past and a responsible attitude towards the future can guide us to a proper and responsible life.

NOTES

Today I shall . . .

. . . try to derive wisdom from the study of the past and act responsibly in consideration of the future.

Sept. 26, 1992
Sept. 14, 1993
Sept. 4, 1994
Sept. 23, 1995
Sept. 12, 1996
Sept. 30, 1997
Sept. 19, 1998

From תְּמֵהַּ אֲנִי אִם יֵשׁ בַּדּוֹר הַזֶּה מִי שֶׁיָּכוֹל לְהוֹכִיחַ
the I wonder if there is anyone in this genera-
Sages tion capable of giving reprimand (*Arachin*
according to reading of *Shitah Mekubetzes* 16b).

This statement appears strange. Many people seem ready and willing to offer constructive criticism.

Criticism is a sharp instrument. It can cut us as deeply as a surgeon's scalpel. A medical student must undergo many years of training before he or she can become a surgeon and make an incision which will lead to the improvement of someone's health. Even the most carefully calculated and well-performed surgical incision is a painful wound, and if the surgeon cannot apply himself to alleviating the patient's suffering and restoring his health, he has no right to make a cut.

Before we criticize someone, even if we have the finest intentions for that person's betterment, we should give serious thought to what we are doing. We must be aware that our remarks will inevitably cause emotional pain, and unless we are ready to assume responsibility for helping the person cope with the pain and assist him or her in making the changes we recommend, we should refrain from criticizing.

Already in the days of the Talmud, the existence of the unique ability to criticize constructively was questioned. We have little reason to believe that we are more competent in this respect today.

Parents who discipline their children are also ready to invest themselves in their children's betterment. This attitude is required before providing constructive criticism.

NOTES

_____
_____
_____
_____
_____
_____
_____
_____
_____

Today I shall . . .

. . . try to realize that offering constructive criticism can be painful and refrain from doing so unless I am ready to help the person cope with the pain.

כִּי יִפְגָּשְׁךָ עֵשָׂו אָחִי וּשְׁאֵלְךָ לֵאמֹר לְמִי *From the*
אַתָּה וְאָנָה תֵלֵךְ וּלְמִי אֵלֶּה לְפָנֶיךָ *Scriptures*

If my brother Esau encounters you and asks you, "To whom do you belong, and whither are you going, and what are these things before you?" (*Genesis* 32:18).

ELUL

29

אלול

Erev Rosh Hashanah
[Eve of Rosh Hashanah]
Sept. 27, 1992
Sept. 15, 1993
Sept. 5, 1994
Sept. 24, 1995
Sept. 13, 1996
Oct. 1, 1997
Sept. 20, 1998

In the homiletic writings, Jacob symbolizes the spiritual, and Esau the secular. Esau tries to seduce a person by saying, "Who do you think you are, anyway? Just where do you think spirituality will get you?"

The spiritual person poses these same questions, but in a different tone. "Where do I belong? Am I but part of the animal kingdom, differing from lower forms of life only by virtue of intellect, or do I belong to a higher order of being? Where am I headed with my life? Do I have an ultimate goal? And what are all these things before me? Am I using objects of the physical world as tools that I can use to reach my goal, or are they ends in themselves to me?"

The very arguments that can draw us away from a spiritual life can be turned back and serve as reasons for embracing spirituality. The physical world has abundant glitter, but emptiness lies beneath its superficial shine. True substance to living lies beyond these temporary pleasures.

Today is the last day of the year, a time for reckoning and asking, "What have I done during the past year that still has value for me today? All the transitory enjoyments of which I partook in the past — what value do they have today?"

A reasonable person chooses things that are of lasting value.

NOTES
_____
_____
_____
_____
_____
_____
_____
_____
_____
_____

Today I shall . . .

. . . think about the past year and consider what I would prefer the coming year to be.

Index

ঙ§ Index

Effort, not Results   19 Teves; 16 Adar;
                                    13 Iyar

Ego   14 Cheshvan; 18 Teves;
            1, 19, 22 Sivan; 18, 25 Av;
      see Humility, Self-Centeredness,
                                Self-Worth

Elders   15 Teves; 10 Sivan, 10 Av

Elevation of the Physical   15 Shevat

Embarrassing Others   2 Adar

Emulating God   25 Nissan

"Enabling"   22 Elul

Escape   4 Tishrei; 4 Shevat;
      2, 3, 25 Iyar; see Self-Awareness

Eternal Life   15 Tishrei

Excess   19 Tammuz

Expressing Emotions   29 Tammuz

Faith   28 Tishrei; 9 Cheshvan;
            4 Kislev; 11, 25, 26 Teves;
      28, 29 Shevat; 24 Adar; 8 Iyar;
            11, 17 Tammuz; 3, 11 Elul;
                       see Trust in God

Falsehood   see Truth

"Farginning"   3 Cheshvan;
                              14 Tammuz

Faults of Others   8, 25 Tammuz

Fear   12 Cheshvan; 26 Sivan

Feelings   11 Nissan

Festivals   24 Tammuz

Finding the Positive   29 Adar

Firmness   27 Iyar

Flattery   16 Kislev

Flexibility   26 Iyar

"Following Instructions"   21 Tammuz

Foresight   29 Kislev

Forgiveness   17 Shevat; 21 Elul

Free Will   15, 21 Nissan;
                       see Responsibility

Freedom   11 Kislev; 8 Teves;
                              16 Tammuz

Friendship   15, 19 Cheshvan;
      14 Teves; 13 Nissan; 13 Elul

Friendship of God   21 Kislev

Frustration   9 Teves

Fulfilling God's Will   7 Adar;
                       see Will of God

Future   7 Shevat

Giving   3, 8, 24 Cheshvan; 2 Shevat;
      20 Iyar; 12 Sivan; see Tzedakah

Goals   16 Cheshvan; 24 Teves;
            9 Shevat; 23 Adar; 21 Iyar;
                       5 Tammuz; 6 Av

Gossip   see Speech

Gratitude   10 Adar; 5 Av

Greatness   20 Kislev

Greeting Pleasantly   26 Av

Growth   7 Tishrei; 10 Cheshvan;
      7, 30 Kislev; 25, 26 Teves;
            23, 24 Shevat; 25 Adar;
      2, 14, 19 Iyar; 5 Sivan;
      22 Tammuz; see Teshuvah

Guidance   3, 20, 22 Shevat; 3 Adar;
            19, 22 Tammuz; 11 Av

Habits   23 Kislev

Happiness   2, 4, 6, Nissan;
            11 Tammuz; 6, 17 Av;
                       18 Elul; see Joy

Helping   8, 18 Shevat; 24 Nissan

Heroes   7 Nissan

Honesty   2, 28 Cheshvan; 12 Teves;
                 28 Iyar; 28 Sivan;
      7, 12, 17 Av; 2, 15 Elul

Honoring/Dishonoring God's Name
            11 Teves; 17 Av; 15 Elul

Honor, Seeking   18 Elul; see Ego,
                              Self-Worth

Hope   11 Elul

Hospitality   5 Tammuz

Humility   13 Tishrei; 1 Cheshvan;
            18 Teves; 1, 19, 24 Sivan;
                 7 Tammuz; see Ego

Identity   25 Tishrei

Impressing Others   18 Kislev

Inner Strength   4 Kislev

"Instant Spirituality"   9 Tammuz